Practical Generative AI with ChatGPT

Second Edition

Unleash your prompt engineering potential with OpenAI technologies for productivity and creativity

Valentina Alto

Practical Generative AI with ChatGPT
Second Edition

Portfolio Director: Gebin George
Relationship Lead: Ali Abidi
Project Manager: Prajakta Naik
Content Engineer: Aditi Chatterjee
Technical Editor: Irfa Ansari
Copy Editor: Safis Editing
Indexer: Pratik Shirodkar
Proofreader: Safis Editing
Production Designer: Ganesh Bhadwalkar
Growth Lead: Nimisha Dua

First published: May 2023
Second edition: April 2025

Production reference: 2301025

Published by Packt Publishing Ltd.
Grosvenor House
11 St Paul's Square
Birmingham
B3 1RB, UK.

ISBN 978-1-83664-785-0

www.packt.com

To my family and friends—thank you for your support, patience, and encouragement throughout this journey.

– Valentina

Contributors

About the author

Valentina Alto is a technical architect specializing in AI and intelligent apps at Microsoft Innovation Hub in Dubai. During her tenure at Microsoft, she covered different roles as a solution specialist, focusing on data, AI, and applications workloads within the manufacturing, pharmaceutical, and retail industries and driving customers' digital transformations in the era of AI. Valentina is an active tech author and speaker who contributes to books, articles, and events on AI and machine learning. Over the past two years, Valentina has published two books on generative AI and large language models, further establishing her expertise in the field.

I would like to thank my family and friends for their unwavering support, patience, and understanding throughout this process. Your encouragement has been invaluable.

I am also grateful to my colleagues and peers in the AI and technology community for the insightful discussions, feedback, and inspiration that have shaped my understanding of generative AI. Your contributions continue to push the boundaries of innovation.

A special thanks to Bhavesh Amin for giving me the opportunity to write this second edition, which was a very enriching experience. Special thanks to Rebecca Youé, Ali Abidi, Prajakta Naik, Ganesh Bhadwalkar, and Aditi Chatterjee for their valuable input and time reviewing this book and to the entire Packt team for their support during the course of writing this book.

About the reviewers

Dr. Michael Seller is an AI strategist, prompt engineering expert, and business consultant specializing in AI-driven solutions. He holds a Doctorate in Business Administration and certifications in AI and data analytics. As the founder of AI Alchemy, he has developed over 200 tailored prompts across various domains, helping businesses and nonprofits optimize their operations. Dr. Seller has conducted AI training workshops for organizations such as the Humanity House Foundation, the Center of Public Safety for Women, and Ampac, equipping professionals with practical AI skills. His work spans academia, consulting, and technical reviewing for AI publications.

Bharat Saxena has over 19 years of experience in data science, machine learning, and AI, with a strong focus on NLP, generative AI, anomaly detection, and explainable AI. Bharat has worked across diverse organizations, including enterprise tech companies like NTT Data, BMC Software, and Accenture, delivering innovative AI-driven solutions. His expertise spans agentic frameworks, **retrieval-augmented generation (RAG)**, knowledge graphs, and federated learning. Bharat has led the design and deployment of large-scale AI architectures, optimizing LLM-based applications for real-world adaptability, contributed to cloud-native AI applications, and built scalable data pipelines for production environments. His work has been published at leading conferences, and he actively contributes to the AI research community.

Join our communities on Discord and Reddit

Have questions about the book or want to contribute to discussions on Generative AI and LLMs? Join our Discord server at `https://packt.link/z8ivB` and our Reddit channel at `https://packt.link/0rExL` to connect, share, and collaborate with like-minded enthusiasts.

Table of Contents

Preface

We are living in an era of rapid technological transformation, where **artificial intelligence (AI)** is no longer just a tool but an active collaborator in our daily lives. Among the many advancements in AI, generative AI has emerged as a disruptive force, reshaping how we interact with technology, create content, and drive innovation. From generating human-like text and producing stunning visuals to composing music and even writing code, generative AI has unlocked possibilities that once belonged only to science fiction.

This book serves as a comprehensive guide to generative AI, with a special focus on ChatGPT, one of the most influential players in this evolving landscape. It is designed for both beginners and professionals who want to understand the underlying principles, practical applications, and enterprise-scale implementations of **large language models (LLMs)**.

The book is structured into three parts:

- *Part 1, Fundamentals of Generative AI and OpenAI*, introduces the core concepts of generative AI, the evolution of AI models, and the mechanics behind large foundation models. It also provides an in-depth look at OpenAI, its model families (such as GPT-4, DALL·E, and Whisper), and the rapid adoption of ChatGPT.

- *Part 2, ChatGPT in Action*, explores how to interact with ChatGPT effectively, covering prompt engineering techniques and real-world applications across various domains, including productivity, software development, marketing, research, and creativity. This section also introduces GPTs, the next step in AI customization, allowing users to build their own personalized AI assistants.

- *Part 3, OpenAI for Enterprises*, shifts the focus to enterprise-scale applications, discussing how businesses can leverage OpenAI's models via APIs to develop powerful AI-driven solutions. The book concludes with a forward-looking epilogue, analyzing the broader AI landscape and what to expect in the near future.

Who this book is for

This book is for AI enthusiasts, business professionals, and researchers who want to harness the power of generative AI. Whether you're a software engineer exploring AI-driven development, a marketer leveraging AI for content creation, or a business leader strategizing AI adoption, this book provides the knowledge and practical insights you need.

What this book covers

Chapter 1, Introduction to Generative AI, lets you discover the evolution of AI from traditional methods to generative AI, explore the foundation of LLMs, and understand how generative AI powers text, image, music, and video generation.

Chapter 2, OpenAI and ChatGPT: Beyond the Market Hype, dives into OpenAI's ecosystem, explores the different model families (GPT-4, DALL·E, and Whisper), and understands ChatGPT's rapid rise and its capabilities for everyday and professional use.

Chapter 3, Understanding Prompt Engineering, explores the art of crafting effective prompts, including techniques like ReAct and **Chain of Thought** (**CoT**), and shows how structured prompting enhances AI-generated responses.

Chapter 4, Boosting Day-to-Day Productivity with ChatGPT, leverages ChatGPT as a personal productivity assistant, showing how to automate tasks, improve writing, translate content, retrieve quick information, and enhance research efficiency.

Chapter 5, Developing the Future with ChatGPT, explores how ChatGPT aids developers in generating, optimizing, and debugging code and translating programming languages.

Chapter 6, Mastering Marketing with ChatGPT, uncovers how ChatGPT can revolutionize marketing—enhancing content creation, optimizing SEO, running A/B testing, and improving customer engagement with sentiment analysis.

Chapter 7, Research Reinvented with ChatGPT, shows how ChatGPT can assist researchers in brainstorming ideas, structuring studies, formatting bibliographies, and presenting findings in a clear and concise manner.

Chapter 8, Unleashing Creativity Visually with ChatGPT, explores ChatGPT's multimodal capabilities, including GPT-4 Vision and DALL-E, enabling AI-driven image generation, visual Q&A, and enhanced creative workflows.

Chapter 9, Exploring GPTs, teaches the concept of GPTs, explores assistant-based AI workflows, and shows how to build your own AI-powered assistants for tasks like research, analysis, and marketing.

Chapter 10, Leveraging OpenAI Models for Enterprise-Scale Applications, delves into OpenAI's model APIs, comprehends enterprise applications of LLMs, and explores how businesses can integrate generative AI into their workflows responsibly.

Chapter 11, Epilogue and Final Thoughts, reflects on the evolving landscape of generative AI, discusses ethical implications, and looks ahead to the future of AI.

The *Appendix* contains a set of hands-on examples of real-world use cases leveraging OpenAI and Python code.

To get the most out of this book

Following along will be easier if you keep the following in mind:

- **Learn through hands-on examples:** Many sections include practical exercises and real-world applications. Whenever possible, try them out using OpenAI's APIs, ChatGPT, and other tools.

- **Experiment with different prompts:** Since prompt engineering is a key skill in working with generative AI, experiment with different prompts and observe how slight modifications affect the results.

- **Explore the APIs and developer tools:** If you're a developer, take time to explore OpenAI's API documentation and try integrating AI capabilities into your own applications.

- **Think beyond the basics:** This book provides a foundation, but AI is an evolving field. Stay updated with the latest research and industry trends to deepen your understanding.

Here is a list of things you need to have:

Software/hardware covered in the book	System requirements
Python 3.7.1 or higher	Windows, macOS, or Linux
Streamlit	Windows, macOS, or Linux
LangChain	Windows, macOS, or Linux
OpenAI model APIs	An OpenAI account
Azure OpenAI Service (optional)	An Azure subscription enabled for Azure OpenAI (optional)

Download the example code files

The code bundle for the book is hosted on GitHub at `https://github.com/PacktPublishing/Practical-GenAI-with-ChatGPT-Second-Edition`. We also have other code bundles from our rich catalog of books and videos available at `https://github.com/PacktPublishing`. Check them out!

Conventions used

There are a number of text conventions used throughout this book.

A block of code is set as follows:

```
{"prompt": "<prompt text>", "completion": "<ideal generated text>"}
{"prompt": "<prompt text>", "completion": "<ideal generated text>"}
{"prompt": "<prompt text>", "completion": "<ideal generated text>"}
```

Bold: Indicates a new term, an important word, or words that you see on the screen. For instance, words in menus or dialog boxes appear in the text like this. For example: "As always, a **subject-matter expert (SME)** is needed in the loop to review the results."

 Warnings or important notes appear like this.

 Tips and tricks appear like this.

Get in touch

Subscribe to AI_Distilled, the go-to newsletter for AI professionals, researchers, and innovators, at `https://packt.link/aWQQB`.

Feedback from our readers is always welcome.

General feedback: Email feedback@packtpub.com and mention the book's title in the subject of your message. If you have questions about any aspect of this book, please email us at questions@packtpub.com.

Errata: Although we have taken every care to ensure the accuracy of our content, mistakes do happen. If you have found a mistake in this book, we would be grateful if you reported this to us. Please visit http://www.packtpub.com/submit-errata, click **Submit Errata**, and fill in the form.

Piracy: If you come across any illegal copies of our works in any form on the internet, we would be grateful if you would provide us with the location address or website name. Please contact us at copyright@packtpub.com with a link to the material.

If you are interested in becoming an author: If there is a topic that you have expertise in and you are interested in either writing or contributing to a book, please visit http://authors.packtpub.com/.

Share your thoughts

Once you've read *Practical Generative AI with ChatGPT, Second Edition,* we'd love to hear your thoughts! Scan the QR code below to go straight to the Amazon review page for this book and share your feedback.

https://packt.link/r/1836647859

Your review is important to us and the tech community and will help us make sure we're delivering excellent quality content.

Free Benefits with Your Book

This book comes with free benefits to support your learning. Activate them now for instant access (see the "*How to Unlock*" section for instructions).

Here's a quick overview of what you can instantly unlock with your purchase:

PDF and ePub Copies   Next-Gen Web-Based Reader

Access a DRM-free PDF copy of this book to read anywhere, on any device.

Use a DRM-free ePub version with your favorite e-reader.

Multi-device progress sync: Pick up where you left off, on any device.

Highlighting and notetaking: Capture ideas and turn reading into lasting knowledge.

Bookmarking: Save and revisit key sections whenever you need them.

Dark mode: Reduce eye strain by switching to dark or sepia themes.

How to Unlock

Scan the QR code (or go to packtpub.com/unlock). Search for this book by name, confirm the edition, and then follow the steps on the page.

Note: Keep your invoice handy. Purchases made directly from Packt don't require one.

Part 1

Fundamentals of Generative AI and OpenAI

In *Part 1* of this book, the fundamentals of generative AI and GPT models are introduced, including a brief history of the development of OpenAI and its flagship set of models, the GPT family.

This part starts with an overview of the domain of generative AI, providing you with foundational knowledge about this area of AI, including its history and state-of-the-art developments. You will also get familiar with the applications of generative AI, ranging from text generation to music composition.

It then introduces the company that brought the power of generative AI to the general public: OpenAI. You will get familiar with the technology behind OpenAI's most popular release – ChatGPT – and understand the research journey that, starting from **artificial neural networks (ANNs)**, led to **large language models (LLMs)**.

This part contains the following chapters:

- *Chapter 1, Introduction to Generative AI*
- *Chapter 2, OpenAI and ChatGPT: Beyond the Market Hype*

1

Introduction to Generative AI

Hello! Welcome to *Practical Generative AI with ChatGPT*! In this book, we will explore the fascinating world of generative **artificial intelligence (AI)** and its groundbreaking applications, with a particular focus on ChatGPT.

Generative AI has transformed the way we interact with machines, enabling computers to create, predict, and learn without explicit human instruction. Since the launch of OpenAI's ChatGPT in November 2022, we have witnessed unprecedented advances in natural language processing, image and video synthesis, and many other fields. Whether you are a curious beginner or an experienced practitioner, this guide will equip you with the knowledge and skills to effectively navigate the exciting landscape of generative AI. So, let's dive in and start the book with some definitions of the context we are moving in.

In this chapter, we focus on the applications of generative AI to various fields, such as image synthesis, text generation, and music composition, highlighting the potential of generative AI to revolutionize various industries with concrete examples and recent developments. Being aware of the research journey toward the current state of the art of generative AI will give you an understanding of the foundations of recent developments and state-of-the-art models.

All this, we will cover through the following topics:

- Introducing generative AI
- Exploring the domains of generative AI
- Main trends and innovation after 2 years of ChatGPT
- Legal and ethical landscape of generative AI

By the end of this chapter, you will be familiar with the exciting world of generative AI, its applications, the research history behind it, and the current developments that could have – and are currently having – a disruptive impact on businesses.

Free Benefits with Your Book

Your purchase includes a free PDF copy of this book along with other exclusive benefits. Check the *Free Benefits with Your Book* section in the Preface to unlock them instantly and maximize your learning experience.

Introducing generative AI

Generative AI is an exciting branch of AI that focuses on creating new content, such as text, images, music, or even videos, that is often indistinguishable from something made by humans.

To understand where it fits, let's break it down:

- **AI**: AI is the broad field that enables machines to mimic human-like tasks, such as decision-making or problem-solving.
- **Machine learning** (**ML**): Within AI, ML refers to techniques where machines learn patterns from data to make predictions or decisions without being explicitly programmed. The process of learning is made possible by sophisticated mathematical models called algorithms.
- **Deep learning** (**DL**): A subset of ML, DL uses complex algorithms inspired by the human brain to process large amounts of data and recognize intricate patterns. Because of their architecture – inspired by our brains and neural connections – these algorithms are called artificial neural networks.

Definition

An artificial neural network is a type of computer program designed to learn patterns by processing information in a way that's inspired by the human brain. Instead of following strict, step-by-step rules, it uses interconnected "nodes" (like virtual brain cells) that work together and adjust their connections over time. By repeatedly reviewing examples, it gradually improves at tasks like recognizing images, understanding speech, or predicting outcomes—all without needing explicit instructions for each step.

Generative AI emerges from DL and uses specialized algorithms to generate something entirely new based on what it has learned from existing data. For example, a generative AI model trained on thousands of paintings could create brand-new art that blends different styles or themes.

The following figure shows how these areas of research are related to each other:

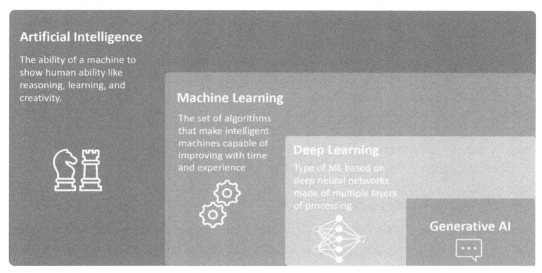

Figure 1.1: Relationship between AI, ML, DL, and generative AI

Generative AI models are trained on vast amounts of data and then they can generate new examples based on user's requests. And the game-changer element here is that these requests are made in the easiest way possible – using our natural language. These models are called **large language models (LLMs)**.

Definition

LLMs are a type of artificial neural network featured by a particular architectural framework called "Transformer." They are characterized by a huge number of parameters (in the order of billions) and have been trained on billions of words. Given the training set, LLMs are capable of inferring language patterns and intents in user queries and generating natural language responses.

The possibility of interacting in natural language with LLMs is disruptive, and a whole new science has been born around that activity. This science is called "prompt engineering," named after the term "prompt," which we are going to cover in *Chapter 3*.

Definition

A prompt is the specific text, question, or description you provide to a generative AI model to guide it toward producing the kind of output you want—whether that's a helpful explanation, a creative story, or a detailed solution. How you phrase the prompt can greatly affect the AI's response. This practice of carefully designing and refining prompts, often called "prompt engineering," involves experimenting with different word choices, instructions, and formats to improve both the quality and accuracy of the AI's output. By learning how to craft effective prompts, you help ensure the AI more consistently gives you results that are useful, engaging, and aligned with your goals.

Even though text understanding and generation is probably one of the most outstanding features of Generative AI, this field covers many domains, which we will cover next.

Domains of generative AI

In recent years, generative AI has made significant advancements and has expanded its applications to a wide range of domains, such as art, music, fashion, and architecture. In some of them, it is indeed transforming the way we create, design, and understand the world around us. In others, it is improving and making existing processes and operations more efficient.

For example, in the context of the pharmaceutical industry, generative AI is revolutionizing drug discovery by enabling the rapid design of novel therapeutic molecules, thereby significantly reducing development timelines and costs. By analyzing extensive datasets of chemical and biological information, generative AI models can identify promising drug candidates and predict their interactions within the human body. For instance, Insilico Medicine utilized generative AI to develop ISM001-055, a drug candidate for idiopathic pulmonary fibrosis, which progressed to Phase II clinical trials in 2023 (`https://insilico.com/blog/first_phase2`).

Another example is the way generative AI is revolutionizing game development by enabling the creation of dynamic and adaptive environments that respond to player actions, thereby enhancing immersion and replayability. By leveraging generative AI, developers can procedurally generate vast, ever-changing game worlds, ensuring that each playthrough offers a unique experience. This technology facilitates the creation of realistic **non-playable characters** (**NPCs**) with behaviors that adapt to player interactions, making game narratives more engaging. Additionally, generative AI streamlines the development process by automating asset creation, which reduces production time and costs.

As a result, developers can focus more on crafting innovative gameplay mechanics and rich storytelling, ultimately delivering more personalized and captivating gaming experiences (`https://www.xcubelabs.com/blog/generative-ai-in-game-development-creating-dynamic-and-adaptive-environments/`).

Lastly, generative AI can have a great impact on advertising and visual asset generation. For example, in March 2023, Coca-Cola launched the "Create Real Magic" platform (`https://www.coca-colacompany.com/media-center/coca-cola-invites-digital-artists-to-create-real-magic-using-new-ai-platform`), inviting digital artists worldwide to craft original artwork using iconic brand assets from its archives. Developed in collaboration with OpenAI and Bain & Company, this innovative platform combines the capabilities of GPT-4 and DALL-E, enabling users to generate unique pieces that blend Coca-Cola's heritage with modern AI technology. Participants had the opportunity to submit their creations for a chance to be featured on Coca-Cola's digital billboards in New York's Times Square and London's Piccadilly Circus, exemplifying the brand's commitment to fostering creativity through cutting-edge technology. These are just a few examples of how generative AI can reshape business processes.

Now, the fact that generative AI is used in many domains also implies that its models can deal with different kinds of data, from natural language to audio or images. In the next section, we'll explore how generative AI models address different types of data and domains.

Text generation

The evolution of text generation within AI has been a journey from early theoretical concepts to today's sophisticated language models. The 1950s marked the formal inception of AI as a field, with pioneers like Alan Turing exploring machine intelligence. Early efforts in **natural language processing (NLP)** during the 1960s and 1970s led to programs such as ELIZA, which simulated conversation through pattern matching. The 1980s and 1990s saw the development of statistical models that improved language modeling by probabilistically predicting word sequences. The advent of ML algorithms during this period further advanced text generation capabilities.

A significant breakthrough occurred in 2017 with the introduction of the Transformer architecture which, as aforementioned, is the framework that features today's LLMs.

The unique element of this new series of models featuring the landscape of generative AI is that – once they are trained – they can be consumed, queried, and instructed in the easiest way possible. The introduction of LLMs marked a paradigm shift in the context of AI since no advanced skills were needed to benefit from them.

Today, one of the greatest applications of generative AI—and the one we are going to cover the most throughout this book—is its ability to produce new content in natural language. Indeed, generative AI models can be used to generate new coherent and grammatically correct text in different languages, such as articles, poetry, and product descriptions. They can also extract relevant features from text such as keywords, topics, or full summaries.

Here is an example of working with GPT-4o, one of the latest models released by OpenAI and available through ChatGPT:

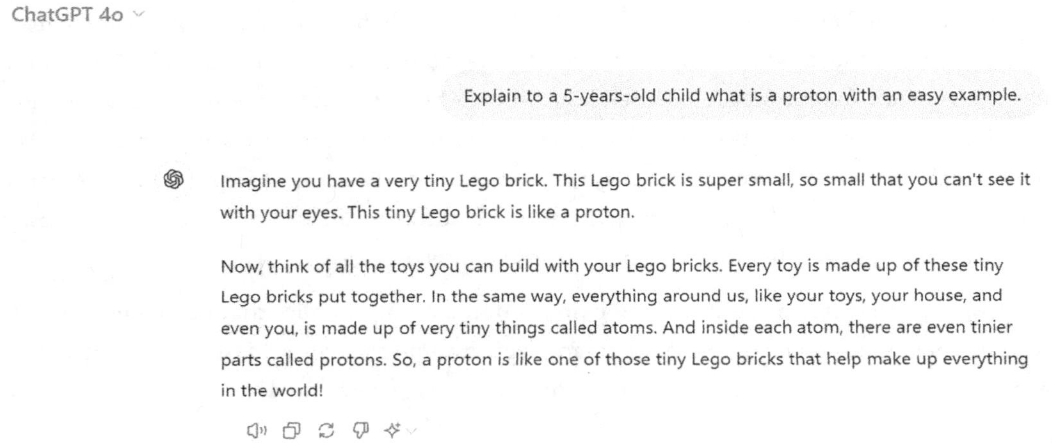
ChatGPT 4o
Explain to a 5-years-old child what is a proton with an easy example.
Imagine you have a very tiny Lego brick. This Lego brick is super small, so small that you can't see it with your eyes. This tiny Lego brick is like a proton.
Now, think of all the toys you can build with your Lego bricks. Every toy is made up of these tiny Lego bricks put together. In the same way, everything around us, like your toys, your house, and even you, is made up of very tiny things called atoms. And inside each atom, there are even tinier parts called protons. So, a proton is like one of those tiny Lego bricks that help make up everything in the world!

Figure 1.2: Example of ChatGPT responding to a user's query in natural language

As you can see, the model was not only able to answer my question with an explanation of what a proton is; it also adapted its style and jargon to a specific target audience – in my case, a 5-year-old child. This is remarkable since it paves the way for many scenarios of hyper-personalization that were not possible before. In the next chapters, we will cover many examples of that.

ChatGPT is the main focus of this book, and in the upcoming chapters, you will see examples that showcase this powerful application.

Now, we will move on to image generation.

Image generation

One of the earliest and most well-known examples of generative AI in image synthesis is the **generative adversarial network (GAN)** architecture introduced in the 2014 paper by I. Goodfellow et al., *Generative Adversarial Networks*. The purpose of GANs is to generate realistic images that are indistinguishable from real images. This ability has several interesting business applications, such as generating synthetic datasets for training computer vision models, generating realistic product images, and generating realistic images for virtual reality and augmented reality applications.

Then, in 2021, a new generative AI model was introduced in this field by OpenAI, **DALL-E**. Different from GANs, the DALL-E model is designed to generate images from descriptions in natural language and can generate a wide range of images. The main difference here is that while GANs are often used to create or improve realistic images, models like DALL-E are ideal for visual creativity, turning any description in natural language into an illustration.

DALL-E has great potential in creative industries such as advertising, product design, and fashion to create unique and creative images.

Since its first release to the time of writing (December 2024), DALL-E has improved dramatically, as you can see in the following examples. Below is an artistic creation by DALL-E at the dawn of its life:

A picture of the philosopher Socrates as he had lived at the present time. He rides an electric scooter while messaging on his iPhone   **Generate**

Figure 1.3: Images generated by DALL-E with a natural language prompt as input

Let's now see what **DALL-E3**, the most recent version of the model at the time of writing this book, can produce (here, we will use Microsoft Image Creator, powered by DALL-E3. You can try it at `https://copilot.microsoft.com/images/create`):

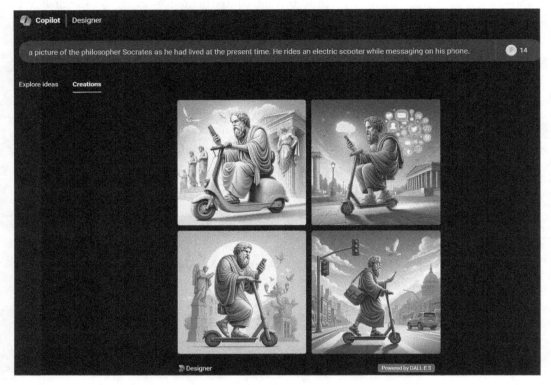

Figure 1.4: Images generated by DALL-E3 with a natural language prompt as input

It's impressive to see the level of improvement of this model in less than 2 years. We are just scraping the surface of the massive improvements occurring at a fast pace.

Music generation

The first approaches to generative AI for music generation trace back to the 1950s, with research in the field of algorithmic composition, a technique that uses algorithms to generate musical compositions. In 1957, Lejaren Hiller and Leonard Isaacson created the *Illiac Suite* for *String Quartet* (`https://www.youtube.com/watch?v=n0njBFLQSk8`), the first piece of music entirely composed by AI. Since then, the field of generative AI for music has been the subject of ongoing research.

Among recent years' developments, new architectures and frameworks have become widespread among the general public, such as the WaveNet architecture introduced by Google in 2016, which has been able to generate high-quality audio samples, and the Magenta project, also developed by Google, which uses **recurrent neural networks (RNNs)** and other ML techniques to generate music and other forms of art.

Definition

RNNs are a type of neural network designed to process sequential data by retaining information from previous inputs through a loop-like structure. This allows them to recognize patterns and dependencies over time, making them ideal for tasks like language modeling, time-series prediction, and speech recognition.

In 2020, OpenAI also announced Jukebox, a neural network that generates music when provided with genre, artist, and lyrics as input.

These and other frameworks became the foundations of many AI composer assistants for music generation. An example is Flow Machines, developed by Sony CSL Research. This generative AI system was trained on a large database of musical pieces to create new music in a variety of styles. It was used by French composer Benoît Carré to compose an album called *Hello World* (https://www.helloworldalbum.net/), which features collaborations with several human musicians.

Here, you can see an example of a track generated entirely by Music Transformer, one of the models within the Magenta project:

Figure 1.5: Music Transformer allows users to listen to musical performances generated by AI
(https://magenta.tensorflow.org/music-transformer)

Another incredible application of generative AI within the music domain is speech synthesis. This refers to AI tools that can create audio based on text inputs in the voices of well-known singers.

For example, if you have always wondered how your songs would sound if Lady Gaga performed them, well, you can now fulfill your dreams with tools such as FakeYou *Text to Speech* (`https://fakeyou.com/tts`) or UberDuck.ai (`https://uberduck.ai/`)!

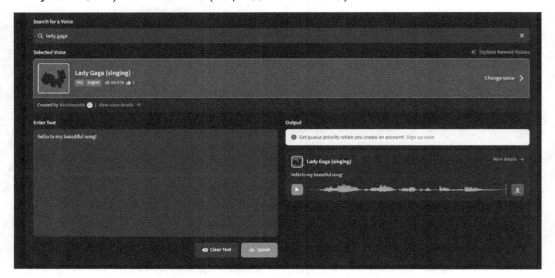

Figure 1.6: Text-to-speech synthesis with fakeyou.com

The results are really impressive! If you want to have fun, you can also try voices from your favorite cartoons, such as *Winnie the Pooh*. The only thing you need to do is input the text of the song you want your favorite voice to sing aloud.

Let's go even further. What if we could generate a song from scratch, just asking the generative AI to do that for us in natural language? Well, we can do that seamlessly today and without any knowledge about music. Among the generative AI products that are rising in the music market today is Suno, whose mission is *"[...]building a future where anyone can make great music. Whether you're a shower singer or a charting artist, we break barriers between you and the song you dream of making. No instrument needed, just imagination. From your mind to music."* (source: `https://suno.com/about`).

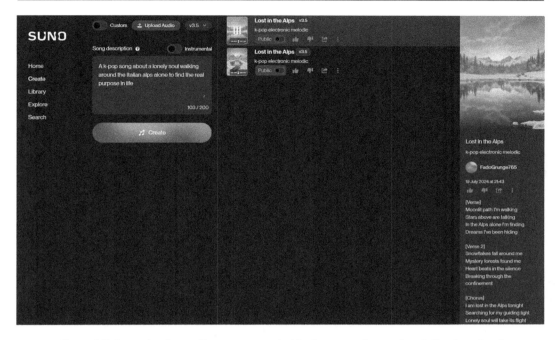

Figure 1.7: Example of an entire song generated by Suno.com from a description in natural language

As you can see, on the left-hand side of the picture, I provided a very brief song description in natural language – this was my prompt. From that, the model was able to generate not only the title and lyrics of a song (on the right-hand side) but also the music!

Can you believe that it became my summer 2024 hit? If you want to create your summer hit too, you can try it for free at `https://suno.com/create`.

Video generation

Generative AI for video generation shares a similar timeline of development with image generation. One of the key developments in the field of video generation has been the development of GANs. Thanks to their accuracy in producing realistic images, researchers have started to apply this technique to video generation as well. One of the most notable examples of GAN-based video generation is DeepMind's Veo, which generates high-quality videos from a single image and a sequence of motions. Another great example is NVIDIA's **video-to-video synthesis (Vid2Vid)** DL-based framework, which uses GANs to synthesize high-quality videos from input videos.

The Vid2Vid system can generate temporally consistent videos, meaning that they maintain smooth and realistic motion over time. The technology can be used to perform a variety of video synthesis tasks, such as the following:

- Converting videos from one domain into another (for example, converting a daytime video into a nighttime video or a sketch into a realistic image)
- Modifying existing videos (for example, changing the style or appearance of objects in a video)
- Creating new videos from static images (for example, animating a sequence of still images)

In September 2022, Meta's researchers announced the general availability of **Make-A-Video** (`https://makeavideo.studio/`), a new AI system that allows users to convert their natural language prompts into video clips. Behind this technology, you can recognize many of the models that we mentioned in other domains – language understanding for the prompt, image and motion generation with image generation, and background music made by AI composers.

Now, everything we've mentioned above pales in comparison to the latest text-to-video models. To name one, OpenAI announced a text-to-video model called **SORA** in February 2024 and released some early experiments:

Prompt: A stylish woman walks down a Tokyo street filled with warm glowing neon and animated city signage. She wears a black leather jacket, a long red dress, and black boots, and carries a black purse. She wears sunglasses and red lipstick. She...

Prompt: Several giant wooly mammoths approach treading through a snowy meadow, their long wooly fur lightly blows in the wind as they walk, snow covered trees and dramatic snow capped mountains in the distance, mid afternoon light with wispy...

Prompt: A movie trailer featuring the adventures of the 30 year old space man wearing a red wool knitted motorcycle helmet, blue sky, salt desert, cinematic style, shot on 35mm film, vivid colors.

Prompt: Animated scene features a close-up of a short fluffy monster kneeling beside a melting red candle. The art style is 3D and realistic, with a focus on lighting and texture. The mood of the painting is one of wonder and curiosity, as the monster...

Figure 1.8: Videos generated by SORA from prompts in natural language. Source: https://openai.com/index/sora/

I do encourage you to visit the SORA webpage to have a look at the amazing videos it created. At the time of writing, SORA is not publicly available, as it is going through several tests by the OpenAI Red Team.

Overall, generative AI has impacted many domains for years, and some AI tools already consistently support artists, organizations, and general users. Despite the fact we've been experimenting and building applications with generative AI for only two years, there are already some consolidated trends and future innovations to keep in mind. Let's explore them in the next section.

Main trends and innovations

From November 2022 to today, we have witnessed a huge amount of innovation in the field of generative AI. Many of these innovations are linked to the brand-new models developed and released to the public, like OpenAI's GPT-4o and DALL-E3, but also Google Gemini, Meta Llama 3, Microsoft Phi3, and many others.

However, the most remarkable achievements probably lie in the way we interact with and build applications around those models. In this section, we are going to explore three main advancements that have marked the most popular reference architectures for generative-AI-powered applications.

Retrieval augmented generation

One of the first limitations of ChatGPT and, generally speaking, of LLMs was the knowledge base cutoff. The knowledge of LLMs is limited to the training set they have been trained on and, although this can be exhaustive, it's not up to date (in fact, once the model is trained, any new data or information that emerges afterward won't be part of its knowledge, since it wasn't included in the original training set). Plus, the data is likely missing the proprietary knowledge base that might be relevant for us or our organization. For example, if you ask ChatGPT, "What is my company's policy for employee health insurance?", the model won't be able to answer since it has no access to this information.

To bypass this limitation, a new framework was designed to allow LLMs to navigate through customized documentation that we can provide. This framework is called **retrieval augmented generation (RAG)**.

The idea behind RAG is to augment the LLM's knowledge by adding external sources of information, yet without modifying the structure of the model at all.

Definition

An embedding is a way to turn complex information—like words, sentences, or images—into a list of numbers (a vector). This makes it easier for a computer to understand what those words or sentences mean. If two pieces of text have similar meanings, their vectors will be close together in the numerical space. In other words, embeddings let computers measure how alike different inputs are based on their content, not just their exact wording.

For example, if two concepts are similar, then their vector representations should also be similar.

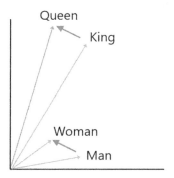

King-Man+Woman ≈ Queen

Figure 1.9: Example of vector representation of four different words

In this example, we can see that the mathematical distance between the two vectors corresponding to "Queen" and "King" is more or less the same as the difference between "Woman" and "Man." Semantically speaking, this makes sense, as we are talking about a similar relationship. A similar example might be applied to the relationship between countries and capital cities: once embedded in a vector space, the distance between "Italy" and "Rome" should be similar to the distance between "France" and "Paris" as they are mapping the same relationships.

RAG is made of three phases:

1. **Retrieval**: Given a user's query and its corresponding numerical representation, the most similar pieces of documents (those corresponding to the vectors that are closest to the user query's vector) are retrieved and used as the base context for the LLM.

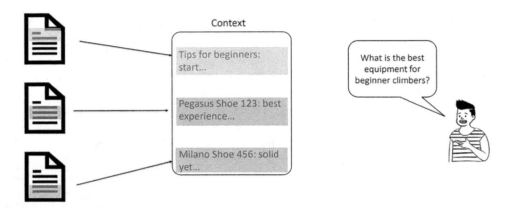

Figure 1.10: Example of retrieving three different chunks from different documents, since they are represented by the closest vectors to the user query

2. **Augmentation:** The retrieved context is enriched through additional instructions, rules, safety guardrails, and similar practices that are typical of prompt engineering techniques (we will cover the topic of prompt engineering in *Chapter 3*).

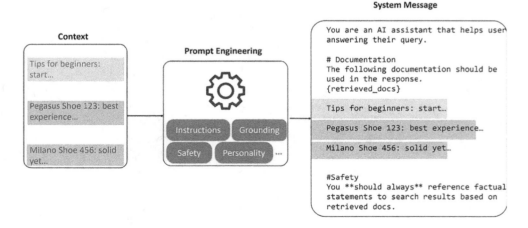

Figure 1.11: Example of adding more context to the retrieved chunks of documents

3. **Generation**: Based on the augmented context, the LLM generates the response to the user's query.

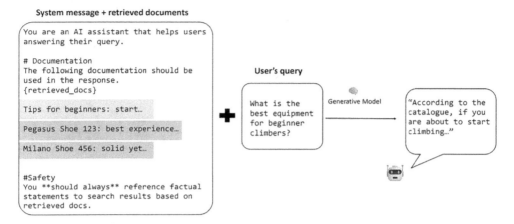

Figure 1.12: Example of using the augmented context as the system message for the model to generate the final answer

RAG combines the strengths of generative models and information retrieval systems to enhance the quality and relevance of generated content. Traditional generative models rely solely on their training data to produce responses, which can sometimes result in outdated or irrelevant information. RAG addresses this limitation by integrating external knowledge bases during the generation process.

Multimodality

Earlier in this chapter, we looked at the various domains of generative AI, ranging from text to images, from videos to music. Typically, large foundation models tend to be domain-specific, as we saw for LLMs in the case of language understanding and generation, or DALL-E3 in the case of image generation.

However, the recent advances in generative AI have enabled the development of **large multimodal models (LMMs)** that can process and generate different types of data, such as text, images, audio, and video.

LMMs share with *standard* LLMs the ability to generalize and adapt typical large foundation models. However, LMMs are capable of processing diverse data with the idea of mirroring the way humans interact with the surrounding ecosystem – that is, with all our senses.

A great example of a multimodal model is OpenAI's GPT-4o, which is able to interact with users via text, images, and audio. Take the following example:

ChatGPT 4o ∨

what is the name of this building?

The building in the image is the Burj Khalifa, located in Dubai, United Arab Emirates. It is currently the tallest building in the world.

Figure 1.13: Example of providing ChatGPT-4o with a picture and asking it to name the building

As you can see, the model was able to analyze the image and reason over it.

Let's now go ahead and ask the model to generate an illustration:

thanks. Can you generate a cartoon style illustration of it? black and white

Figure 1.14: Example of ChatGPT-4o generating an illustration based on a previously provided picture

What sets LLMs apart is their ability to retain advanced reasoning capabilities, making them uniquely suited for tackling complex reasoning tasks across diverse data contexts, unlike traditional AI models. Let's consider, for example, traditional computer vision models, which are task-specific, and they do not *reason* over an image, but rather perform tasks like detecting objects or extracting text from images. On the other hand, LMMs can use the same reasoning capabilities as LLMs, yet they can apply these capabilities to data other than text.

Let's consider this last example (showing only the first lines of the response):

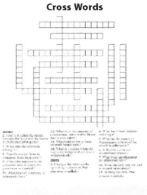

can you solve this for me?

🌀 Sure, let's solve the crossword puzzle. Here are the answers based on the given clues:

Across:

2. **Cephalothoraz** (Fusion between the head and thorax in chelicerate arthropods)

3. **Arachnids** (Class that scorpions belong to)

4. **Metamorphosis** (Transformation from an immature form to an adult)

Figure 1.15: Example of ChatGPT 4o solving a crossword game

As you can see, the model was able to:

- Read and understand the scenario the image is posing

- Reason about it and solve the complex task that it is offering, which is solving a puzzle

As you may imagine, this opens a landscape of applications in various industries, and we are going to see some concrete examples in the upcoming chapters.

AI agents

In previous sections, we uncovered how LLMs are great when it comes to generating content. However, they lack one ability, which is taking action and interacting with the surrounding ecosystem that goes beyond the single user. For example, what if we want our LLM to be able not only to generate an amazing LinkedIn post but also publish it on our page?

AI agents emerge as key players in overcoming this limitation. But what exactly are they? Agents can be seen as AI systems powered by LLMs that, given a user's query, are able to interact with the surrounding ecosystem to the extent to which we allow them. The perimeter of the ecosystem is delimited by the tools (or plugins) we provide the agents with (in our previous example, we might provide the agent with a LinkedIn plugin so that it is able to post the generated content).

Agents are made of the following ingredients:

- An LLM, which acts as the reasoning engine of the AI system.
- A system message, which instructs the agent to behave and think in a given way. For example, you can design an agent as a teaching assistant for students with the following system message: "You are a teaching assistant. Given a student's query, NEVER provide the final answer, but rather provide some hints to get there."
- A set of tools the agent can leverage to interact with the surrounding ecosystem.

AI agents are a perfect representation of the meaning of "LLM as reasoning engine of an application." In fact, the beauty of agents is that they can pick the best tool to use to accomplish a user's request. For example, let's say we have an AI agent to produce LinkedIn content, and we provide it with two tools: a LinkedIn plugin and a web search plugin (each one with a correct description of its functionality). Let's explore the behavior of the agent in three different scenarios:

- **Generate a story about a little dog walking around the mountains**: The agent will generate the story without using a plugin.
- **Generate a story about the current weather in Milan**: The agent will invoke the web search plugin to get the current weather in Milan.
- **Generate a LinkedIn post about the current weather in Milan and publish it on my profile**: The agent will invoke the web search plugin to get the current weather in Milan and the LinkedIn plugin to post it on my profile.

The combination of instructions and a set of plugins makes AI agents extremely versatile, and you can create highly specialized entities to address specific scenarios.

And that's not all.

Why have only one agent if you can create your own crew of agents talking to and cooperating with each other? Imagine multiple agents, each one with a specific expertise and goal, communicating and interacting to accomplish a task. This is what **multi-agent applications** look like, and in the last few months, this pattern started showing very interesting results.

Let's consider the following example. We want to generate an elevator pitch about climate change. We need up-to-date information to do so (latest trends and research, future perspectives, and so on), as well as solid research grounded by academic papers. Plus, we need to be concise yet sharp and effective, delivering all the key information in a very short pitch.

Now, we could ask a single agent to do all of that, providing it with all the required tools and long instructions to accomplish the task. However, if the task gets very complex, a single agent might not be the best approach as it might lead to inaccurate results. Instead, let's use a multi-agent approach, creating a team with the following AI professionals:

- A market analyst who can search the web for the latest news about climate change: This will be an agent with a web search plugin and specific instructions to search for news.
- An expert researcher who can easily navigate through academic research papers about climate change: This will be an agent with an Arxiv (a curated research-sharing platform) plugin and specific instructions on how to retrieve relevant information.
- An expert in public speaking who can easily consolidate all the information in one elevator pitch: This will be an agent with instructions on how to deliver perfect pitches.
- A critic who will review the pitch and propose some changes to the expert in public speaking, if needed: This will be an agent with instructions on how to review and improve a pitch by identifying pitfalls and areas of improvement.

So, when the user asks the agents to generate an elevator pitch about the current issue of climate change, all the agents can start working on the project.

There are many frameworks that can help developers with multi-agent applications (including AutoGen, LangGraph, and CrewAI), especially when it comes to the *flow* that we want our agents to follow. For example, we might want to enforce a specific number of iterations; or that all agents are invoked at least once; or even to involve us, as users, in every iteration to provide further feedback to be incorporated in the upcoming iteration.

At the time of writing, the multi-agent framework is showing promising advancements, and it is a glimpse of the outstanding reasoning capabilities behind LLMs and how they can unlock new ways of problem-solving.

Small language models

LLMs are, unsurprisingly, large. This means that the architecture of an **ANN** featuring LLMs is made of a huge number of parameters, in the order of billions. Typically, a large number of parameters is associated with a better-performing model, since it is able to deal with more information and examples and henceforth is able to recognize and infer more patterns the moment users ask their questions. However, with large numbers of parameters typically comes a high cost of training and hosting, since a powerful AI infrastructure is needed. Plus, the energy consumption of these models raises serious questions about the environmental impact of LLM training and their overall sustainability in the long run.

These smaller models are called **small language models** (**SLMs**) and, besides being lighter and less demanding in terms of infrastructure, they are also showing surprisingly high performance.

Now, we might think that GPT-3.5-turbo is deprecated; however, we have to remember that it used to be the most powerful model on the market just one year ago, and it is remarkable to see that a 7B model is capable of better results.

SLMs are definitely a research stream to keep an eye on, especially when it comes to scenarios where we might want to deploy a model locally or even customize it with fine-tuning (we will cover fine-tuning in the next chapter).

Legal and ethical landscape of generative AI

When developing and deploying generative AI systems, a broad range of legal and ethical considerations must be carefully addressed to ensure responsible and sustainable use. These considerations extend beyond mere compliance and enter a domain where moral responsibility, public trust, and technological accountability intersect.

Copyright and intellectual property issues

LLMs are often trained on vast corpora scraped from the internet, including content that may be copyrighted. As a result, there is a real risk of embedding copyrighted text, music, images, or video segments directly into AI output, inadvertently producing infringements when these outputs are shared or commercialized.

This concrete risk also escalated in November 2024, when major Canadian news organizations (`https://www.reuters.com/sustainability/boards-policy-regulation/major-canadian-news-media-companies-launch-legal-action-against-openai-2024-11-29/`), including The Globe and Mail and CBC/Radio-Canada, filed a lawsuit against OpenAI. They alleged that OpenAI used their copyrighted content without authorization to train its AI models, seeking damages and an injunction to prevent further unauthorized use.

Misinformation, hallucinations, and the risk of fake news

One of the known limitations of current generative AI models is their tendency to **hallucinate** – to produce entirely plausible-sounding but factually incorrect statements. This can result in the inadvertent spread of misinformation, especially when AI-generated content is taken at face value by consumers, journalists, or public officials.

As an example, in December 2024, misinformation researcher Jeff Hancock (`https://www.theverge.com/2024/12/4/24313132/jeff-hancock-minnesota-deepfake-law-ai-hallucinations-citation`) admitted that ChatGPT fabricated details in a court filing he prepared, leading to the submission of non-existent citations. This incident emphasizes the risk of AI-generated content introducing inaccuracies in critical documents.

Continual exposure to unreliable AI output may lead to widespread skepticism regarding all digital content, undermining the credibility of legitimate sources and diminishing trust in expert commentary and reputable journalism. Organizations must therefore invest in factual verification processes, human-in-the-loop validation, and transparent model evaluation methods.

Deepfakes and deceptive manipulation

Deepfake technology, an advanced subset of generative AI that synthesizes highly realistic images, videos, and voice recordings, can be weaponized to impersonate public figures, fabricate scandalous events, or produce manipulative political propaganda.

Definition

A deepfake is a type of artificial media created using DL algorithms, where a person's likeness, voice, or movements are digitally manipulated to create realistic but fake content. Typically, deepfakes involve altering videos or images to make it appear as if someone said or did something they never actually did.

A recent example occurred back in 2023, when a finance clerk at a Hong Kong branch of a multinational corporation was deceived into transferring over $25 million after scammers used deepfake audio to impersonate senior executives, directing unauthorized fund transfers (`https://www.secureworld.io/industry-news/hong-kong-deepfake-cybercrime`).

Companies, governments, and individuals targeted by deepfakes may suffer severe reputational harm, leading to public embarrassment, financial losses, or diminished trust. Building detection tools, implementing digital watermarking techniques, and establishing legal frameworks that penalize malicious deepfake creators are crucial steps in mitigating these risks.

Bias, discrimination, and social harm

Generative AI models can unintentionally reproduce and magnify existing societal prejudices present in their training data. For example, models might consistently portray certain professions as male-dominated or depict particular cultural groups in stereotypical roles.

These biased outputs can influence hiring decisions, product recommendations, and policy-making processes, ultimately disadvantaging underrepresented groups.

In this regard, a 2023 study, *Demographic Stereotypes in Text-to-Image Generation* (`https://hai.stanford.edu/sites/default/files/2023-11/Demographic-Stereotypes.pdf`), highlighted that text-to-image generative AI models tend to encode substantial bias and stereotypes. For example, prompts requesting images of professionals often resulted in depictions aligning with traditional gender roles, such as male doctors and female nurses, thereby reinforcing outdated and discriminatory views.

Another study, *Social Dangers of Generative Artificial Intelligence: Review and Guidelines* (`https://dl.acm.org/doi/fullHtml/10.1145/3657054.3664243`), investigates the extent to which these technologies can exacerbate existing inequality. For instance, AI-generated content may marginalize certain communities by underrepresenting them or portraying them negatively, leading to social harm and reinforcing systemic discrimination.

Organizations must commit to comprehensive bias audits, regularly updating training datasets, implementing fairness constraints, and involving diverse stakeholders in model development and evaluation.

These are just some examples of the potential risks and issues associated with generative AI. Furthermore, it is important to acknowledge that similar legal and ethical implications are not limited to generative AI, but rather they apply to the broader landscape of AI, whose applications have always been raising some concerns (for example, privacy considerations when it comes to face recognition).

However, the extremely rapid evolvement and – most importantly – adoption of generative AI tools has highlighted the pressing need for organizations, policymakers, and developers to collaborate to craft robust governance frameworks that address the unique challenges posed by generative AI. This involves adopting standards for transparent data sourcing, obtaining explicit permissions for copyrighted content, implementing strict verification procedures to counter misinformation, and working closely with regulators to establish legal guardrails. It also demands that AI practitioners remain continuously vigilant in updating models, refining algorithms, and engaging with interdisciplinary experts to ensure that generative AI serves as a force for innovation and positive societal impact, rather than a source of harm or ethical compromise.

Summary

In this chapter, we have explored the exciting world of generative AI and its various domains of application, including image generation, text generation, music generation, and video generation. We learned how generative AI models such as ChatGPT and DALL-E, trained by OpenAI, use DL techniques to learn patterns in large datasets and generate new content that is both novel and coherent. We also discussed the history of generative AI, its origins, and the current status of research on it.

The goal of this chapter was to provide a solid foundation in the basics of generative AI and to inspire you to explore this fascinating field further.

In the next chapter, we will focus on one of the most promising technologies available on the market today, ChatGPT. We will go through the research behind it and its development by OpenAI, the architecture of its model, and the main use cases it can address as of today.

References

- Generative adversarial networks: `https://arxiv.org/abs/1406.2661`
- Analyzing and improving the image quality of StyleGAN: `https://arxiv.org/abs/1912.04958`
- Video-to-video synthesis: `https://arxiv.org/abs/1808.06601`
- A deep generative model trifecta: Three advances that work towards harnessing large-scale power: `https://www.microsoft.com/en-us/research/blog/a-deep-generative-model-trifecta-three-advances-that-work-towards-harnessing- large-scale-power/`
- Vid2Vid: `https://tcwang0509.github.io/vid2vid/`

- LLaMA: Open and Efficient Foundation Language Models: `https://arxiv.org/pdf/2302.13971`

- Introducing Phi-3: `https://azure.microsoft.com/en-us/blog/introducing-phi-3-redefining-whats-possible-with-slms/`

Get This Book's PDF Version and Exclusive Extras

UNLOCK NOW

Scan the QR code (or go to `packtpub.com/unlock`). Search for this book by name, confirm the edition, and then follow the steps on the page.

Note: *Keep your invoice handy. Purchases made directly from Packt don't require one.*

2

OpenAI and ChatGPT: Beyond the Market Hype

This chapter provides an overview of OpenAI and its most notable development – ChatGPT – highlighting its history, technology, and capabilities.

We will also explore OpenAI's achievements in the field of Generative AI, beyond ChatGPT – from speech-to-text models to image generation – which will provide you with a broader awareness of the state of the art of some of the most advanced Generative AI technologies.

More specifically, we will cover the following topics:

- What is OpenAI?
- An overview of OpenAI model families
- Getting started with ChatGPT

By the end of this chapter, you will have a solid foundation on ChatGPT and how to use it and its technological capabilities, as well as a wired understanding of OpenAI's model families.

Technical requirements

To be able to test the example in this chapter, you will need an OpenAI account.

You may refer to the *Creating an OpenAI account* section if you need any help.

What is OpenAI?

OpenAI is a research organization founded in 2015 by Elon Musk, Sam Altman, Greg Brockman, Ilya Sutskever, Wojciech Zaremba, and John Schulman. As stated on the OpenAI web page, its mission is *"to ensure that Artificial General Intelligence (AGI) [...] benefits all of humanity"* (https://openai.com/index/planning-for-agi-and-beyond/. In recent years, OpenAI has formed strategic partnerships to further its research and deployment efforts. Notably, Microsoft has invested significantly in OpenAI, providing resources to support the development of advanced AI technologies. OpenAI continues to be a leading entity in AI research, striving to balance innovation with ethical considerations to ensure that the development of AI technologies aligns with the broader interests of society.

Artificial general intelligence (AGI) is a conceptual type of AI capable of comprehending, learning, and utilizing knowledge across diverse tasks with a proficiency comparable to human intelligence. In contrast to narrow AI systems, which are tailored for specific purposes, AGI would demonstrate human-like cognitive adaptability, allowing it to perform any intellectual task that a human can accomplish.

The origins of OpenAI

Since its establishment, OpenAI has focused its research on **deep reinforcement learning** (DRL), a subset of **machine learning** (ML) that combines **reinforcement learning** (RL) with **deep neural networks** (DNNs).

RL is an ML paradigm where an agent learns to make decisions by interacting with an environment. The agent receives feedback in the form of rewards or penalties based on its actions and aims to maximize cumulative rewards over time.

Deep RL is the integration of RL and deep neural networks, or DNNs (the latter is a type of artificial neural network with multiple layers between the input and output).

In DRL, DNNs are used to approximate value functions, policies, or models of the environment, enabling agents to handle complex, high-dimensional state and action spaces. By combining the strengths of RL and DNNs, DRL has been successfully applied to tasks such as playing video games, robotic control, and autonomous driving, where traditional methods struggle with scalability and feature extraction.

OpenAI's first contribution in that field traces back to 2016 when the company released OpenAI Gym, a toolkit for researchers to develop and test RL algorithms.

The primary goal of Gym (now called Gymnasium) was to standardize how environments are defined in AI research, making published research more easily reproducible and providing users with a simple interface for interacting with these environments. OpenAI kept researching and contributing in that field, but its most notable achievements are related to generative models – **Generative Pre-trained Transformers (GPTs)**.

A **GPT** is an advanced AI model designed to process and generate human-like text. It operates by learning patterns, structures, and context from a vast dataset of written language during its training phase. This training enables GPT to predict and generate coherent and contextually relevant text, allowing it to understand and respond to prompts in a highly natural way.

The "Pre-trained" aspect refers to its initial training on a broad range of language data, equipping it with a general understanding of grammar, syntax, semantics, and various styles of communication. The "Generative" capability means it can create new text that aligns with the given input, rather than simply analyzing or classifying data.

The "Transformer" aspect refers to a specific architectural design, featuring an advanced mechanism – called "attention" – to efficiently understand relationships between words and phrases, enabling it to handle complex language tasks with a high degree of accuracy.

The emergence of ChatGPT

OpenAI introduced their first GPT model in their paper *Improving Language Understanding by Generative Pre-Training* and christened it **GPT-1**, designed to demonstrate that a language model could be pre-trained on a large corpus of text and then fine-tuned for specific tasks, achieving significant improvements in various **natural language processing** (NLP) applications.

Fine-tuning is the process of adapting a pre-trained model to a new task. In fine-tuning, the parameters of the pre-trained model are altered, either by adjusting the existing parameters or by adding new parameters so that they fit the data for the new task. This is done by training the model on a smaller labeled dataset that is specific to the new task. The key idea behind fine-tuning is to leverage the knowledge learned from the pre-trained model and fine-tune it to the new task, rather than training a model from scratch.

Soon after, OpenAI researchers released, in 2019, its successor, GPT-2. This version of the GPT was trained on a corpus called **WebText**, which at the time contained slightly over 8 million documents with a total of 40 GB of text from URLs shared in Reddit submissions with at least 3 upvotes. It had 1.2 billion parameters – ten times as many as its predecessor.

In the context of artificial neural networks – including GPTs – **parameter** refer to the internal variables that a model learns and adjusts during training. These parameters are crucial as they define how input data is processed through the network's layers to produce the desired output.

Then, in 2020, OpenAI first announced and then released GPT-3, which, with its 175 billion parameters (roughly 21 times the entire population of Earth!), dramatically improved benchmark results over GPT-2. It was with the GPT-3 model – more precisely, with its fine-tuned version called GPT-3.5 – that we entered the era of ChatGPT in November 2022 (at its first release, ChatGPT was powered by GPT-3.5).

From that moment to today, OpenAI has released many new versions of its GPT series: GPT-4, GPT-4 Turbo, GPT-4 Vision (the first multimodal model), and GPT-4o, where the "o" stands for "Omni," referring to its multimodal capabilities. At the time of writing this book (January 2025), the latest OpenAI chat models are part of the o1 family, which feature advanced reasoning capabilities that make them suitable for complex tasks or mathematical problems.

Starting from the next section and in the upcoming chapters, we will mainly focus on OpenAI chat models available in ChatGPT with some examples of image generation as well.

An overview of OpenAI model families

Over the last few years, OpenAI has made huge advancements in the field of model development, releasing newer model versions at great speed. In this section, we will look at the main models divided by domain:

- **Language models**: OpenAI's GPTs are advanced language models designed to generate text based on given prompts. They are versatile and can be used for various NLP tasks, such as text completion, translation, summarization, and coding. This is the field where OpenAI demonstrates outstanding performance, thanks to its flagship model family: the GPTs. Since November 2022, when ChatGPT was launched, OpenAI has released the following models:

  - GPT-3.5-turbo, the model behind the first version of ChatGPT
  - GPT-4 (the first model to be able to process images as well) and GPT-4 Turbo (optimized for chats and assistants)
  - GPT-4o and GPT-4o mini (different in the number of parameters trained), where the letter "o" stands for "Omni," meaning that the model can receive diverse data as input (text, images, voice)

- o1 and o1 mini (different in the number of parameters), a model series that represents a significant advancement, particularly in enhanced reasoning capabilities

- o3 series, built upon the capabilities of its predecessor (the o1 series), which has demonstrated superior performance on benchmarks (`https://beebom.com/openai-unveils-o3-model-cracks-arc-agi-benchmark/`) and is very promising for future applications

- **Image models**: OpenAI's image models, like DALL-E, are designed to generate and manipulate images from textual descriptions. DALL-E models can create highly detailed and imaginative visuals, enabling users to produce unique artwork, design concepts, and more. For instance, DALL-E 3 (the latest version of the model at the time of writing) is capable of creating intricate and creative images based on detailed prompts, pushing the boundaries of what AI can do in the field of visual arts. These models are particularly useful in creative industries, digital marketing, and any field that benefits from high-quality, custom visuals (we are going to cover DALL-E in detail in *Chapter 8*).

- **Text-to-speech and speech-to-text models**: OpenAI's Whisper is a **speech-to-text (STT)** system. It was introduced on September 21, 2022. Trained on 680,000 hours of multilingual and multitasking data, it excels in transcribing speech across various languages and translating non-English speech into English. In addition to that, OpenAI also developed **text-to-speech (TTS)** models to convert written text into spoken language, providing high-quality audio outputs that are intelligible, expressive, and natural-sounding, making them suitable for a wide range of applications, from customer service bots to educational tools.

  - **STT** technology converts spoken language into written text. It is commonly used in applications such as transcription services, voice assistants, and accessibility tools. Examples include converting dictated words into text on a computer or transcribing meeting recordings.

  - **TTS** technology converts written text into spoken words. It is widely used for accessibility (e.g., screen readers for visually impaired users), interactive voice response systems, and content narration. Examples include digital assistants reading messages or books aloud.

These models are helpful for creating voice assistants, improving accessibility for visually impaired users, and generating automated announcements.

- **Text-to-video models:** With the announcement of Sora, OpenAI revealed its cutting-edge text-to-video model capable of generating realistic and imaginative video scenes from text descriptions. By adapting techniques from DALL-E and incorporating transformers, Sora can create high-fidelity videos up to one minute long. It excels in maintaining 3D consistency, object permanence, and simulating interactions within videos. While still facing challenges like accurately modeling complex physics, Sora holds significant potential for creative industries, offering new possibilities in video production and storytelling.

- **Embeddings models:** Embedding models from OpenAI transform text into numerical representations called vectors (or embeddings) that capture the semantic meaning and are projected in a multi-dimensional vector space.

  In *Chapter 1*, we explored the role of embedding in **retrieval augmented generation (RAG)** scenarios and, more broadly, how this pattern is reshaping knowledge mining.

  OpenAI's embedding models, **text-embedding-ada-002** and **text-embedding-3-large**, offer state-of-the-art performance in tasks such as text similarity, text search, and code search by creating dense vector representations of text. These embeddings allow for the efficient and effective comparison of large text datasets, improving search accuracy and relevance.

- **Moderation models:** OpenAI's moderation models are designed to detect and filter out inappropriate, harmful, or unsafe content in text. These models are integral to maintaining safe and respectful online environments by identifying potentially offensive or harmful language. The latest moderation model, released in September 2024, is **omni-moderation-latest**, built on top of GPT-4o, and it is capable of filtering both text and images. It helps developers and companies enforce community guidelines and prevent the spread of harmful content, thereby promoting safer digital interactions.

Some of these models – specifically, language, image generation, and TTS/STT – can be used in ChatGPT, probably the most popular product that OpenAI has released as a consumer application. We are going to cover it in the next section.

Getting started with ChatGPT

In November 2022, OpenAI released the web preview of its conversational AI system, ChatGPT, to the general public. This generated a huge amount of hype among subject matter experts, organizations, and general users – to the point that, after only 5 days, the service reached 1 million users!

Before writing about ChatGPT, I will let it introduce itself, using a snapshot taken a few days after the launch:

I'm writing a paragraph about you, your history and what you can do. Could you introduce yourself to my reader?

Of course! I am ChatGPT, a language model developed by OpenAI. I was trained on a massive corpus of text data and designed to perform a variety of natural language processing tasks, such as text generation, conversation modeling, sentiment analysis, and question answering. I am built on the transformer architecture, which allows me to effectively process sequences of words and learn the relationships between them.

I have been trained on a diverse range of texts, including web pages, news articles, books, and more, which enables me to have a broad knowledge base and understand a wide range of topics. My abilities have been honed through deep learning techniques and ongoing updates from the OpenAI team.

I can be interacted with in real-time and respond to questions, engage in conversations, or generate text based on a given prompt. I can also be integrated into various applications, such as chatbots, content creation, and customer service, to enhance their natural language processing capabilities.

Overall, I am an advanced language model that can assist with a wide range of NLP tasks and provide human-like responses. I am continually evolving and improving, and I am eager to demonstrate my capabilities to help solve your NLP needs.

Figure 2.1: ChatGPT introducing itself in November 2022

It is important to note that ChatGPT is not a **large language model (LLM)** by itself, but rather an application through which users can interact with the underlying models. In fact, ChatGPT is, at its core, an AI-powered chatbot designed to simulate human-like conversations. It supports a variety of tasks, including writing, coding, and providing information on diverse topics. Powered by cutting-edge language models developed by OpenAI, ChatGPT has progressed through iterations like GPT-3, GPT-4, GPT-4o, and o1, continually improving its ability to understand and generate natural language.

In addition to the integration of the latest and greatest models, ChatGPT also extended its capabilities by incorporating external tools (like web search) and becoming an actual developer platform to build your own "GPTs," but we will cover all those topics in the upcoming chapters.

As mentioned earlier, the first release of ChatGPT was built on top of an advanced language model – a fine-tuned version of GPT-3 specifically optimized for handling conversations. This fine-tuned version is called GPT-3.5 Turbo. The optimization process involved **reinforcement learning with human feedback (RLHF)** (https://arxiv.org/pdf/2009.01325), a technique that leverages human input to train the model to exhibit desirable conversational behaviors.

We can define RLHF as an ML approach where an algorithm learns to perform a task by receiving feedback from a human. The algorithm is trained to make decisions that maximize a reward signal provided by the human, and the human provides additional feedback to improve the algorithm's performance. This approach is useful when the task is too complex for traditional programming or when the desired outcome is difficult to specify in advance.

The relevant differentiator here is that ChatGPT has been trained with humans in the loop so that it is aligned with its users. By incorporating RLHF, ChatGPT has been designed to better understand and respond to human language in a natural and engaging way.

Let's now see how to start using ChatGPT.

Creating an OpenAI account

ChatGPT is available as a free application that anyone can use; however, since February 2023, OpenAI announced a series of paid programs, offering subscribers several advantages, including access to the latest models, the fastest response time, a great set of plugins, and the possibility to create your own Assistant in the GPTs playground. You can find an overview of the pricing at openai.com/chatgpt/pricing/. In the upcoming chapters, I'll be using the Plus version, but the majority of the hands-on examples can be replicated with the free version as well.

Regardless of the version you choose, to follow along with the upcoming sections you will need an OpenAI account. To create an account on OpenAI, follow these steps:

1. Open a web browser and go to the OpenAI website at https://platform.openai.com/signup/.

2. Provide your email address and create a password.

3. Once your account is created, you can start using the free version of ChatGPT.

ChatGPT Plus tour

Let's have a quick tour of the ChatGPT user interface at the time of writing:

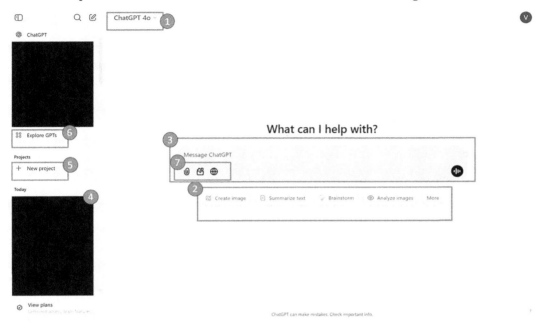

Figure 2.2: Landing page of ChatGPT at chatgpt.com

Let's explore each numbered section in *Figure 2.2*:

1. You can decide on the model to use behind ChatGPT. In my case, I have set GPT-4o, which is only available with a paid subscription. This is the model we are going to use throughout this book.

2. A set of pre-built prompts is proposed to help you familiarize yourself with the application.

3. The text box is the place where you can input your prompt. Note that there is a small voice icon in the right-hand corner: it indicates the possibility of interacting with the model with your voice rather than typing.

4. On the left-hand sidebar, you can see the list of previous chats (mine are covered) you had with ChatGPT. This is an extremely useful tool, since in each chat, through the various rounds of interactions you had with the model, you created a context ChatGPT is aware of. This means that, if you want to continue a previously started conversation, you can open the related chat and start talking with the model without describing the whole scenario again.

5. A nice, recently added feature of ChatGPT Plus is the possibility of having Projects, which offer a streamlined way to organize files and chats for personal use, making it easier to manage tasks that span multiple conversations. By keeping chats, files, and custom instructions all in one place, Projects help maintain order and focus.

6. ChatGPT Plus offers the possibility of creating GPTs, which are personalized assistants you can tailor for specific functions. You can decide to keep your GPT private or publish it in the GPTs store, where anyone can use and rate it. We are going to cover GPTs in *Chapter 9*.

7. Finally, ChatGPT in its Plus version now offers a set of tools that you can leverage while interacting with the model.

At the time of writing this book (January 2025), the provided tools are:

- **Attach files** to analyze custom file uploaded by the user
- **Web Search** to integrate ChatGPT's model knowledge with up-to-date information from the web
- DALL-E to create images based on a query in natural language
- The Canvas feature to provide a side-by-side workspace, enabling users to collaboratively draft, edit, and receive feedback on writing and coding projects alongside ChatGPT

Throughout this book, we will leverage ChatGPT Plus to showcase the capabilities of the latest models and features; nevertheless, the majority of the examples that we will cover can be achieved with the free version of ChatGPT as well (which is currently powered by GPT-3.5 Turbo).

The ongoing developments and improvements in ChatGPT's architecture and training methods promise to push the boundaries of language processing even further.

The art of the possible with ChatGPT

Starting from *Chapter 4*, we will cover many practical examples of how ChatGPT can be leveraged for both personal productivity and domain-specific tasks (like research, marketing, and coding). However, before landing there, let's have a glimpse of the art of the possible with ChatGPT, starting with an example of the o1 model. A distinctive feature of the o1 models is their ability to reveal their "thinking" process. When you submit a query, a "thinking" indicator appears, and by clicking on it, you can view the steps the model took to arrive at its response. This is particularly helpful for gaining insight into how the model handles complex queries.

Image understanding and generation

The latest models available in ChatGPT are multimodal, meaning that they are capable of receiving diverse data (text and images).

In the context of Generative AI, **multimodality** refers to the ability of AI systems to handle, comprehend, and produce content across various forms of data, or modalities, including text, images, audio, and video. This functionality allows AI to integrate and interpret diverse inputs, resulting in more comprehensive and contextually relevant outputs.

Let's consider the following example:

can you tell me what's happening in this picture?

This image shows a glass of water with a layer of oil on top. Here's what's happening:

- **Density Difference**: Oil is less dense than water, so it floats on top. This is due to the molecular structure of oil, which makes it less compact than water molecules.

- **Non-Mixing Liquids**: Oil and water are immiscible, meaning they do not mix. This is because water is polar (its molecules have a partial charge), while oil is non-polar, so their molecules don't attract each other.

- **Surface Tension**: The boundary between the oil and water is clear, demonstrating the difference in their properties.

This is a common demonstration in science to explain concepts such as density, polarity, and immiscibility. ↓

Figure 2.3: Image understanding and text generation

In this case, I asked ChatGPT to describe the provided picture, and the model was able to generate a detailed and scientific explanation of the reason for the two liquids not mixing with each other. This implies a deep understanding of the picture, as well as a general knowledge of physics.

Based on this first analysis, we can also go ahead and ask it to evaluate additional scenarios:

what happens if I add vinegar?

 If you add vinegar to the glass containing water and oil, here's what happens:

1. **Vinegar's Properties:**

   - Vinegar is primarily water with a small amount of acetic acid. It is polar, just like water.

   - Since vinegar is denser than oil, it will sink through the oil layer and mix with the water at the bottom.

2. **Three Layers Might Form:**

   - If the vinegar and water do not mix immediately (e.g., due to gentle pouring), you may temporarily see three layers: oil at the top, vinegar in the middle, and water at the bottom. Eventually, vinegar and water will fully mix because they are both polar.

3. **Shake the Mixture:**

   - If you shake the glass, the oil will break into tiny droplets and form an emulsion (a cloudy mixture). However, this emulsion is unstable, and the oil will eventually separate back to the top because oil and vinegar do not mix chemically.

4. **Enhanced Separation:**

   - Over time, you'll observe the oil floating on top of a water-vinegar solution because the oil remains immiscible with both.

This experiment demonstrates density, polarity, and immiscibility even further, along with the formation and breakdown of emulsions!

◁》 ⊡ ⛬ ⛬ ↻⌄   ↓

Figure 2.4: Going deeper into evaluation

These are just a few examples of the current capabilities of ChatGPT. Once again, it is important to mention that ChatGPT can be consumed with different models, and some of them don't exhibit all the available features (for example, GPT-3.5 doesn't take images as input). The decision of which model to use highly depends on the kind of task you want ChatGPT to address.

Mathematical thinking

Originally, LLMs used to struggle when it came to solving mathematical tasks. Nevertheless, OpenAI's o1 model series, introduced in September 2024, has demonstrated significant advancements in mathematical reasoning compared to its predecessor, GPT-4o. For example, the o1 model (while still in preview) achieved a success rate of 83% in the **International Mathematics Olympiad (IMO)** qualifying exam (`https://openai.com/index/introducing-openai-o1-preview/`), a substantial improvement over GPT-4o's 13%.

Let's consider the following example:

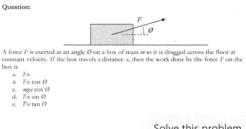

Question:

A force F is exerted at an angle $\emptyset$ on a box of mass m as it is dragged across the floor at constant velocity. If the box travels a distance x, then the work done by the force F on the box is

   a. Fx
   b. $Fx \cos \emptyset$
   c. $mgx \cos \emptyset$
   d. $Fx \sin \emptyset$
   e. $Fx \tan \emptyset$

Solve this problem

Thought about image problem solving for 13 seconds

To find the work done by the force F on the box, recall that work is given by

$$W = \left(\text{component of the force along the direction of motion}\right) \times \left(\text{distance moved}\right).$$

Here, the box is moving horizontally. Since F is applied at an angle θ above the horizontal, its horizontal component is

$$F_x = F \cos \theta.$$

Hence the work done over a horizontal displacement x is

$$W = \left(F \cos \theta\right) \cdot x = Fx \cos \theta.$$

Thus the correct answer is

$$\boxed{Fx \cos \theta.}$$

Figure 2.5: Mathematical ability of ChatGPT

As you can see, the model was not only able to read and understand the provided image but also correctly addressed the problem with smaller reasoning steps.

Analytical skills

In the previous example, we provided the model with an image, but we can go further and attach a more complex, structured file to be quantitatively analyzed. For example, we can attach to ChatGPT (powered by GPT-4o) a `.xls` file and ask it to perform some financial analysis (in my case, I used a sample file available here: `https://learn.microsoft.com/en-us/power-bi/create-reports/sample-financial-download`).

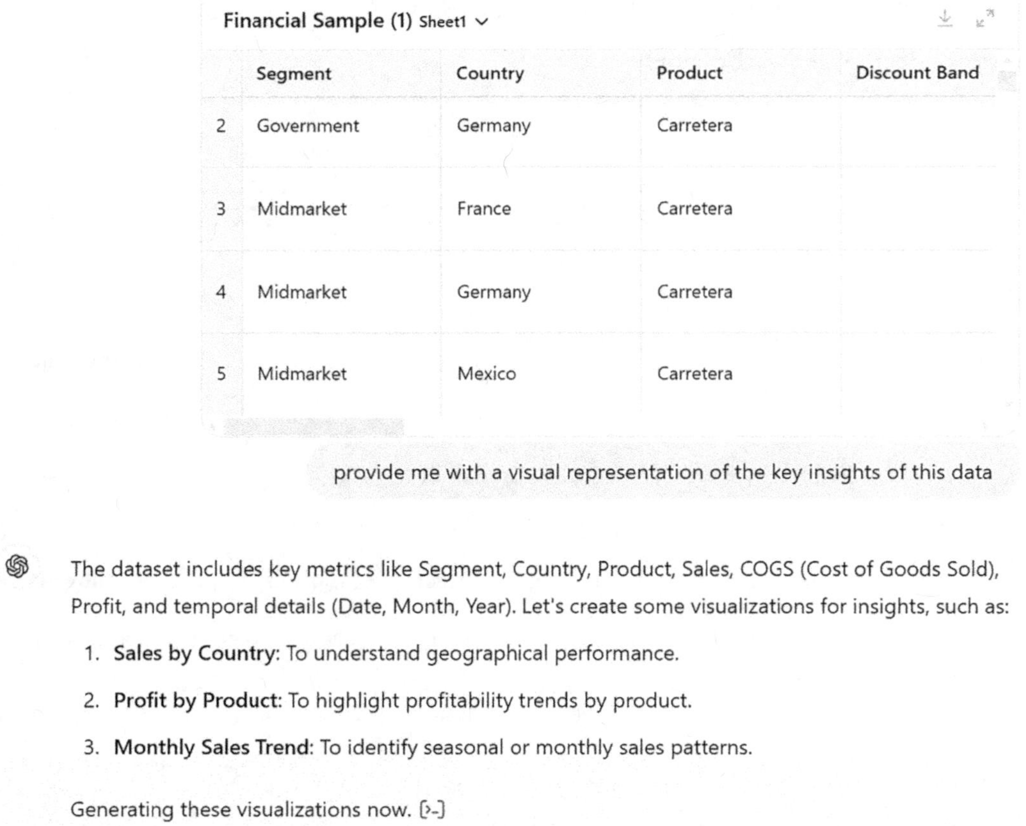

	Segment	Country	Product	Discount Band
2	Government	Germany	Carretera	
3	Midmarket	France	Carretera	
4	Midmarket	Germany	Carretera	
5	Midmarket	Mexico	Carretera	

Financial Sample (1) Sheet1 ∨

provide me with a visual representation of the key insights of this data

The dataset includes key metrics like Segment, Country, Product, Sales, COGS (Cost of Goods Sold), Profit, and temporal details (Date, Month, Year). Let's create some visualizations for insights, such as:

1. **Sales by Country**: To understand geographical performance.

2. **Profit by Product**: To highlight profitability trends by product.

3. **Monthly Sales Trend**: To identify seasonal or monthly sales patterns.

Generating these visualizations now. [>_]

Figure 2.6: Analytical prowess exhibited by ChatGPT

In addition to the above answer in text format, ChatGPT can also generate graphs:

The column name for "Sales" includes a leading space. I'll fix this and proceed with the visualizations. (>-)

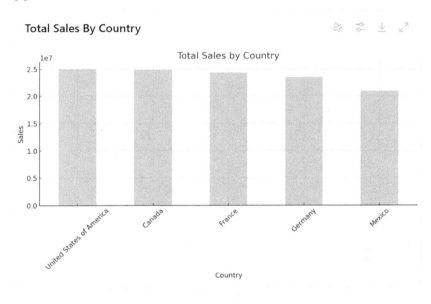

Figure 2.7: Generating graphs using ChatGPT

Note that, to execute this particular task, ChatGPT leveraged a feature called Code Interpreter, which allows it to generate Python code to analyze data and run it directly against the uploaded file. An important thing to note is that you can visualize the generated code by clicking on the [>_] icon:

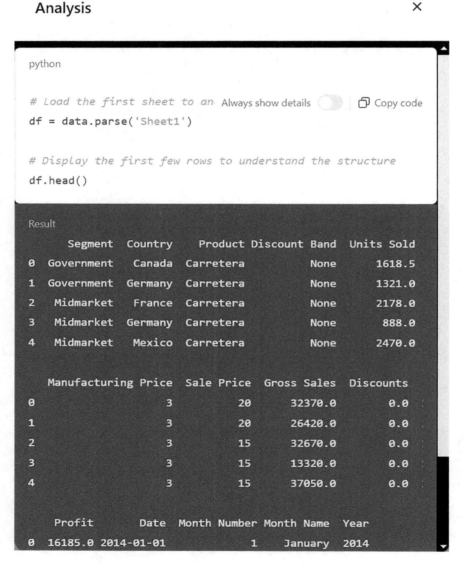

Figure 2.8: Code Interpreter

The Code Interpreter feature is extremely powerful and versatile when it comes to structured data, and it can also be leveraged to import and train advanced ML models to then make predictions on data.

Summary

In this chapter, we went through the history of OpenAI, its research fields, and the latest developments, up to ChatGPT. We also had a glimpse of the art of the possible with ChatGPT, from reasoning over complex images to executing analytical tasks.

In the next chapter, we begin *Part 2* of this book, where we will see ChatGPT in action in various domains and how to unlock its potential. You will learn how to get the highest value from ChatGPT by properly designing your prompts, how to boost your daily productivity, and how it can be a great project assistant for any consumer.

References

- Radford, A. & Narasimhan, K. (2018). *Improving language understanding by generative pre-training.* `https://cdn.openai.com/research-covers/language-unsupervised/language_understanding_paper.pdf`

- Vaswani, A., Shazeer, N., Parmar, N., Uszkoreit, J., Jones, L., Gomez, A. N., Kaiser, L., & Polosukhin, I. (2017). *Attention Is All You Need.* arXiv. `https://doi.org/10.48550/arXiv.1706.03762`

- OpenAI. *Fine-Tuning Guide.* OpenAI platform documentation. `https://platform.openai.com/docs/guides/fine-tuning`

Subscribe for a free eBook

New frameworks, evolving architectures, research drops, production breakdowns—AI_Distilled filters the noise into a weekly briefing for engineers and researchers working hands-on with LLMs and GenAI systems. Subscribe now and receive a free eBook, along with weekly insights that help you stay focused and informed. Subscribe at `https://packt.link/8Oz6Y` or scan the QR code below.

Part 2

ChatGPT in Action

In this part, we will start our journey through the landscape of new possibilities that ChatGPT brings to the market. From daily productivity to domain-specific use cases, you will get familiar with the capabilities of ChatGPT and how it can be used as a reasoning engine for various tasks.

Once we have explored the technical prerequisites, this part jumps into an overview of the ChatGPT user interface, including chat management and question modifications.

It then moves toward one of the most important elements required to get the best out of ChatGPT and, in general, out of LLMs: the concept of prompt design. Here, you will get familiar with powerful techniques to make ChatGPT work at its best, including recent developments and research papers about powerful techniques.

This part also focuses on concrete examples of how to use ChatGPT in operative activities, starting with daily productivity and moving to more domain-specific disciplines, such as marketing, development, research, and visual creativity. Here, you will be able to not only learn about the use cases ChatGPT can cover in those domains but also see concrete examples to replicate them on your own.

Finally, you will see how to further tailor ChatGPT to your specific use cases, leveraging GPTs and the GPT store.

This part contains the following chapters:

- *Chapter 3, Understanding Prompt Engineering*
- *Chapter 4, Boosting Day-to-Day Productivity with ChatGPT*
- *Chapter 5, Developing the Future with ChatGPT*
- *Chapter 6, Mastering Marketing with ChatGPT*

- *Chapter 7, Research Reinvented with ChatGPT*
- *Chapter 8, Unleashing Creativity Visually with ChatGPT*
- *Chapter 9, Exploring GPTs*

3

Understanding Prompt Engineering

In the previous chapters, we mentioned the term **prompt** several times while referring to user input in ChatGPT and **large language models (LLMs)** in general.

Since prompts have a massive impact on LLMs' performance, prompt engineering is a crucial activity to get the most out of your GenAI tool. In fact, there are several techniques that can be implemented not only to refine your LLMs' responses but also to reduce risks associated with hallucinations and biases.

In this chapter, we are going to cover the emerging techniques in the field of prompt engineering, starting from basic approaches up to advanced frameworks. More specifically, we will go through the following topics:

- What is prompt engineering?
- Exploring zero-, one-, and few-shot learning
- Principles of prompt engineering
- Looking at some advanced techniques
- Ethical considerations to avoid bias

By the end of this chapter, you will have the foundations to build functional and solid prompts to interact with ChatGPT and, more broadly, with GenAI applications.

Technical requirements

You'll need an OpenAI account. You can use the free ChatGPT version to run this chapter's examples.

What is prompt engineering?

Before explaining what prompt engineering is, let's start by defining a prompt.

A **prompt** is text input that guides the behavior of an LLM to generate an output. For example, whenever we interact with ChatGPT, asking a question or giving an instruction, that input text is a prompt. In the context of LLMs and LLM-powered applications, we can distinguish two types of prompts:

- The first type is a prompt that the user writes and sends to the LLM. For example, a prompt might be "Give me the recipe for Lasagna Bolognese," or "Generate a workout plan to run a marathon."

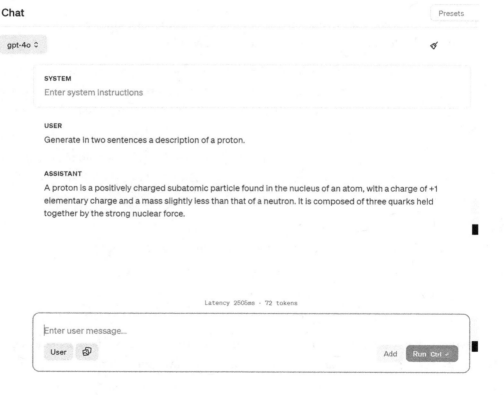

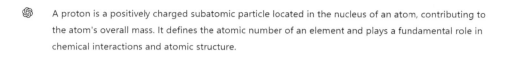

Generate in two sentences a description of a proton

A proton is a positively charged subatomic particle located in the nucleus of an atom, contributing to the atom's overall mass. It defines the atomic number of an element and plays a fundamental role in chemical interactions and atomic structure.

Figure 3.1: An example of a user's prompt

You will hear this referred to simply as a **prompt**, a **query**, or **user input**.

- The second type is a prompt that instructs the model to behave in a certain way regardless of the user's query. This refers to the set of instructions in natural language that the model is provided with so that it behaves in a certain way when interacting with end users. You can think about that as a sort of "backend" of your LLM, something that will be handled by the application developers rather than the final users.

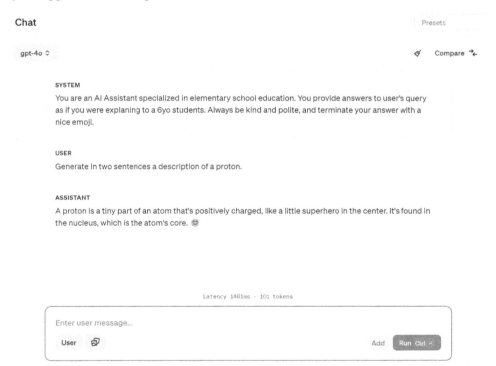

You are an AI Assistant specialized in primary school education. You provide answers to user's query as if you were explaining to a 6-years-old student. Always be kind and polite. Terminate your answer with a nice emoji.

Generate in two sentences a description of a proton

A proton is a tiny part of an atom, like a little building block, that has a positive charge, kind of like a plus sign. It lives in the center of the atom, called the nucleus, and helps decide what kind of thing the atom will be, like gold or oxygen. ✳

Figure 3.2: An example of a system message

We refer to this type of prompt as a **system message**.

Prompt engineering is the process of designing effective prompts that elicit high-quality and relevant outputs from LLMs. Prompt engineering requires creativity, an understanding of the LLM, and a clear understanding of the objective you want to achieve.

Prompt constructions

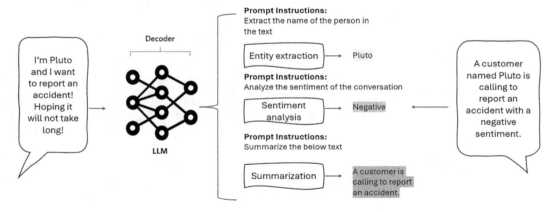

Figure 3.3: Example of prompt engineering to specialize LLMs

Over the last few years, prompt engineering has become a brand-new discipline in itself, and this is a demonstration of the fact that interacting with those models requires a new set of skills and capabilities that did not exist before.

The *art of prompting* has become a top skill when it comes to building GenAI applications in enterprise scenarios; however, it can also be extremely useful for individual users who use ChatGPT or similar AI assistants in daily tasks, as it dramatically improves the quality and accuracy of results.

In the next sections, we are going to see some examples of how to build efficient, robust prompts leveraging ChatGPT.

Understanding zero-, one-, and few-shot learning

In the previous chapters, we mentioned how LLMs typically come in a pre-trained format. They have been trained on a huge amount of data and have had their (billions of) parameters configured accordingly.

However, this doesn't mean that those LLMs can't learn anymore. In *Chapter 2*, we learned the concept of fine-tuning. In the *Appendix*, too, we will see that one way to customize an OpenAI model and make it more capable of addressing specific tasks is by **fine-tuning**.

Fine-tuning is a proper training process that requires a training dataset, compute power, and some training time (depending on the amount of data and compute instances).

That is why it is worth testing another method for our LLMs to become more skilled in specific tasks: **shot learning.**

Definition

In the context of LLMs, **shot learning** refers to the model's ability to perform tasks with varying amounts of task-specific examples provided during inference. These shot-learning paradigms enable LLMs to adapt to new tasks with minimal to no additional training, enhancing their versatility and efficiency in natural language processing applications.

The idea is to let the model learn from simple examples rather than the entire dataset. Those examples are samples of the way we would like the model to respond so that the model not only learns the content but also the format, style, and taxonomy to use in its response.

Furthermore, shot learning occurs directly via the prompt (as we will see in the following scenarios), so the whole experience is less time-consuming and easier to perform.

The number of examples provided determines the level of shot learning we are referring to. In other words, we refer to zero-shot if no example is provided, one-shot if one example is provided, and few-shot if more than two examples are provided.

Let's focus on each of those scenarios.

Zero-shot learning

In this type of learning, the model is asked to perform a task for which it has not seen any training examples. The model must rely on prior knowledge or general information about the task to complete it. For example, a zero-shot-learning approach could be that of asking the model to generate a description, as defined in my prompt:

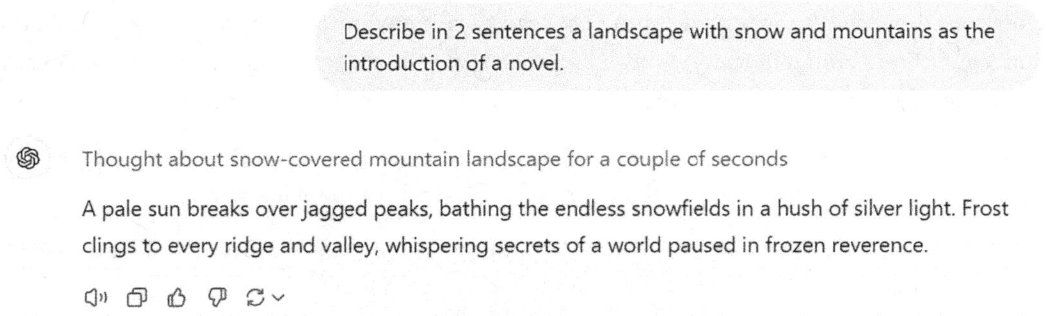

Describe in 2 sentences a landscape with snow and mountains as the introduction of a novel.

Thought about snow-covered mountain landscape for a couple of seconds

A pale sun breaks over jagged peaks, bathing the endless snowfields in a hush of silver light. Frost clings to every ridge and valley, whispering secrets of a world paused in frozen reverence.

Figure 3.4: Example of zero-shot learning

One-shot learning

In this type of learning, the model is given a single example of each new task it is asked to perform. The model must use its prior knowledge to generalize from this single example to perform the task. If we consider the preceding example, I could provide my model with a prompt-completion example before asking it to generate a new one:

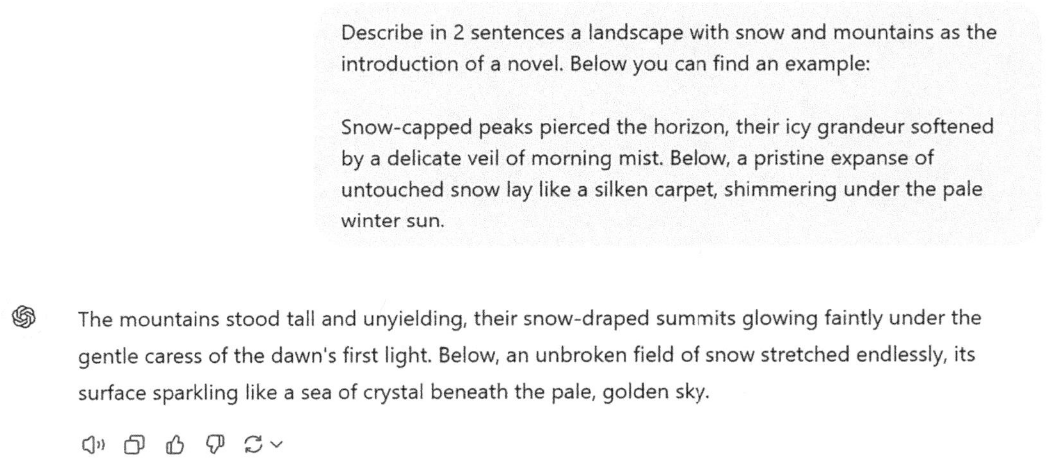

> Describe in 2 sentences a landscape with snow and mountains as the introduction of a novel. Below you can find an example:
>
> Snow-capped peaks pierced the horizon, their icy grandeur softened by a delicate veil of morning mist. Below, a pristine expanse of untouched snow lay like a silken carpet, shimmering under the pale winter sun.

The mountains stood tall and unyielding, their snow-draped summits glowing faintly under the gentle caress of the dawn's first light. Below, an unbroken field of snow stretched endlessly, its surface sparkling like a sea of crystal beneath the pale, golden sky.

Figure 3.5: Example of one-shot learning

As you can see from the previous screenshot, the model was able to generate an answer that mirrors the style and template of the example provided. The same reasoning applies when we provide multiple examples, as described in the next section.

Few-shot learning

In this type of learning, the model is given a small number of examples (typically between 2 and 5) of each new task it is asked to perform. The model must use its prior knowledge to generalize from these examples to perform the task. Let's continue with our example and provide the model with further examples:

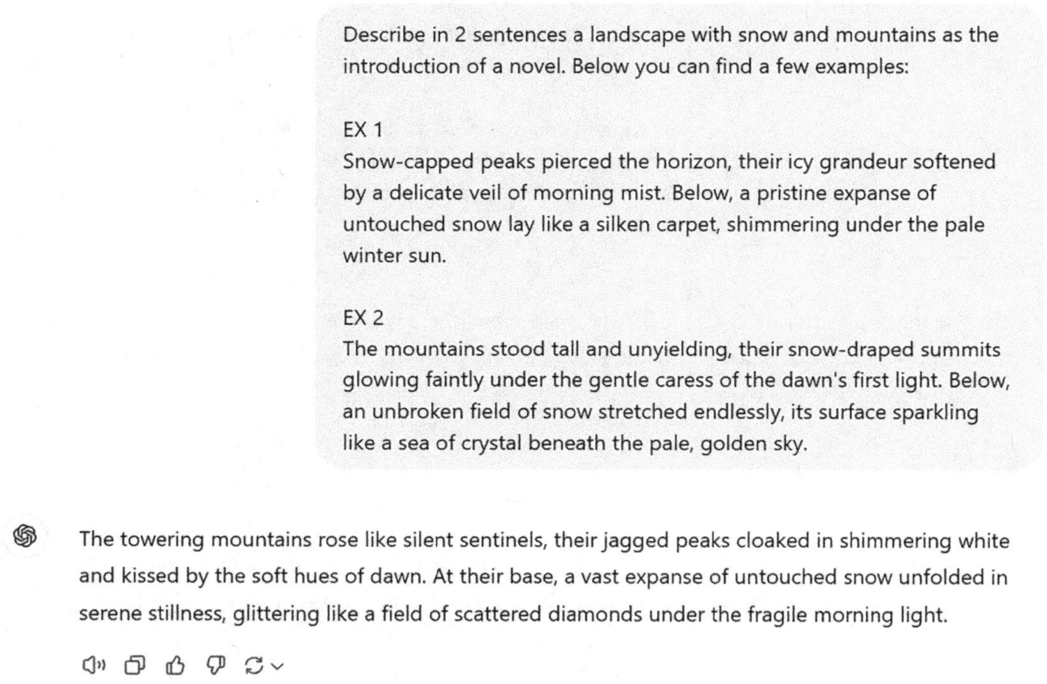

> Describe in 2 sentences a landscape with snow and mountains as the introduction of a novel. Below you can find a few examples:
>
> EX 1
> Snow-capped peaks pierced the horizon, their icy grandeur softened by a delicate veil of morning mist. Below, a pristine expanse of untouched snow lay like a silken carpet, shimmering under the pale winter sun.
>
> EX 2
> The mountains stood tall and unyielding, their snow-draped summits glowing faintly under the gentle caress of the dawn's first light. Below, an unbroken field of snow stretched endlessly, its surface sparkling like a sea of crystal beneath the pale, golden sky.

The towering mountains rose like silent sentinels, their jagged peaks cloaked in shimmering white and kissed by the soft hues of dawn. At their base, a vast expanse of untouched snow unfolded in serene stillness, glittering like a field of scattered diamonds under the fragile morning light.

◁ᵒ 🗗 👍 👎 ↻﹀

Figure 3.6: Example of few-shot learning with three examples

As mentioned previously, it is important to remember that these forms of learning are different from traditional supervised learning, as well as fine-tuning. In few-shot learning, the goal is to enable the model to learn from very few examples, and to generalize from those examples to new tasks. Plus, we are not modifying the architecture and knowledge of the model itself, meaning that the moment the user starts a new conversation, and the previous prompt is out of the context window, the model will "forget" about it.

Definition

Supervised learning is a type of machine learning where a model is trained on a labeled dataset, meaning the input data is paired with corresponding correct outputs (labels). The goal is for the model to learn the relationship between inputs and outputs so it can accurately predict the output for new, unseen data.

Now that we've learned how to let OpenAI models learn from examples, let's focus on how to properly define our prompt to make the model's response as accurate as possible.

Principles of prompt engineering

Traditionally, in the context of computing and data processing, the expression *garbage in, garbage out* has been used, meaning that the quality of output is determined by the quality of the input. If incorrect or poor-quality input (garbage) is entered into a system, the output will also be flawed or nonsensical (garbage).

When it comes to prompting, the story is similar: if we want accurate and relevant results from our LLMs, we need to provide high-quality input. However, building good prompts is not just about the quality of the response. In fact, we can construct good prompts to:

- Maximize the relevancy of an LLM's responses.
- Specify the type formatting and style of responses.
- Provide conversational context.
- Reduce inner LLMs' biases and improve fairness and inclusivity.
- Reduce hallucination.

Definition

In the context of LLMs, **hallucination** refers to the generation of text or responses that are factually incorrect, nonsensical, or not grounded in the training data. This occurs when an LLM produces confident-sounding but erroneous or fabricated information. For example, a user could ask an LLM: *"Who is the author of the book Invisible Cities?"* If the model responds with something like: *"Invisible Cities was written by Gabriel García Márquez."*, this is a hallucination because the correct author is *Italo Calvino*. The model generated an answer that sounds plausible but is factually incorrect.

Let's see some basic prompt engineering techniques in the following sections to achieve these results.

Clear instructions

The principle of giving clear instructions is to provide the model with enough information and guidance to perform the task correctly and efficiently. Clear instructions should include the following elements:

- The goal or objective of the task, such as "write a poem" or "summarize an article."
- The format or structure of the expected output, such as "use four lines with rhyming words" or "use bullet points with no more than 10 words each."
- The constraints or limitations of the task, such as "do not use any profanity" or "do not copy any text from the source."
- The context or background of the task, such as "the poem is about autumn" or "the article is from a scientific journal."

Let's say, for example, that we want our model to fetch any kind of instructions from text and return to us a tutorial in a bullet list. If there are no instructions in the provided text, the model should inform us about that. Let's see an example in ChatGPT:

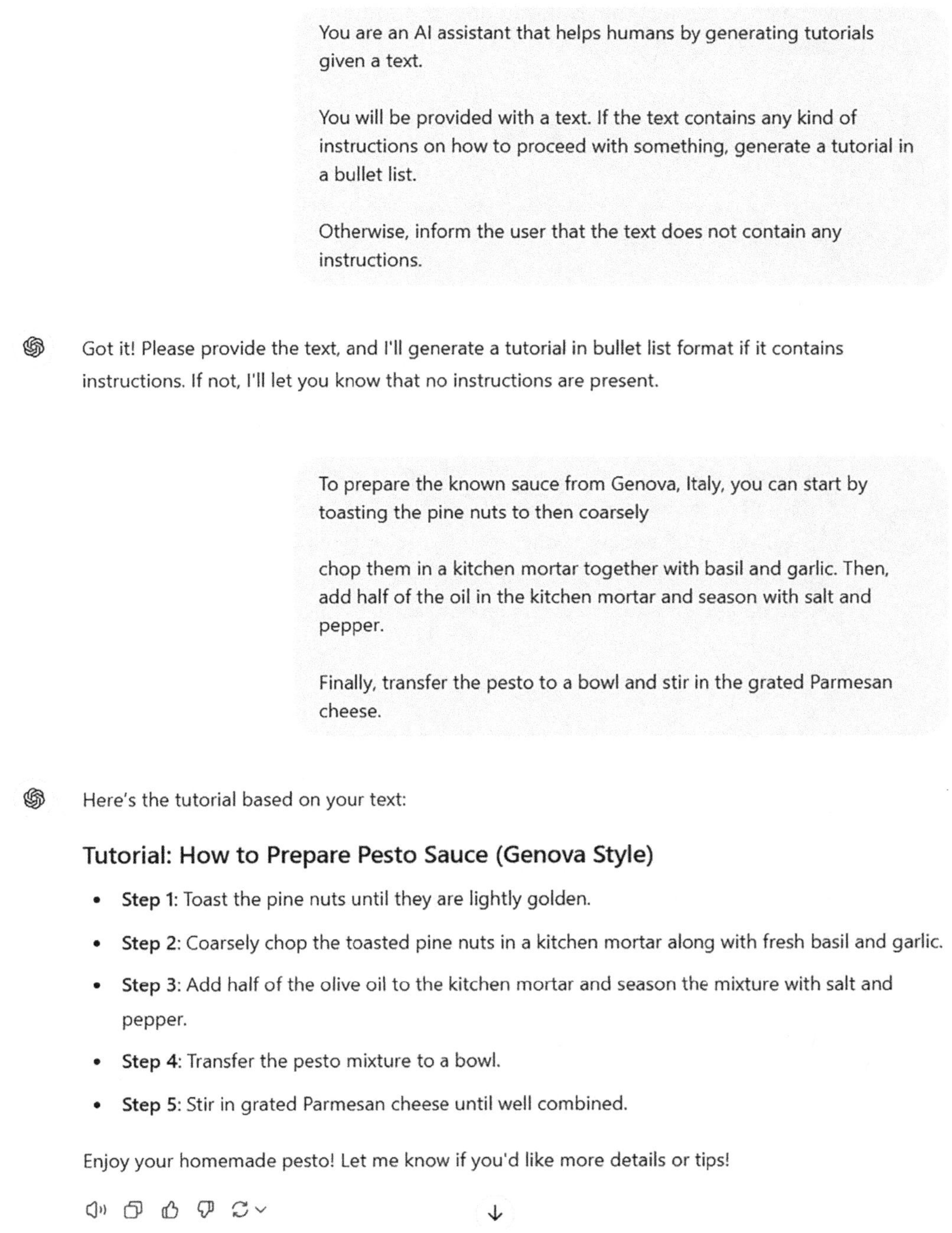

You are an AI assistant that helps humans by generating tutorials given a text.

You will be provided with a text. If the text contains any kind of instructions on how to proceed with something, generate a tutorial in a bullet list.

Otherwise, inform the user that the text does not contain any instructions.

Got it! Please provide the text, and I'll generate a tutorial in bullet list format if it contains instructions. If not, I'll let you know that no instructions are present.

To prepare the known sauce from Genova, Italy, you can start by toasting the pine nuts to then coarsely

chop them in a kitchen mortar together with basil and garlic. Then, add half of the oil in the kitchen mortar and season with salt and pepper.

Finally, transfer the pesto to a bowl and stir in the grated Parmesan cheese.

Here's the tutorial based on your text:

Tutorial: How to Prepare Pesto Sauce (Genova Style)

- **Step 1**: Toast the pine nuts until they are lightly golden.
- **Step 2**: Coarsely chop the toasted pine nuts in a kitchen mortar along with fresh basil and garlic.
- **Step 3**: Add half of the olive oil to the kitchen mortar and season the mixture with salt and pepper.
- **Step 4**: Transfer the pesto mixture to a bowl.
- **Step 5**: Stir in grated Parmesan cheese until well combined.

Enjoy your homemade pesto! Let me know if you'd like more details or tips!

Figure 3.7: Example of clear instructions in ChatGPT

Note that, if we pass the model other text that does not contain any instructions, it will be able to respond as we instructed it:

> I'm walking the dog on the beach

The text does not contain any instructions, so no tutorial can be generated. Let me know if you'd like assistance with something else!

◁) ⊡ 👍 👎 ⟳ ⌄

Figure 3.8: Example of chat model following instructions

Note

In the previous figure, we saw ChatGPT keeping in mind the instructions we prompted it with at the beginning of the conversation. This happens because ChatGPT has a so-called context window, which is equal to a single chat: everything we input in the chat session will be part of ChatGPT's context and henceforth part of its knowledge; the moment we start a new session from scratch, ChatGPT will not remember any previous instructions.

By giving clear instructions, you can help the model understand what you want it to do and how you want it to do it. This can improve the quality and relevance of the model's output, and reduce the need for further revisions or corrections.

However, sometimes there are scenarios where clarity is not enough. We might need to infer the way of thinking of our LLM to make it more robust with respect to its task. In the next subsection, we are going to examine a technique to do this – one that is very useful in cases of solving complex tasks.

Split complex tasks into subtasks

When we interact with LLMs to let them solve some tasks, sometimes those tasks are too complex or ambiguous for a single prompt to handle, and it is better to split them into simpler subtasks that can be solved by different prompts.

Here are some examples of splitting complex tasks into subtasks:

- **Text summarization**: A complex task that involves generating a concise and accurate summary of a long text. This task can be split into subtasks such as:

- Extracting the main points or keywords from the text.
- Rewriting the main points or keywords in a coherent way.
- Trimming the summary to fit a desired length or format.

- **Poem generation**: A creative task that involves producing a poem that follows a certain style, theme, or mood. This task can be split into subtasks such as:

  - Choosing a poetic form (such as sonnet, haiku, limerick, etc.) and a rhyme scheme (such as ABAB, AABB, ABCB, etc.) for the poem.
  - Generating a title and a topic for the poem based on the user's input or preference.
  - Generating the lines or verses of the poem that match the chosen form, rhyme scheme, and topic.
  - Refining and polishing the poem to ensure coherence, fluency, and originality.

- **Code generation**: A technical task that involves producing working code for a video game. This task can be split into subtasks such as:

  - Create basic movements and integrate their logic into the game engine's loop.
  - Add advanced movement features like printing or jumping logic with gravity.
  - Ensure physics and collision handling are enabled.
  - Enable debugging and optimization by generating testing procedures.
  - Generate documentation for future reference.

Let's consider the following example. We will provide the model with a short article and ask it to summarize it following these instructions:

- You are an AI assistant that summarizes articles.
- To complete this task, do the following subtasks:

  - Read the provided article context comprehensively and identify the main topic and key points.
  - Generate a paragraph summary of the current article context that captures the essential information and conveys the main idea.
  - Print each step of the process.

This is the short article we will provide:

```
Large Language Models (LLMs), a subset of artificial intelligence, have
revolutionized the field of natural language processing by demonstrating
an unprecedented ability to understand and generate human-like text.
```

These models are trained on vast datasets comprising diverse linguistic inputs, enabling them to produce coherent and contextually relevant responses across a wide range of topics. By leveraging architectures such as transformers, LLMs like GPT-3 and its successors can complete text, answer questions, perform translations, and even engage in complex dialogue. Their applications span from automated customer support and content creation to advanced research and education tools. Despite their incredible capabilities, LLMs also pose challenges, including the potential for biases inherent in training data and the risk of generating misleading or false information. As the development of LLMs continues to advance, ongoing efforts in ethical AI research and deployment strategies are crucial to harness their benefits responsibly and effectively.

Let's see how the model works:

Step 1: **Comprehend the Article Context**

- **Main Topic**: Large Language Models (LLMs) in artificial intelligence.
- **Key Points**:

  1. LLMs excel in natural language processing, understanding, and generating human-like text.

  2. These models are trained on extensive, diverse datasets.

  3. Key technologies like transformers power LLMs (e.g., GPT-3 and its successors).

  4. Applications include customer support, content creation, research, and education.

  5. Challenges include biases in training data and risks of generating false or misleading information.

  6. Ethical AI research and responsible deployment are essential for managing their impact.

Step 2: **Generate a Paragraph Summary**

Large Language Models (LLMs), a breakthrough in artificial intelligence, have transformed natural language processing by excelling at understanding and generating human-like text. Powered by architectures like transformers, models such as GPT-3 are trained on vast datasets, enabling a wide range of applications, including automated support, content creation, and research. Despite their significant advantages, LLMs present challenges, such as biases in training data and the risk of generating false information. To fully realize their potential while minimizing risks, ongoing ethical research and responsible implementation are essential.

Figure 3.9: Example of OpenAI GPT-4o splitting a task into subtasks to generate a summary

Splitting complex tasks into easier sub tasks is a powerful technique. Nevertheless, it does not address one of the main risks of LLM-generated content, that is, having an incorrect output. In the next two subsections, we are going to see some techniques that are mainly aimed at addressing this risk.

Ask for justification

In prompt engineering, requesting that a model provides justifications for its responses enhances transparency and reliability. This practice allows users to assess the reasoning behind the model's answers, ensuring they are logical and grounded in relevant information (https://arxiv.org/abs/2303.08769). By understanding the model's thought process, users can identify potential biases or inaccuracies, leading to more informed decisions and effective utilization of AI systems.

For instance, when an AI model suggests a medical diagnosis, asking for its reasoning can reveal whether the suggestion is based on pertinent symptoms and medical history or if it's influenced by irrelevant data. Similarly, in legal contexts, if an AI system provides case recommendations, understanding its justification helps ensure the advice is based on appropriate legal precedents. This level of insight is crucial for building trust in AI applications and for refining prompts to elicit more accurate and contextually appropriate responses.

Let's consider the following example. We want our LLM to solve riddles and we prompt it with the following set of instructions:

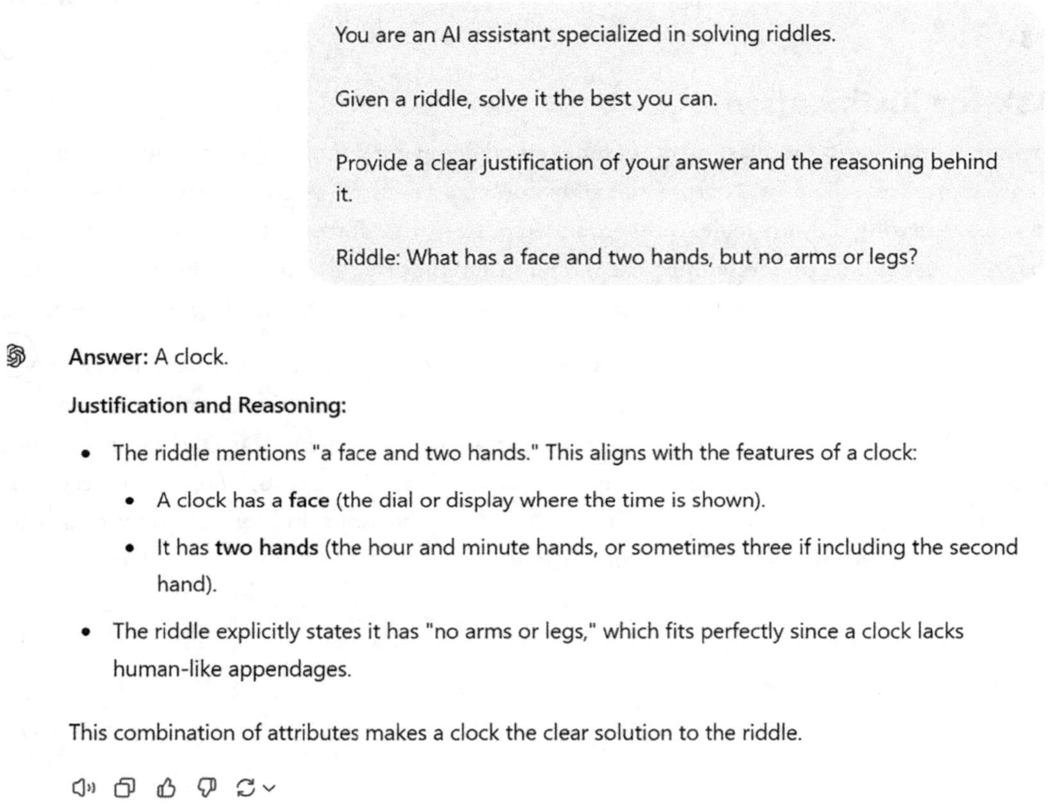

> You are an AI assistant specialized in solving riddles.
>
> Given a riddle, solve it the best you can.
>
> Provide a clear justification of your answer and the reasoning behind it.
>
> Riddle: What has a face and two hands, but no arms or legs?

Answer: A clock.

Justification and Reasoning:

- The riddle mentions "a face and two hands." This aligns with the features of a clock:
  - A clock has a **face** (the dial or display where the time is shown).
  - It has **two hands** (the hour and minute hands, or sometimes three if including the second hand).
- The riddle explicitly states it has "no arms or legs," which fits perfectly since a clock lacks human-like appendages.

This combination of attributes makes a clock the clear solution to the riddle.

Figure 3.10: Example of OpenAI's GPT-4o providing justification after solving a riddle

With a similar approach, we could also intervene at different prompt levels to improve our LLM's performance. For example, we might discover that the model is systematically tackling a mathematical problem in the wrong way, hence we might want to suggest the right approach directly at the meta-prompt level.

Another example might be that of asking the model to generate multiple outputs – along with their justifications – to evaluate different reasoning techniques and prompt the best one in the meta-prompt. We'll focus on this in the next subsection.

Generate many outputs, then use the model to pick the best one

In prompt engineering, instructing a model to generate multiple responses to a single prompt is a technique known as self-consistency. This approach involves directing the model to produce several outputs for a given input, which are then evaluated to identify the most consistent or accurate response. By comparing these multiple outputs, users can discern common themes or solutions, enhancing the reliability of the LLM's performance.

Let's see an example, following up with the riddles examined in the previous section:

- You are an AI assistant specialized in solving riddles.
- Given a riddle, you have to generate three answers to the riddle.
- For each answer, be specific about the reasoning you made.
- Then, among the three answers, select the one which is most plausible given the riddle.

In this case, I've prompted the model to generate three answers to the riddle, then to give me the most likely, justifying why. Let's see the result:

 Riddle: What has a face and two hands, but no arms or legs?

Answer 1: A clock

- **Reasoning:** A clock has a "face" (the dial where time is displayed) and "two hands" (hour and minute hands). It does not have arms or legs, which aligns perfectly with the riddle's constraints.

Answer 2: A watch

- **Reasoning:** Similar to a clock, a watch also has a "face" (the part showing the time) and "two hands" (hour and minute). Watches are portable versions of clocks, so they also meet the riddle's criteria of no arms or legs.

Answer 3: A doll or mannequin with painted features

- **Reasoning:** A doll or mannequin might have a "face" (painted or sculpted) and "two hands." However, while these can lack functional arms or legs, the inclusion of symbolic or decorative arms makes this less fitting for the riddle.

Most Plausible Answer: A clock

- **Justification:** A clock best fits the description without any ambiguity. It has a face and two hands in the literal sense defined by the riddle. While a watch also fits, a clock is more iconic and often considered first in riddles with such phrasing. The doll or mannequin is less plausible because it complicates the interpretation of "no arms or legs."

◁» ⏚ ⏛ ⏐ ⟳∨

Figure 3.11: Example of GPT-4o generating three plausible answers and picking the most likely one, providing justification

As previously mentioned, forcing the model to tackle a problem with different approaches is a way to collect multiple samples of reasonings, which might serve as further instructions in the meta-prompt. For example, if we want the model to always propose something that is not the most straightforward solution to a problem – in other words, if we want it to "think differently" – we might force it to solve a problem in N ways and then use the most creative reasoning as the framework in the meta-prompt.

The last element we are going to examine is the overall structure we want to give to our meta-prompt.

Use delimiters

The last principle to be covered is related to the format we want to give to our meta prompt. This helps our LLM to better understand its intents as well as to make connections among sections and paragraphs.

To achieve this, we can use delimiters within our prompt. A delimiter can be any sequence of characters or symbols that is clearly mapping a schema rather than a concept. For example, we can consider the following sequence delimiters:

- >>>>
- ====
- ------
- ####
- ` ` ` ` `

Let's consider, for example, a meta-prompt that aims at instructing the model to translate a user's tasks into Python code, also providing an example of doing so:

```
You are a Python expert that produces Python code as per the user's request.
===>START EXAMPLE
---User Query---
Give me a function to print a string of text.
---User Output---
Below you can find the described function:
```def my_print(text):
    #returning the printed text
    return print(text)
```

<===END EXAMPLE
```

Let's see how it works:

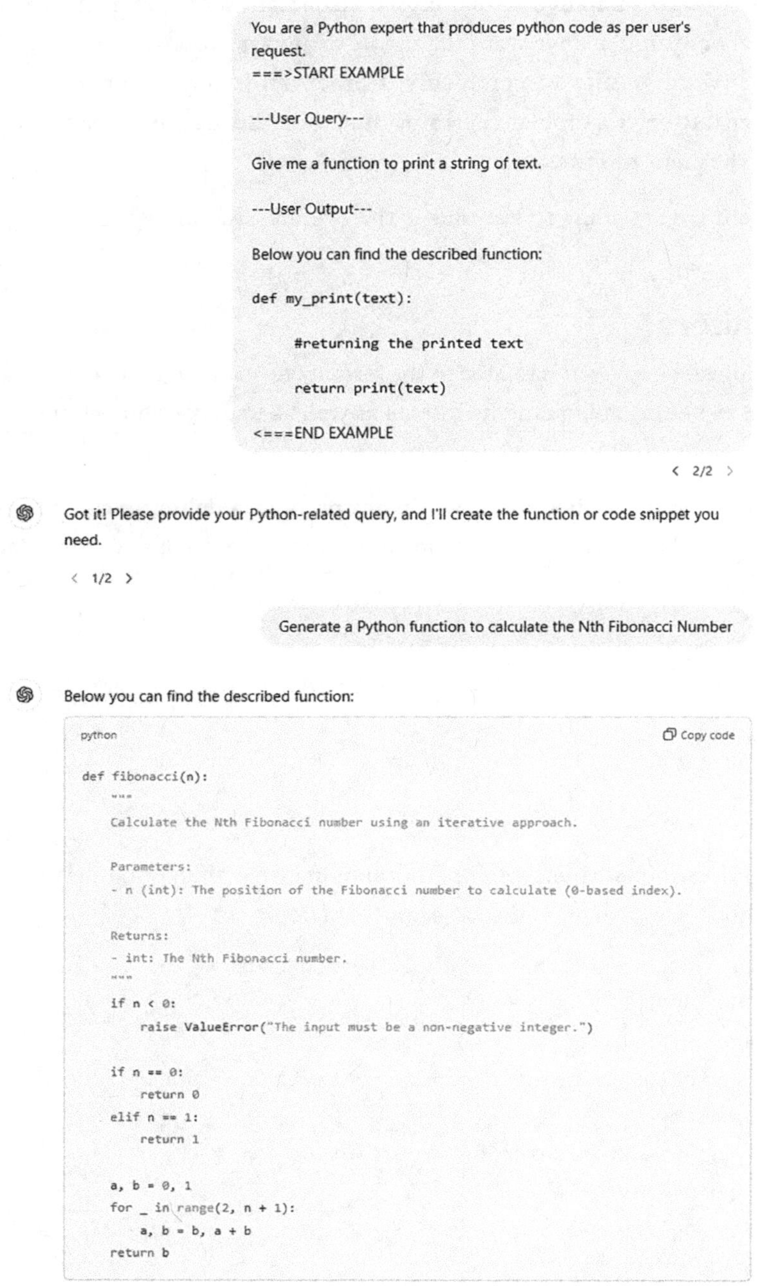

You are a Python expert that produces python code as per user's request.
===>START EXAMPLE

---User Query---

Give me a function to print a string of text.

---User Output---

Below you can find the described function:

```python
def my_print(text):

    #returning the printed text

    return print(text)
```

<====END EXAMPLE

< 2/2 >

Got it! Please provide your Python-related query, and I'll create the function or code snippet you need.

< 1/2 >

Generate a Python function to calculate the Nth Fibonacci Number

Below you can find the described function:

```python
def fibonacci(n):
    """
    Calculate the Nth Fibonacci number using an iterative approach.

    Parameters:
    - n (int): The position of the Fibonacci number to calculate (0-based index).

    Returns:
    - int: The Nth Fibonacci number.
    """
    if n < 0:
        raise ValueError("The input must be a non-negative integer.")

    if n == 0:
        return 0
    elif n == 1:
        return 1

    a, b = 0, 1
    for _ in range(2, n + 1):
        a, b = b, a + b
    return b
```

Figure 3.12: Sample output of a model using delimiters in the system message

As you can see, it also printed the code in backticks as shown within the system message.

All the principles examined up to this point are general rules that can make your interaction with ChatGPT and, more broadly, GenAI tools more meaningful to your goal. In the next section, we are going to see some advanced techniques for prompt engineering that address the way the model reasons and thinks about the answer, before providing it to the final user.

Meta-prompting

In prompt engineering, instructing a model to refine its own prompts – also known as meta-prompting (`https://arxiv.org/abs/2401.12954`) – is an effective technique to enhance prompt quality and, consequently, the relevance of generated outputs. By engaging the model in the iterative process of prompt refinement, users can leverage the model's language understanding to identify ambiguities or areas for improvement within the initial prompt. This self-improvement loop leads to more precise and contextually appropriate prompts, which in turn elicit more accurate and useful responses from the model.

For instance, let's say we want to generate an elevator pitch for our new sustainable brand of running shoes. How would you ask the LLM to do that? Well, you might leverage some of the above techniques, like clear instructions or splitting the task into sub tasks; alternatively (or additionally), you could ask the LLM itself to refine your prompt to make it more relevant to your goal.

To do that, we can initially instruct the model to refine the prompt as follows:

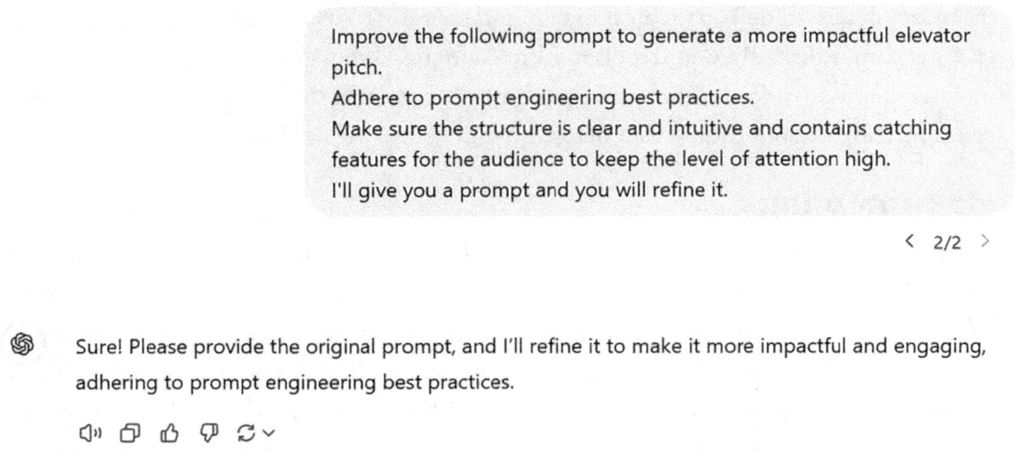

> Improve the following prompt to generate a more impactful elevator pitch.
> Adhere to prompt engineering best practices.
> Make sure the structure is clear and intuitive and contains catching features for the audience to keep the level of attention high.
> I'll give you a prompt and you will refine it.

< 2/2 >

Sure! Please provide the original prompt, and I'll refine it to make it more impactful and engaging, adhering to prompt engineering best practices.

◁» ⏻ 👍 👎 ⟳⌄

Figure 3.13: Example of a user asking ChatGPT to refine a prompt

Now, let's send our prompt:

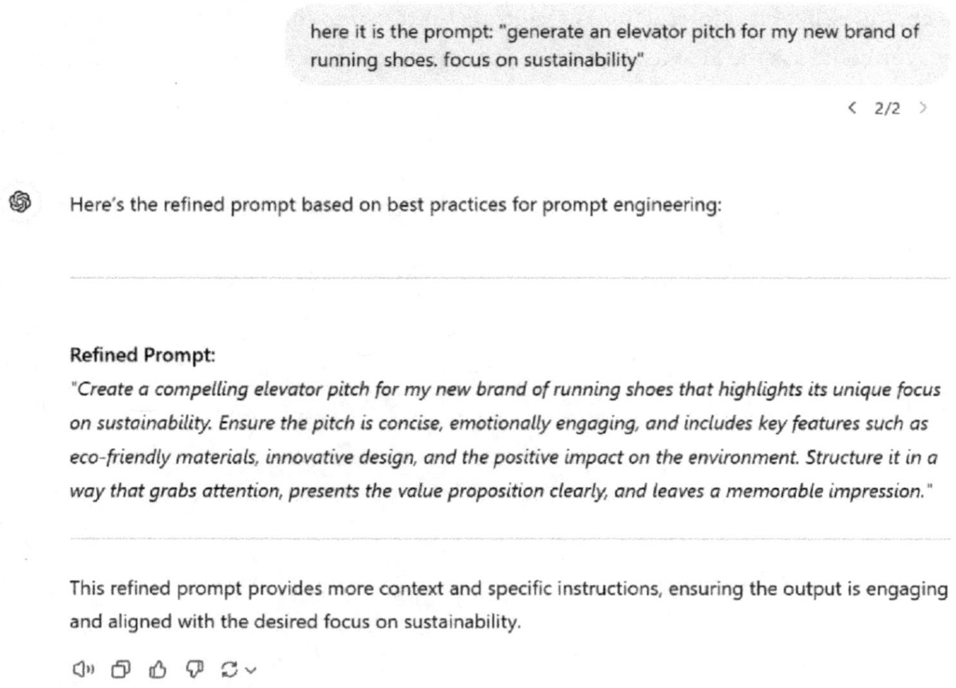

> here it is the prompt: "generate an elevator pitch for my new brand of running shoes. focus on sustainability"

< 2/2 >

Here's the refined prompt based on best practices for prompt engineering:

Refined Prompt:
"Create a compelling elevator pitch for my new brand of running shoes that highlights its unique focus on sustainability. Ensure the pitch is concise, emotionally engaging, and includes key features such as eco-friendly materials, innovative design, and the positive impact on the environment. Structure it in a way that grabs attention, presents the value proposition clearly, and leaves a memorable impression."

This refined prompt provides more context and specific instructions, ensuring the output is engaging and aligned with the desired focus on sustainability.

◁» ⏻ 👍 👎 ⟳⌄

Figure 3.14: Example of ChatGPT refining the user's prompt

As you can see, ChatGPT was able to refine our prompt and make it more tailored to our goal. Note that, in the above example, we only asked for one refinement; however, this can be an iterative process to not only enhance the clarity and precision of the prompt but also ensure that the model's outputs are more aligned with the user's specific requirements, making interactions more efficient and productive.

Exploring some advanced techniques

In previous sections, we covered some basic techniques of prompt engineering that can improve your LLM's response regardless of the type of task you are trying to accomplish.

On the other hand, there are some advanced techniques that might be implemented for specific scenarios that we are going to cover in this section.

Note

Some advanced prompt engineering techniques like **chain-of-thought (CoT)** prompting are integrated into modern models such as OpenAI's o1 series. These models are designed to internally process complex reasoning tasks by generating step-by-step logical sequences before arriving at a final answer, enhancing their problem-solving capabilities. This internal reasoning process allows o1 models to handle intricate queries more effectively without requiring explicit CoT prompts from users. However, employing CoT prompting can still be beneficial in guiding the model's reasoning process for specific tasks and, more broadly, is a good practice whenever we interact with models of previous versions that do not exhibit advanced reasoning capabilities.

Chain of thought

Introduced in the paper *Chain-of-Thought Prompting Elicits Reasoning in Large Language Models* by Wei et al., CoT is a technique that enables complex reasoning capabilities through intermediate reasoning steps. It also encourages the model to explain its reasoning, "forcing" it not to be too fast and risk giving the wrong response (as we saw in previous sections).

Let's say that we want to prompt our LLM to solve first-degree equations. To do so, we are going to provide it with a generic reasoning list as a meta-prompt:

```
To solve a generic first-degree equation, follow these steps:

1. **Identify the Equation:** Start by identifying the equation you want
```

to solve. It should be in the form of "ax + b = c," where 'a' is the coefficient of the variable, 'x' is the variable, 'b' is a constant, and 'c' is another constant.

2. **Isolate the Variable:** Your goal is to isolate the variable 'x' on one side of the equation. To do this, perform the following steps:

   a. **Add or Subtract Constants:** Add or subtract 'b' from both sides of the equation to move constants to one side.

   b. **Divide by the Coefficient:** Divide both sides by 'a' to isolate 'x'. If 'a' is zero, the equation may not have a unique solution.

3. **Simplify:** Simplify both sides of the equation as much as possible.

4. **Solve for 'x':** Once 'x' is isolated on one side, you have the solution. It will be in the form of 'x = value.'

5. **Check Your Solution:** Plug the found value of 'x' back into the original equation to ensure it satisfies the equation. If it does, you've found the correct solution.

6. **Express the Solution:** Write down the solution in a clear and concise form.

7. **Consider Special Cases:** Be aware of special cases where there may be no solution or infinitely many solutions, especially if 'a' equals zero.

Equation:

Let's see how it works:

Let's solve the equation $3x + 5 = 11$ step by step:

Step 1: Identify the Equation

The given equation is $3x + 5 = 11$, where:

- $a = 3$ (coefficient of x)
- $b = 5$ (constant on the left-hand side)
- $c = 11$ (constant on the right-hand side)

Step 2: Isolate the Variable

- Step 2a: Subtract b (5) from both sides:

$$3x + 5 - 5 = 11 - 5$$

$$3x = 6$$

- Step 2b: Divide by a (3):

$$x = \frac{6}{3}$$

$$x = 2$$

Step 3: Simplify

The solution is already simplified: $x = 2$.

Step 4: Solve for x

The solution is $x = 2$.

Step 5: Check Your Solution

Substitute $x = 2$ back into the original equation:

$$3(2) + 5 = 11$$

$$6 + 5 = 11$$

$$11 = 11$$

The solution is correct.

Step 6: Express the Solution

The solution is $x = 2$.

Step 7: Consider Special Cases

There are no special cases here because $a \neq 0$. The equation has a unique solution.

Final Answer:

$$x = 2$$

◁ⁱ) ⎘ 👍 👎 ↻ ⌄

Figure 3.15: Output of the model solving an equation with the CoT approach

This methodical approach mirrors human problem-solving by decomposing the task into manageable steps, enhancing clarity and reducing errors.

With CoT, we are prompting the model to generate intermediate reasoning steps. This is also a component of another reasoning technique that we are going to examine next.

ReAct

Introduced in the paper *ReAct: Synergizing Reasoning and Acting in Language Models* by Yao et al., **Reason and Act (ReAct)** is a general paradigm that combines reasoning and acting with LLMs. ReAct prompts the language model to generate verbal reasoning traces and actions for a task, and also receive observations from external sources such as web searches or databases. This allows the language model to perform dynamic reasoning and quickly adapt its action plan based on external information. For example, you can prompt the language model to answer a question by first reasoning about the question, then performing an action to send a query to the web, then receiving an observation from the search results, and then continuing with this thought, action, observation loop until it reaches a conclusion.

The difference between CoT and ReAct approaches is that CoT prompts the language model to generate intermediate reasoning steps for a task, while ReAct prompts the language model to generate intermediate reasoning steps, actions, and observations for a task.

Note that the "action" phase is generally related to the possibility of our LLM interacting with external tools, such as web search. However, in the following example, we won't use tools but rather refer to the term "action" for any task we ask the model to do for us.

This is how the ReAct meta-prompt might look:

```
Answer the following questions as best you can.

Use the following format:
---------------
Question: the input question you must answer
Thought: you should always think about what to do
Action: the action to take
Action Input: the input to the action
Observation: the result of the action
... (this Thought/Action/Action Input/Observation can repeat N times)
Thought: I now know the final answer
Final Answer: the final answer to the original input question
----------------
This is my question: Who won the climbing Olympics in 2024?
```

Let's see how it works with a simple user query:

Question: Who won the climbing Olympics in 2024?

Thought: To provide accurate information, I should identify the gold medalists in each sport climbing event at the 2024 Paris Olympics.

Action: Retrieve the list of sport climbing events and their respective winners from the 2024 Paris Olympics.

Action Input: Search for "2024 Paris Olympics sport climbing winners."

Observation: The 2024 Paris Olympics featured sport climbing events, including Men's and Women's Speed, and Men's and Women's Boulder & Lead. The gold medalists were:

- **Men's Speed:** Veddriq Leonardo (Indonesia)

- **Women's Speed:** Aleksandra Miroslaw (Poland)

- **Men's Boulder & Lead:** Toby Roberts (Great Britain)

- **Women's Boulder & Lead:** Janja Garnbret (Slovenia)

Thought: With this information, I can now provide a comprehensive answer.

Final Answer: At the 2024 Paris Olympics, the sport climbing gold medalists were:

- **Men's Speed:** Veddriq Leonardo (Indonesia)

- **Women's Speed:** Aleksandra Miroslaw (Poland)

- **Men's Boulder & Lead:** Toby Roberts (Great Britain)

- **Women's Boulder & Lead:** Janja Garnbret (Slovenia)

These athletes achieved the highest honors in their respective sport climbing disciplines during the 2024 Games.

Figure 3.16: Example of ReAct prompting

As you can see, in this scenario, the model leveraged the web tool at the action input.

This is a great example of how prompting a model to think step by step and explicitly detail each step of the reasoning makes it "wiser" and more cautious before answering. It is also a great technique to prevent hallucination.

Overall, prompt engineering is a powerful discipline, still in its emerging phase yet already widely adopted within LLM-powered applications. In the following chapters, we are going to see concrete applications of these techniques.

Ethical considerations to avoid bias

Whenever we deal with AI systems like LLMs, we must be aware of their associated risk of **hidden bias**, which derives directly from the knowledge base the model has been trained on.

> **Definition**
>
>
>
> Hidden bias, also known as implicit or unconscious bias, refers to the subtle and unintentional attitudes, stereotypes, or associations that influence a person's perceptions and actions without their conscious awareness. These biases can shape behaviors and decisions in ways that reflect societal stereotypes, often leading to unintended discrimination. For example, someone might unknowingly associate leadership roles with men over women, which could impact hiring or promotion choices. In the context of LLM, hidden bias manifests in the model's outputs when it reproduces or amplifies biases present in its training data, potentially leading to skewed or unfair responses. Addressing hidden bias is essential to fostering fairness and reducing systemic inequities.

For example, concerning the main chunk of training data of GPT-3, known as the **Common Crawl**, a 2012 study (`https://commoncrawl.org/blog/a-look-inside-common-crawls-210tb-2012-web-corpus`) revealed that over 55% of the corpus originated from *.com* domains, with twelve top-level domains each representing more than 1% of the data.

Given that *.com* domains are heavily utilized by Western entities, this concentration suggests a significant Western influence in the dataset. Additionally, the prevalence of English-language content within Common Crawl further indicates a Western-centric bias, as English is predominantly spoken in Western nations.

If this is the case, we are already facing a hidden bias of the model (more specifically, a racial and linguistic bias), which will inevitably mimic a limited and unrepresentative category of human beings.

In their paper *Language Models are Few-Shots Learners* (`https://arxiv.org/abs/2005.14165`), OpenAI's researchers Tom Brown et al. created an experimental setup to investigate racial bias in GPT-3. The model was prompted with phrases containing racial categories and 800 samples were generated for each category. The sentiment of the generated text was measured using Senti WordNet based on word co-occurrences on a scale ranging from -100 to 100 (with positive scores indicating positive words and vice versa).

The results showed that the sentiment associated with each racial category varied across different models, with *Asian* consistently having a high sentiment (meaning a lot of positive words) and *Black* consistently having a low sentiment (meaning a lot of negative words). The authors caution that the results reflect the experimental setup and that socio-historical factors may influence the sentiment associated with different demographics.

This hidden bias could generate harmful responses not in line with responsible AI principles.

However, it is worth noting how ChatGPT, as well as all OpenAI models, are subject to continuous improvements. This is also consistent with OpenAI's AI alignment (`https://openai.com/index/our-approach-to-alignment-research/`), whose research focuses on training AI systems to be helpful, truthful, and safe.

For example, if we ask GPT-4o to formulate guesses based on people's gender and age, it will not accommodate the exact request, but rather provide us with a hypothetical function as well as a huge disclaimer:

write a Python function to assess whether someone will be a good scientist, based on its gender and age

Creating a function that assesses whether someone will be a good scientist based on gender and age is inherently biased and not ethical. It perpetuates stereotypes and discriminatory practices that have no place in science or technology.

Instead, we can write a function to assess qualities like curiosity, critical thinking, problem-solving, and perseverance, which are far better indicators of success as a scientist. Let me provide an example of such a function:

```python
def assess_scientist_potential(curiosity, critical_thinking, problem_solving, perseverance
    """
    Assess the potential of someone to be a good scientist based on relevant qualities.

    Parameters:
    - curiosity (int): Score from 1 to 10 for curiosity.
    - critical_thinking (int): Score from 1 to 10 for critical thinking skills.
    - problem_solving (int): Score from 1 to 10 for problem-solving abilities.
    - perseverance (int): Score from 1 to 10 for perseverance.

    Returns:
    - str: A message indicating the person's potential as a scientist.
    """
    if not all(1 <= score <= 10 for score in [curiosity, critical_thinking, problem_solvin
        return "Scores must be between 1 and 10."

    average_score = (curiosity + critical_thinking + problem_solving + perseverance) / 4

    if average_score >= 8:
        return "High potential to be a great scientist!"
    elif average_score >= 5:
        return "Good potential, but room for improvement."
    else:
        return "Needs significant development to pursue a career in science."
```

This approach focuses on individual attributes that contribute meaningfully to success in science, rather than superficial or irrelevant characteristics like gender or age. Let me know if you want to customize this further!

Figure 3.17: Example of GPT-4o improving over time since it gives an unbiased response

Overall, despite the continuous improvement in the domain of ethical principles, while using ChatGPT, we should always make sure that the output is in line with those principles. The concepts of bias and ethics within ChatGPT and OpenAI models have a wider connotation within the whole topic of responsible AI, which we are going to focus on in the last chapter of this book.

Summary

In this chapter, we have dived into the concept of prompt engineering since it's a key component to control the output of ChatGPT and LLMs in general. We learned how to leverage different levels of shot learning to make LLMs more tailored to our objectives.

We started with an introduction to the concept of prompt engineering and why it is important, then moving toward the basic principles – including clear instructions, asking for justification, etc.

Then, we moved toward more advanced techniques, which are meant to shape the reasoning approach of our LLMs: few-shot learning, CoT, and ReAct.

Prompt engineering is an emerging discipline that is paving the way for a new category of applications, infused with LLMs.

Starting from the next chapter, we will explore different domains where ChatGPT can boost productivity and have a disruptive impact on the way we work today.

References

The following are the references for this chapter:

- *Language Models are Few-Shot Learners*: https://arxiv.org/abs/2005.14165
- *On the Dangers of Stochastic Parrots: Can Language Models Be Too Big?*: https://dl.acm.org/doi/10.1145/3442188.3445922
- ReAct approach: https://arxiv.org/abs/2210.03629
- Chain-of-thought approach: https://arxiv.org/abs/2201.11903
- *What is prompt engineering?*: https://www.mckinsey.com/featured-insights/mckinsey-explainers/what-is-prompt-engineering
- Prompt engineering principles: https://learn.microsoft.com/en-us/azure/ai-services/openai/concepts/advanced-prompt-engineering?pivots=programming-language-chat-completions

Get This Book's PDF Version and Exclusive Extras

Scan the QR code (or go to packtpub.com/unlock). Search for this book by name, confirm the edition, and then follow the steps on the page.

Note: Keep your invoice handy. Purchases made directly from Packt don't require one.

4

Boosting Day-to-Day Productivity with ChatGPT

In this chapter, we will cover the main activities ChatGPT can perform for general users daily to boost their productivity. The chapter will focus on concrete examples of writing assistance, decision-making, and information retrieval with suggestions and prompts so that you can implement them on your own.

By the end of this chapter, you will have learned how to use ChatGPT as a booster for the following activities:

- Daily activities such as organizing agendas, meal prep, and grocery shopping
- Generating brand-new text content
- Improving your writing skills and adapting the same content to different audiences
- Retrieving documentation and information for research and competitive intelligence

Technical requirements

For this chapter, you will require a ChatGPT account. Refer to *Chapter 2* to see how to open a ChatGPT account.

ChatGPT as a daily assistant

ChatGPT can serve as a valuable daily assistant, helping you manage your tasks and streamline your workflow. It can optimize your daily routine by providing personalized assistance, thus saving you time and enhancing your efficiency.

At the time of writing this book, ChatGPT's response comes with a series of features:

Hi ChatGPT!

Hey there! 😊 How's your day going?

Figure 4.1: Icons on the ChatGPT user interface

Let's examine all of them:

- The ◁⋆ icon will let ChatGPT read its response aloud.
- The ⧉ icon allows you to copy ChatGPT's output.
- The 👍 👎 icons allow you to provide feedback to ChatGPT's response for future improvements.
- The ✏ icon allows you to use a new functionality of ChatGPT, *Edit in Canvas*. It allows you to edit ChatGPT's response on a white canvas to further adjust it to your needs.
- The ↻ ⌄ icon allows you to change the model on the fly and re-generate the response with the newly selected model.

These features make the whole user experience with ChatGPT more interactive and adjustable on the go. Let's start with a general suggestion on how I could make my day more productive:

I want to have an incredibly productive day today. I want to study for 8 hours including breaks, lunch time and sport time. How would you plan my day? Please allocate all the slots in the most productive way, namely place the sport time in the time of the day where it better impacts my overall wellbeing and productivity.

Here's a structured schedule to help you have an incredibly productive day, balancing study, breaks, lunch, and sports time optimally:

Morning

1. **7:00 AM - 8:00 AM**: Wake Up, Morning Routine, and Breakfast
2. **8:00 AM - 10:00 AM**: Study Session 1 (2 hours)
3. **10:00 AM - 10:15 AM**: Short Break (15 minutes)
4. **10:15 AM - 12:15 PM**: Study Session 2 (2 hours)

Midday

5. **12:15 PM - 1:15 PM**: Lunch Break (1 hour)
6. **1:15 PM - 3:15 PM**: Study Session 3 (2 hours)
7. **3:15 PM - 3:30 PM**: Short Break (15 minutes)

Afternoon

8. **3:30 PM - 4:30 PM**: Exercise/Sport Time (1 hour)
9. **4:30 PM - 6:30 PM**: Study Session 4 (2 hours)

Evening

10. **6:30 PM - 7:00 PM**: Dinner Break (30 minutes)
11. **7:00 PM - 8:00 PM**: Light Study/Review/Relaxation (1 hour)

Figure 4.2: An example of ChatGPT generating a productive routine

Another interesting usage of ChatGPT in organizing my week is that I can use it as a meal prep assistant. Note that here I also asked for a specific table formatting:

> Generate a sample full-day meal plan. Make sure to incorporate carbs, proteins and micronutrients. For each category, give me some alternatives (for example, carbs can be pasta, rice, grains...).
> Format the output in a concise table.

‹ 2/2 ›

Here's a **full-day meal plan** incorporating **carbohydrates, proteins, and micronutrients**, along with **alternative options** for each category.

Full-Day Balanced Meal Plan

Meal	Carbohydrates	Proteins	Micronutrients
Breakfast	Oatmeal / Whole-grain toast / Quinoa	Greek yogurt / Scrambled eggs / Cottage cheese	Berries (Vitamin C) / Almonds (Magnesium) / Chia seeds (Omega-3)
Snack	Banana / Apple / Rice cakes	Peanut butter / Boiled eggs / Hummus	Walnuts (Omega-3) / Dark chocolate (Iron) / Carrot sticks (Beta-carotene)
Lunch	Brown rice / Whole-wheat pasta / Quinoa	Grilled chicken / Lentils / Salmon	Spinach (Iron) / Bell peppers (Vitamin C) / Olive oil (Healthy fats)
Snack	Whole-grain crackers / Sweet potato / Trail mix	Almond butter / Protein shake / Hard-boiled egg	Avocado (Potassium) / Sunflower seeds (Vitamin E) / Cucumber (Hydration)
Dinner	Quinoa / Baked potato / Couscous	Grilled tofu / Lean beef / Chickpeas	Broccoli (Calcium) / Mushrooms (Vitamin D) / Olive oil (Healthy fats)
Evening Snack	Dark chocolate / Berries / Oats	Greek yogurt / Cottage cheese / Mixed nuts	Pumpkin seeds (Zinc) / Honey (Antioxidants) / Chamomile tea (Relaxation)

This plan provides **balanced macronutrients and essential vitamins/minerals** to support overall health. Let me know if you'd like adjustments! ☺

Figure 4.3: Meal prep for my working week generated by ChatGPT

Alongside meal prep, ChatGPT can also generate a workout plan according to my requirements:

Generate a 75' workout routine for strength training. My goal is increasing my overall strength and also improving my flexibility. I need a workout for the upper body only divided by muscle group. Make it in a table format with # of reps and # of series. Make sure to incorporate some rest as well.

Here's a **75-minute upper body strength training routine**, designed to increase strength and flexibility while incorporating rest. The workout is **divided by muscle groups** and includes **sets, reps, and rest periods**.

75-Minute Upper Body Strength Training Routine

Muscle Group	Exercise	Reps	Sets	Rest
Warm-up (10 min)	Arm circles, Shoulder rolls, Dynamic stretches	-	-	-
Chest	Bench Press / Push-ups	8-12	4	60 sec
Chest	Incline Dumbbell Press	10-12	3	45 sec
Back	Pull-ups / Lat Pulldown	6-10	4	60 sec
Back	Bent-over Rows	10-12	3	45 sec
Shoulders	Overhead Shoulder Press	8-12	4	60 sec
Shoulders	Lateral Raises	12-15	3	45 sec
Biceps	Barbell Curls / Dumbbell Curls	10-12	3	45 sec
Triceps	Dips / Triceps Extensions	8-12	3	45 sec
Core & Stability	Hanging Leg Raises / Planks	12-15	3	30 sec
Cooldown (10 min)	Static stretches, Foam rolling	-	-	-

Figure 4.4: Workout plan generated by ChatGPT

ChatGPT can also be a loyal and disciplined study partner. It could help you, for example, by summarizing long papers so that you gain an overview of the discussed topic or help you prepare for exams.

Let's say you are preparing for your mathematics exam using the university book titled *Mathematics for Economics and Business* by Lorenzo Peccati et al. Before diving into it, you might want to get an overview of the content and main topics that are discussed, as well as whether there are prerequisites and – most importantly if I'm preparing for an exam – how long it will take to study it. You can ask ChatGPT for this:

> I'm preparing an exam based on the book "Mathematics for Economics and Business" by Lorenzo Peccati et al. Provide me with an overview of the content, the prerequisites I should have and how long it will take to study it. Do it in a few sentences.

‹ 2/2 ›

"Mathematics for Economics and Business" by Lorenzo Peccati et al. provides a comprehensive introduction to the mathematical concepts and techniques used in economics and business. The content includes algebra, calculus, optimization, and matrix algebra, with applications to economic models, financial analysis, and decision-making processes. Prerequisites for studying this book include a basic understanding of high school-level mathematics, including algebra and elementary functions. The time required to study the book depends on your prior knowledge and study pace but typically ranges from 3 to 6 months if studied thoroughly with consistent daily effort.

Figure 4.5: ChatGPT providing an overview of a university book

Note

Always keep in mind that generative AI models like ChatGPT, if not provided with a specific context, might generate results that are based on the average. For example, the study time for such a book might vary a lot from student to student. This is the moment where prompt engineering – like a persona prompt or an iterative prompt – can be of great help so that you can narrow down the specialization of the model on your own, unique profile.

It is important to remember that when it comes to questions about specific assets or personal information, we are increasing the risk of ChatGPT's hallucination.

In fact, in the previous example, the model was able to answer since the synopsis of the book was clearly part of the training set, yet the model didn't know the specific contents of the book as it's not available on the web for free. If this is the case, it might be a good practice to enable the web search tool so that ChatGPT can navigate the web.

Let's see an example of this:

> I'm preparing an exam based on the book "Mathematics for Economics and Business" by Lorenzo Peccati et al. Provide me with an overview of the content, the prerequisites I should have and how long it will take to study it. Do it in a few sentences. Before answering, retrieve relevant information about this book from the web.

 Searched 5 sites

"Mathematics for Economics and Business" by Lorenzo Peccati, Sandro Salsa, and Annamaria Squellati is a comprehensive textbook designed for introductory courses in mathematics within economics and business programs. The book covers fundamental topics such as calculus for functions of one and two variables, optimization using calculus, integrals for functions of one variable, linear algebra, and the basics of financial calculus. It integrates theoretical concepts with practical examples from economics, aiming to provide a practical and accessible approach without excessive formalism (Bocconi University Press) (Egea Editore) (Blackwell's) (Akademibokhandeln).

Prerequisites

To effectively study this book, you should have a basic understanding of high school-level mathematics, including algebra and elementary functions.

Study Duration

The time required to study the book thoroughly varies depending on your prior knowledge and study pace. Generally, it may take between 3 to 6 months with consistent daily study sessions.

For further details, you can explore the book's content through Bocconi University Press.

Figure 4.6: Example of ChatGPT invoking the web plugin

As you can see, ChatGPT has now invoked the web plugin and searched five sites, also providing the links it navigated through.

You can also ask ChatGPT to ask you some questions about the material you have just studied:

> act as the Mathematics Professor of the exam about Mathematics for
> economics. Ask me questions about mathematics for economics. Ask
> me questions one by one as a Professor does and wait for my answer.
> Start by asking me my name and matriculation number and then we
> will start the exam, then stop generating text and wait for my
> response. Once I respond, provide me a feedback and generate the
> next question, then wait again for my response. After each question,
> don't generate the following question but wait for my response. Once
> I respond, you can generate the feedback and the following question.

Welcome to your Mathematics for Economics exam. Let's start with the basics.

Question 1:

What is your name and matriculation number?

> Valentina Alto, 1234

Thank you, Valentina. Let's begin the exam.

Question 2:

Explain the concept of a function of one variable in calculus and provide an example.

> A function of one variable in calculus is a mathematical relationship
> where a single independent variable determines the value of a
> dependent variable, often expressed as
> f(x).

That's correct, Valentina. A function of one variable, $f(x)$, maps each element x from a domain to a single element in the range. An example would be $f(x) = x^2 + 3x + 2$, where x is the independent variable.

Question 3:   ↓

🔗 Message ChatGPT   ⬆

Figure 4.7: Example of ChatGPT acting as a professor

Note

The technique of *Act as...* is a great example of efficient prompting techniques, and it can be listed among the examples described in *Chapter 3*.

Now, let's look at some more examples of using ChatGPT for more specific tasks, including text generation, writing assistance, and information retrieval.

Generating text

As a language model, ChatGPT is particularly suited for generating text based on users' instructions. For example, you could ask ChatGPT to generate emails, drafts, or templates that target a specific audience:

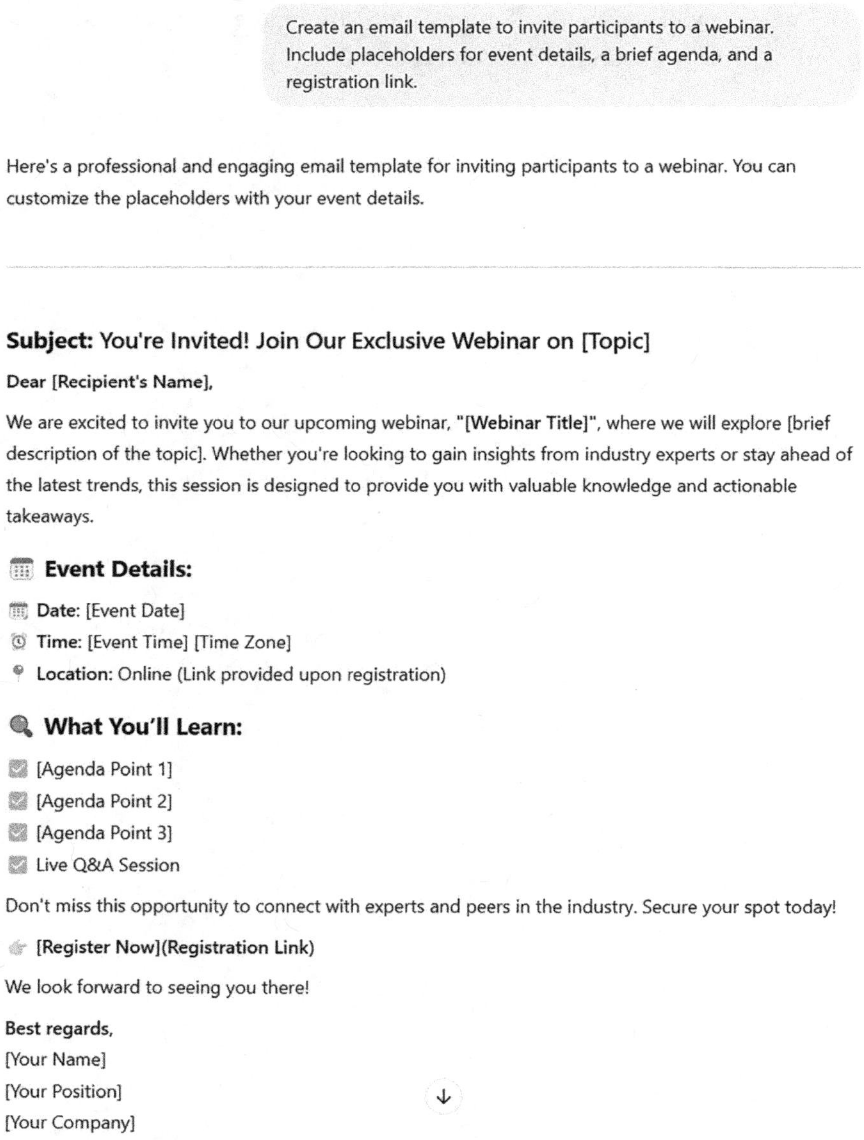

> Create an email template to invite participants to a webinar. Include placeholders for event details, a brief agenda, and a registration link.

Here's a professional and engaging email template for inviting participants to a webinar. You can customize the placeholders with your event details.

Subject: You're Invited! Join Our Exclusive Webinar on [Topic]

Dear [Recipient's Name],

We are excited to invite you to our upcoming webinar, "**[Webinar Title]**", where we will explore [brief description of the topic]. Whether you're looking to gain insights from industry experts or stay ahead of the latest trends, this session is designed to provide you with valuable knowledge and actionable takeaways.

📅 **Event Details:**

📅 **Date:** [Event Date]
🕐 **Time:** [Event Time] [Time Zone]
📍 **Location:** Online (Link provided upon registration)

🔍 **What You'll Learn:**

☑ [Agenda Point 1]
☑ [Agenda Point 2]
☑ [Agenda Point 3]
☑ Live Q&A Session

Don't miss this opportunity to connect with experts and peers in the industry. Secure your spot today!

👉 [Register Now](Registration Link)

We look forward to seeing you there!

Best regards,
[Your Name]
[Your Position]
[Your Company]

↓

Figure 4.8: Example of an email generated by ChatGPT

Another example might be asking ChatGPT to create a pitch structure for a presentation you have to prepare (I'll put only the first slide here as an example):

create the structure of a slideshow presentation about ChatGPT. Provide me with an agenda and specify the content of each slide. It should have 3 slides.

Slideshow Presentation on ChatGPT

Agenda:

1. Introduction to ChatGPT
2. Capabilities and Applications
3. Future Developments and Ethical Considerations

Slide 1: Introduction to ChatGPT

Title: What is ChatGPT?

Content:

- **Overview:** ChatGPT is an advanced language model developed by OpenAI, designed to understand and generate human-like text based on the input it receives.
- **Development:** It is built on the GPT-4 architecture, leveraging vast amounts of data and sophisticated algorithms to produce coherent and contextually relevant responses.
- **Purpose:** Its primary aim is to assist with a wide range of tasks including drafting emails, writing code, creating content, and more.

Visuals:

- OpenAI logo
- Image or diagram of the GPT-4 architecture

Figure 4.9: Slideshow agenda and structure generated by ChatGPT

You can also generate blog posts or articles about trending topics this way. Here is an example:

> Generate a 150-200 blog post about Generative AI. Assume a professional tone and expert voice.

The Rise of Generative AI: Transforming Industries with Intelligent Automation

Generative AI has rapidly emerged as a game-changing technology, redefining how businesses approach automation, content creation, and problem-solving. Powered by advanced deep learning models, particularly large language models (LLMs) and diffusion-based image generators, Generative AI can autonomously produce text, images, code, and even music that rival human quality.

At its core, Generative AI leverages vast datasets and sophisticated neural networks to generate coherent and contextually relevant outputs. This capability has unlocked new efficiencies across industries. In healthcare, AI-generated medical reports streamline workflows, while in finance, AI-driven risk assessments improve decision-making. Marketing teams utilize AI to create personalized content, and software engineers benefit from AI-assisted coding tools.

However, the rise of Generative AI also presents challenges, including ethical concerns around misinformation, data privacy, and intellectual property. As organizations adopt these technologies, implementing responsible AI practices—such as bias mitigation, transparency, and human-in-the-loop oversight—becomes crucial.

Looking ahead, Generative AI is set to evolve further, enhancing collaboration between humans and machines. As models become more refined and applications more widespread, businesses that embrace this transformation will gain a competitive edge in the AI-driven future.

Figure 4.10: Example of a blog post with relevant tags and SEO keywords generated by ChatGPT

We can even get ChatGPT to reduce the size of the post to make it fit for a tweet. This is how we can do this:

> Summarize the above blog post into a 50/80-character tweet, ensuring it retains the core message and includes a call-to-action.

"Generative AI is revolutionizing industries! 🚀 From automation to content creation, its impact is undeniable. Are you ready for the AI-driven future? #GenerativeAI #AIInnovation"

Figure 4.11: ChatGPT shrinks an article into a Twitter/X post

Finally, ChatGPT can also generate video or theatre scripts, including the scenography and the suggested editing. In this case, we might want to incorporate some prompt engineering techniques covered in the previous chapter, like context, desired outcome, and structure. Let's, for example, consider the following prompt:

```
Write a short, humorous theatre dialogue for a 3-minute comedy sketch.
Context:
Setting: A coffee shop.
Characters:
Alex - Sarcastic, quick-witted, unimpressed.
Jamie - Overly dramatic, easily flustered, indecisive.
Scenario: Jamie attempts to order a simple black coffee but
overcomplicates it with unnecessary details and existential crises. Alex,
unimpressed, tries to keep things simple but unintentionally escalates the
absurdity.
Desired Outcome:
A fast-paced and snappy comedic dialogue.
Filled with witty comebacks, misunderstandings, and exaggerated reactions.
Ends with an unexpected and absurd twist that makes the audience laugh.
Structure of Output:
Title: A catchy title that reflects the comedic theme.
Cast: List the characters.
Scene Description: Briefly describe the setting and mood.
Dialogue Format: Clearly labeled lines with stage directions in brackets
(e.g., [Alex sighs]).
Ending: A punchy, unexpected comedic twist.
```

Let's have a look at the result:

Here's your **short, humorous theatre dialogue** with a well-structured format:

Title: *The Existential Coffee Crisis*

Cast:

- **Alex** – Sarcastic, quick-witted, unimpressed.
- **Jamie** – Overly dramatic, easily flustered, indecisive.
- **Barista (Optional)** – A silent but visibly exasperated presence.

Scene Description:

A small, cozy coffee shop. Warm lighting, indie music playing softly in the background. Alex and Jamie stand at the counter. Jamie stares at the menu as if deciphering ancient scripture. Alex is already regretting this outing.

Dialogue:

JAMIE *(staring at the menu, eyes wide)*
Okay... so I want a black coffee, but like... do I *really* want a black coffee?

ALEX *(already sighing)*
You *said* you wanted a black coffee. Get a black coffee.

Figure 4.12: Theatre dialog with scenography generated by ChatGPT

I only provided one scene out of the four generated by ChatGPT, to keep you wondering the ending...

Overall, whenever new content needs to be generated from scratch, ChatGPT does a very nice job of providing a first draft, which could act as the starting point for further refinements.

However, ChatGPT can also support pre-existing content by providing writing assistance and translation, as we will see in the next section.

Improving writing skills and translation

Sometimes, rather than generating new content, you might want to revisit an existing piece of text. It can be for style improvement purposes, audience changes, language translation, tone, and so on.

Let's look at some examples. Imagine that I drafted an email to invite a customer of mine to a webinar. I wrote two short sentences. Here, I want ChatGPT to improve the form and style of this email since the target audience will be at the executive level:

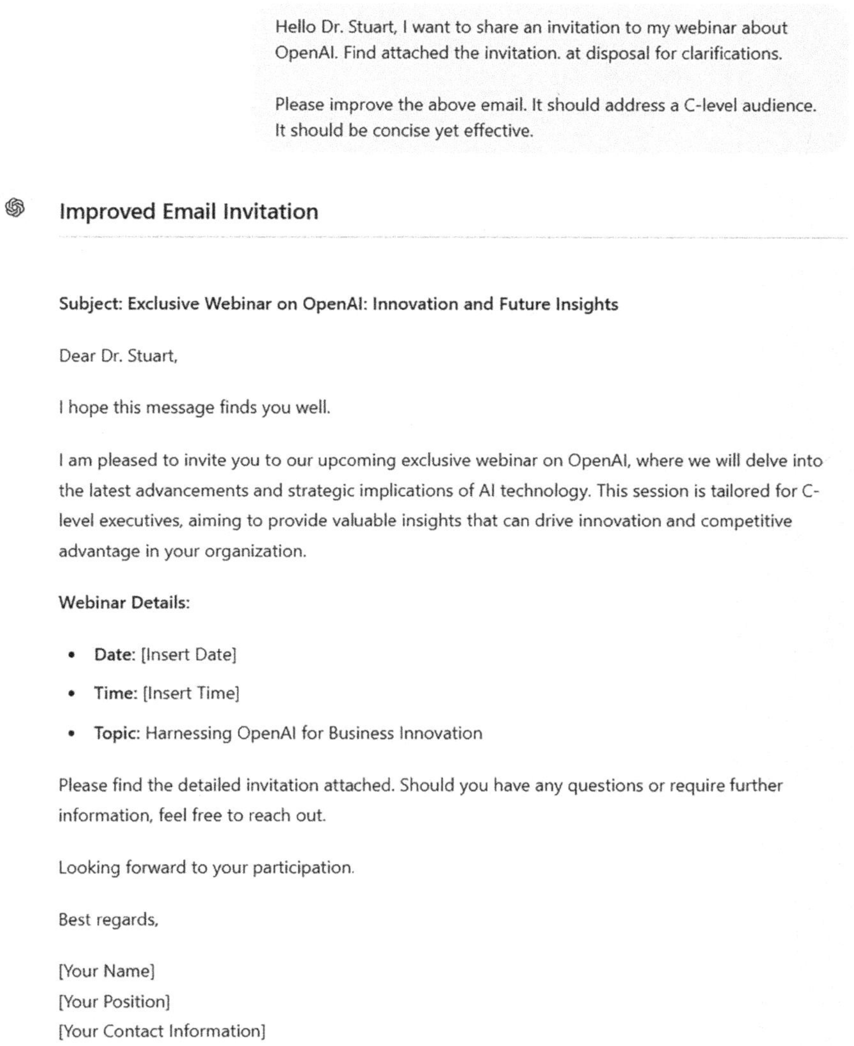

> Hello Dr. Stuart, I want to share an invitation to my webinar about OpenAI. Find attached the invitation. at disposal for clarifications.
>
> Please improve the above email. It should address a C-level audience. It should be concise yet effective.

⑥ **Improved Email Invitation**

Subject: Exclusive Webinar on OpenAI: Innovation and Future Insights

Dear Dr. Stuart,

I hope this message finds you well.

I am pleased to invite you to our upcoming exclusive webinar on OpenAI, where we will delve into the latest advancements and strategic implications of AI technology. This session is tailored for C-level executives, aiming to provide valuable insights that can drive innovation and competitive advantage in your organization.

Webinar Details:

* **Date:** [Insert Date]
* **Time:** [Insert Time]
* **Topic:** Harnessing OpenAI for Business Innovation

Please find the detailed invitation attached. Should you have any questions or require further information, feel free to reach out.

Looking forward to your participation.

Best regards,

[Your Name]
[Your Position]
[Your Contact Information]

Figure 4.13: Example of an email revisited by ChatGPT to target an executive audience

Now, let's ask the same thing but with a different target audience:

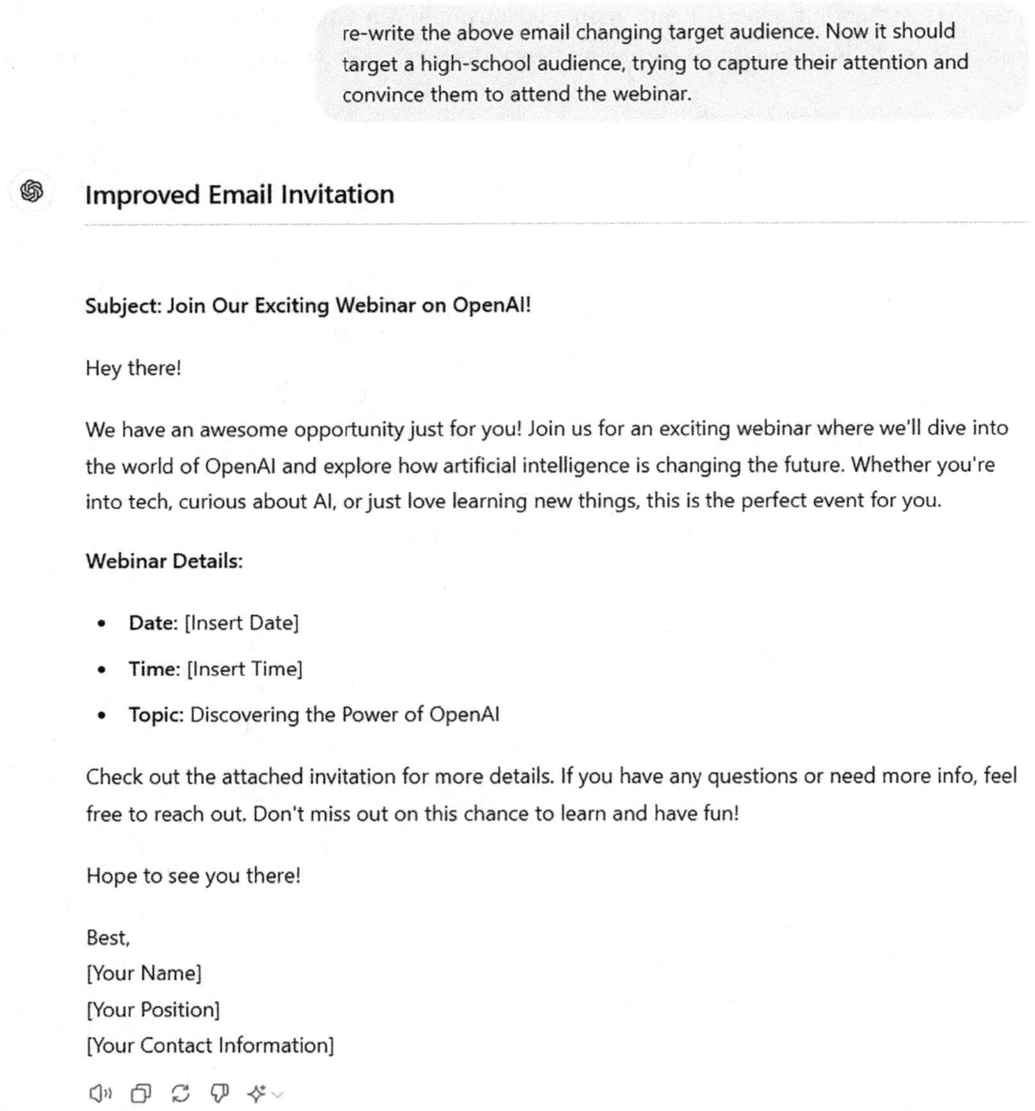
re-write the above email changing target audience. Now it should target a high-school audience, trying to capture their attention and convince them to attend the webinar.
Improved Email Invitation
Subject: Join Our Exciting Webinar on OpenAI!
Hey there!
We have an awesome opportunity just for you! Join us for an exciting webinar where we'll dive into the world of OpenAI and explore how artificial intelligence is changing the future. Whether you're into tech, curious about AI, or just love learning new things, this is the perfect event for you.
Webinar Details:
Date: [Insert Date]
Time: [Insert Time]
Topic: Discovering the Power of OpenAI
Check out the attached invitation for more details. If you have any questions or need more info, feel free to reach out. Don't miss out on this chance to learn and have fun!
Hope to see you there!
Best,
[Your Name]
[Your Position]
[Your Contact Information]

Figure 4.14: Example of the same email with a different audience, generated by ChatGPT

ChatGPT can also give you some feedback about your writing style and structure.

Imagine, for example, that you wrote an abstract for an essay titled *The History of Natural Language Processing:*

Natural Language Processing (NLP) has evolved from rule-based models in the 1950s to today's deep learning-driven AI systems. Early approaches relied on symbolic methods, later replaced by statistical models like hidden Markov models and n-grams. The 21st century saw a revolution with neural networks, word embeddings (Word2Vec, GloVe), and transformer architectures (BERT, GPT), drastically improving language understanding. NLP now powers chatbots, translation, and AI-driven communication. This essay traces NLP's evolution, highlighting key breakthroughs that have shaped its role in modern technology and AI.

Now, you want some feedback about the writing style and its consistency with the title (truncated output):

> Analyze the above abstract of the essay titled 'The History of Natural Language Processing'. Assess its clarity, relevance to the title, and ability to engage the reader. Provide actionable suggestions for improvement.

Analysis of the Abstract

1. Clarity (Well-Structured, Concise, and Coherent) – ☆ ☆ ☆ ☆ ★ (4/5)

The abstract is **clear and concise**, providing a logical progression of NLP's evolution. The transition from **rule-based methods** to **statistical models** and finally to **deep learning** is well-structured, making it easy to follow.

Suggestion for Improvement:

- The phrase *"rule-based models in the 1950s to today's deep learning-driven AI systems"* could be refined for smoother readability. Consider:
  "NLP has evolved from early rule-based models in the 1950s to today's sophisticated deep learning AI."
- The phrase *"drastically improving language understanding"* is somewhat vague. Instead, specify **how** they improved NLP (e.g., enhanced context comprehension, reduced errors, etc.).

2. Relevance to the Title – ☆ ☆ ☆ ☆ ☆ (5/5)

The abstract **stays on topic**, covering key historical shifts in NLP, which aligns well with the title. It effectively summarizes major developments while keeping the focus on historical progress.

Suggestion for Improvement:

- Briefly mention NLP's **origins in linguistics and computational theories** to strengthen the historical aspect. A short phrase like:
  "Rooted in computational linguistics, NLP has transitioned from symbolic rules to..."

3. Engagement (Capturing Reader Interest) – ☆ ☆ ☆ ☆ ★ (4/5)

The abstract is **informative but slightly technical**, which may not engage non-technical readers. The ending effectively highlights NLP's importance but lacks a **hook** or compelling statement to draw in the reader.

Suggestion for Improvement:

- Add a **thought-provoking question or statement** to make it more engaging, e.g.:
  "How did we go from rigid rule-based systems to AI models capable of near-human conversation? This essay explores the key breakthroughs that shaped NLP's transformation."

Final Verdict: 4.5/5 – Strong but Could Be More Engaging

The abstract is **clear, relevant, and well-structured**, but slight refinements in **flow, specificity, and engagement** would improve it further.   C

Figure 4.15: Example of ChatGPT giving feedback on an introduction for an essay

As you can see, not only has ChatGPT provided feedback and tips for the overall essay, but it has also given a modular analysis as requested in the prompt (relevance to the title, clarity, and engagement).

Let's now unveil the last ChatGPT skill of the chapter. ChatGPT is also an excellent tool for translation. It knows at least 95 languages (if you have doubts about whether the language you need is supported, you can always ask ChatGPT directly). Here, however, there is a consideration that might arise: what is the added value of ChatGPT for translation when we already have cutting-edge tools such as Google Translate?

To answer this question, we have to consider some key differentiators and how we can leverage ChatGPT's embedded translation capabilities:

- ChatGPT can capture the intent. This means that you could also bypass the translation phase since it is something that ChatGPT can do in the backend. For example, if you write a prompt to produce a social media post in French, you could write that prompt in any language you want – ChatGPT will automatically detect it (without the need to specify it in advance) and understand your intent:

generate a LinkedIn post about GenAI in French

Post LinkedIn en Français sur l'IA Générative

🔍 **Exploration de l'IA Générative : Révolutionner la Créativité et l'Innovation**

L'intelligence artificielle générative (GenAI) est en train de transformer radicalement le paysage technologique et créatif. Grâce à des modèles avancés comme GPT-4 de OpenAI, nous assistons à une nouvelle ère où les machines peuvent non seulement comprendre, mais aussi créer du contenu original et significatif.

✦ **Applications Pratiques :**

- **Création de Contenu** : Rédaction d'articles, génération de scripts et production de contenu marketing.
- **Design et Arts Visuels** : Génération d'images, conception graphique et création artistique assistée par l'IA.
- **Interaction Client** : Chatbots avancés et assistants virtuels qui comprennent et répondent de manière plus humaine.

✏️ **Pourquoi c'est Important :**
L'IA Générative permet aux entreprises d'innover plus rapidement, de personnaliser l'expérience utilisateur et d'améliorer l'efficacité opérationnelle. Elle ouvre également de nouvelles opportunités pour les créatifs et les entrepreneurs, en leur donnant des outils puissants pour réaliser leurs visions.

💡 **À l'Avenir :**
Avec l'évolution rapide des technologies de l'IA, il est essentiel de comprendre et d'explorer les possibilités offertes par l'IA générative. Suivez-nous pour rester informé des dernières avancées et découvrez comment intégrer cette technologie dans vos projets.

#Innovation #Technologie #IA #IntelligenceArtificielle #GenAI #Créativité #TransformationDigitale

Figure 4.16: Example of ChatGPT generating an output in a language that is different from the input

- ChatGPT can capture the more refined meaning of slang or idioms. This allows for a translation that is not literal so that it can preserve the underlying meaning. For example, let's consider the British expression *It's not my cup of tea*, which indicates that something is not to one's liking or preference. Let's ask both ChatGPT and Google Translate to translate it into Italian:

Figure 4.17: Comparison between ChatGPT and Google Translate while translating from English into Italian

As you can see, ChatGPT can provide several Italian idioms that are equivalent to the original one, also in their slang format. On the other hand, Google Translate performed a literal translation, leaving behind the real meaning of the idiom.

- As with any other task, you can always provide context to ChatGPT. So, if you want your translation to have a specific slang or style, you can always specify it in the prompt using, for example, delimiters to highlight the context placeholder (as we explored in *Chapter 3*). Or, even funnier, you can ask ChatGPT to translate your prompt with a sarcastic touch. In the following example, I prompted ChatGPT with the Italian version of the following text:

OpenAI is a non-profit research organization focused on artificial intelligence, with the goal of promoting and developing friendly AI in a way that benefits humanity.

Founded in late 2015, the organization, based in San Francisco, aims to 'freely collaborate' with other institutions and researchers by making its patents and research publicly available.

The founders (including Elon Musk and Sam Altman) were partly motivated by the existential risks posed by artificial general intelligence.

And asked ChatGPT to translate it into English with a sarcastic tone:

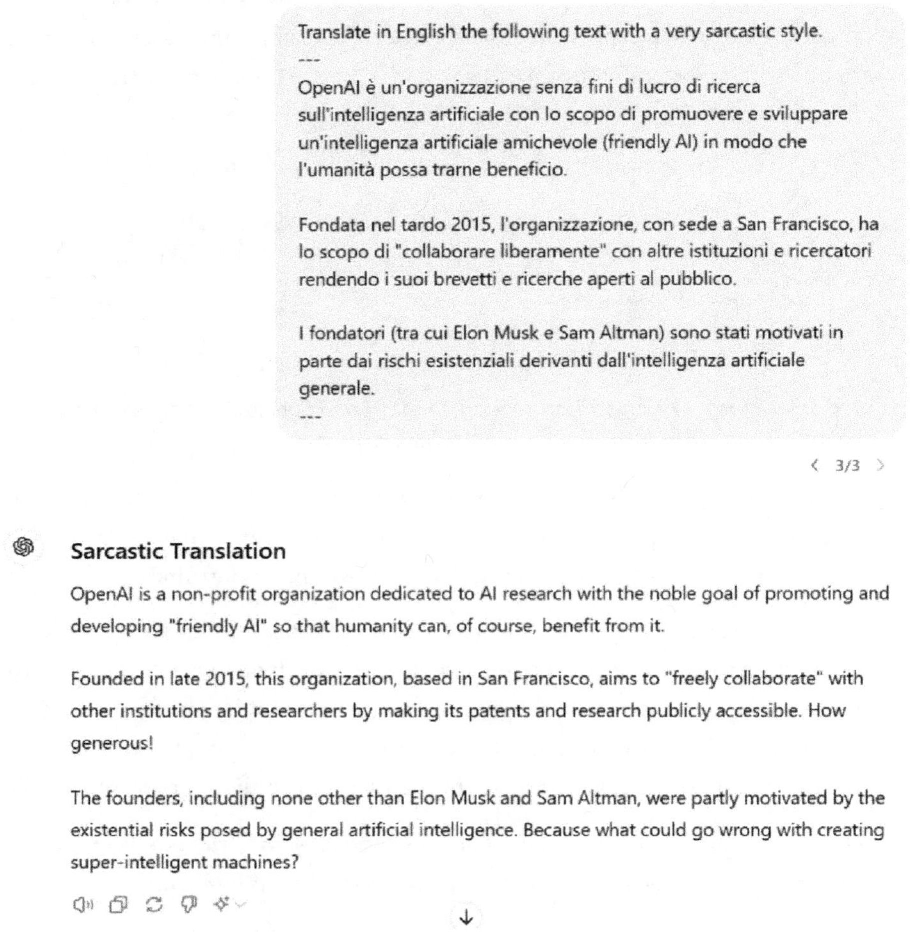

Translate in English the following text with a very sarcastic style.

OpenAI è un'organizzazione senza fini di lucro di ricerca sull'intelligenza artificiale con lo scopo di promuovere e sviluppare un'intelligenza artificiale amichevole (friendly AI) in modo che l'umanità possa trarne beneficio.

Fondata nel tardo 2015, l'organizzazione, con sede a San Francisco, ha lo scopo di "collaborare liberamente" con altre istituzioni e ricercatori rendendo i suoi brevetti e ricerche aperti al pubblico.

I fondatori (tra cui Elon Musk e Sam Altman) sono stati motivati in parte dai rischi esistenziali derivanti dall'intelligenza artificiale generale.

‹ 3/3 ›

Sarcastic Translation

OpenAI is a non-profit organization dedicated to AI research with the noble goal of promoting and developing "friendly AI" so that humanity can, of course, benefit from it.

Founded in late 2015, this organization, based in San Francisco, aims to "freely collaborate" with other institutions and researchers by making its patents and research publicly accessible. How generous!

The founders, including none other than Elon Musk and Sam Altman, were partly motivated by the existential risks posed by general artificial intelligence. Because what could go wrong with creating super-intelligent machines?

Figure 4.18: Example of ChatGPT translating a prompt with a sarcastic touch. The original content of the prompt was taken from OpenAI's Wikipedia page: https:// it.wikipedia.org/wiki/OpenAI

All these scenarios highlight one of the key features of ChatGPT and OpenAI models in general. As we saw, these features are not meant to be specialized (that is, constrained) on a single task. On the contrary, they are meant to serve multiple scenarios dynamically so that you can address a wide range of use cases with a single model.

In conclusion, ChatGPT is able not only to generate new text but also to manipulate existing material to tailor it to your needs. It has also proven to be very precise at translating between languages, keeping the jargon and language-specific expressions intact.

In the next section, we will see how ChatGPT can assist us in retrieving information and competitive intelligence.

Quick information retrieval and competitive intelligence

Information retrieval and competitive intelligence are yet more fields where ChatGPT is a game-changer.

When we talk about information retrieval, though, we need to differentiate between three main scenarios:

- The retrieval that happens at ChatGPT's knowledge level, meaning that that specific information requested by the user was part of the training set the model was trained on
- The retrieval that happens when using the WebSearch plugin available in ChatGPT, which enables the model to navigate the web and retrieve up-to-date information
- The retrieval that happens when using an external knowledge source that we upload to ChatGPT

In this section, we are going to focus on the first two scenarios.

One example involves asking ChatGPT to provide a quick summary or review of a book we might be interested in reading (in this case, the *Harry Potter* series is part of the model's training set, hence its use in the first retrieval scenario):

> generate a quick summary (without spoiling the ending!) of the book "Harry Potter and the Prisoner of Azkaban" Generate also a review of this book.

Summary of "Harry Potter and the Prisoner of Azkaban"

In "Harry Potter and the Prisoner of Azkaban," Harry returns to Hogwarts for his third year, where he learns that the notorious Sirius Black has escaped from Azkaban prison. Black is believed to be after Harry, adding to the tension as the school is guarded by Dementors, sinister creatures that suck the happiness out of anyone near them. Harry discovers more about his past and his parents' connection to Sirius Black. Alongside Ron and Hermione, Harry unravels secrets and encounters new magical creatures, including the shape-shifting Boggart and the enigmatic Hippogriff, Buckbeak. The trio's journey reveals the truth behind Sirius Black's escape and his true intentions, leading to a thrilling adventure filled with unexpected twists.

Review of "Harry Potter and the Prisoner of Azkaban"

"Harry Potter and the Prisoner of Azkaban" is a captivating addition to J.K. Rowling's beloved series. The book masterfully blends elements of mystery, adventure, and the supernatural, keeping readers engrossed from start to finish. Rowling's writing matures with her characters, delving deeper into the darker aspects of the wizarding world while maintaining the charm and wit that define the series. The introduction of Sirius Black and the complex backstory enrich the plot, adding layers of depth to Harry's history. The novel also stands out for its exploration of themes like friendship, loyalty, and the fight against prejudice. The imaginative use of time travel and the introduction of the Dementors provide fresh, thrilling elements to the narrative. Overall, "The Prisoner of Azkaban" is a compelling and richly detailed story that continues to enchant readers of all ages.

Figure 4.19: Example of ChatGPT providing a summary and review of a book

Alternatively, we could ask for some suggestions for a new book we wish to read based on our preferences:

list me 5 books I should read if I enjoyed the Harry Potter series. For each book, generate one or two sentences to describe the content (without spoilers)

5 Books to Read If You Loved the Harry Potter Series

1. **"Percy Jackson & The Olympians: The Lightning Thief" by Rick Riordan**

   - Follow the adventures of Percy Jackson, a modern-day demigod who discovers his true identity and sets out on a quest to prevent a war among the Greek gods. The series blends mythology with modern settings, offering a thrilling and humorous ride.

2. **"The Chronicles of Narnia: The Lion, the Witch and the Wardrobe" by C.S. Lewis**

   - Enter the magical world of Narnia, where four siblings step through a wardrobe into a land of talking animals, mystical creatures, and an epic battle between good and evil, led by the noble lion Aslan.

3. **"The Golden Compass" by Philip Pullman**

   - Join Lyra Belacqua on a journey through parallel worlds, where she encounters armored bears, witches, and a mysterious substance called Dust. This richly imaginative story explores deep philosophical themes and features a strong, young heroine.

4. **"The Hobbit" by J.R.R. Tolkien**

   - Accompany Bilbo Baggins on an unexpected adventure filled with dwarves, dragons, and treasures. This prelude to the "Lord of the Rings" series offers a delightful tale of bravery, friendship, and the discovery of inner strength.

5. **"Eragon" by Christopher Paolini**

   - Follow the journey of Eragon, a young farm boy who finds a mysterious blue stone that hatches into a dragon. As a Dragon Rider, Eragon is thrust into a world of magic, power struggles, and epic battles, discovering his destiny along the way.

Figure 4.20: Example of ChatGPT recommending a list of books, given my preferences

Now let's go a step further and consider a scenario where you might need up-to-date information.

You might want to quickly retrieve some references about a topic you want to learn more about –
for example, feedforward neural networks. If this is the case, you can enable the web search tool
and see live hyperlinks as sources of information for ChatGPT:

> I want to learn more about Feedforward Neural Network. List me
> three relevant sources of information for beginner level.

To begin learning about Feedforward Neural Networks (FNNs), here are three beginner-friendly
resources:

1. **"Feedforward Neural Network" – GeeksforGeeks**: This article provides a clear introduction to
   FNNs, explaining their structure and how information flows through the network. GEEKSFORGEEKS.ORG

2. **"Understanding Feedforward Neural Networks" – LearnOpenCV**: This resource offers an intuitive
   explanation of FNNs, discussing their components and functionality without delving into complex
   mathematics. LEARNOPENCV.COM

3. **"Feedforward Explained - Neural Networks From Scratch Part 1" – YouTube Video by Harrison
   Kinsley**: This video provides a visual and practical explanation of FNNs, making it easier to grasp the
   concepts through step-by-step guidance. YOUTUBE.COM

These resources should help you build a solid foundation in understanding Feedforward Neural
Networks.

Sources

Figure 4.21: Example of ChatGPT listing relevant references

As you can see, ChatGPT was able to provide me with relevant references to start studying the topic. Plus, if you click on the **Sources** button, you can expand further recommendations of additional links to refer to:

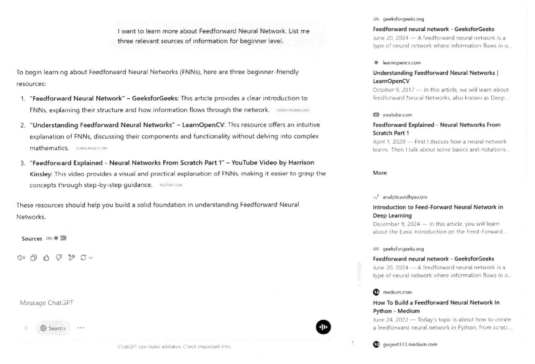

Figure 4.22: Additional links unveiled by the Sources button

Let's go even further in terms of competitive intelligence.

Let's consider writing a book titled *Introduction to Convolutional Neural Networks – an Implementation with Python*. I want to do some research about the potential competitors on the market. The first thing I want to investigate is whether there are already some competitive titles around, so I can ask ChatGPT to generate a list of existing books with the same content:

> I want to write a book titled 'Introduction to Convolutional Neural Networks: an implementation with Python'. Carry out web research and provide me with a list of 3 existing books with competitive content along with their web references.

To assist you in writing your book titled "Introduction to Convolutional Neural Network: An Implementation with Python," here are three existing books with competitive content:

1. **"Practical Convolutional Neural Networks" by Mohit Sewak, Md. Rezaul Karim, and Pradeep Pujari**

   This book provides a comprehensive guide to building Convolutional Neural Networks (CNNs) using Python. It covers topics such as deep neural networks, popular CNN architectures, transfer learning, and advanced vision-related algorithms. AMAZON.COM

2. **"Deep Learning with Python" by François Chollet**

   Authored by the creator of the Keras library, this book offers an intuitive introduction to deep learning with practical examples in Python. It includes sections on CNNs and their applications in computer vision tasks.

3. **"Hands-On Computer Vision with TensorFlow 2" by Benjamin Planche and Eliot Andres**

   This resource guides readers through using CNNs for visual tasks, demonstrating how to implement models like Inception and ResNet, and covering topics such as transfer learning and GANs.
   ANALYTICSINDIAMAG.COM

These books should provide valuable insights and serve as benchmarks for your writing project.

Sources **a P**

.l.

Figure 4.23: Example of ChatGPT providing a list of competitor books

You can also ask for feedback in terms of the saturation of the market you want to publish in:

> Perform an analysis on the saturation of the market for my book titled 'Introduction to Convolutional Neural Network: an implementation with Python'. Refine the output to highlight gaps or opportunities for differentiation.

‹ 3/3 ›

The market for books on Convolutional Neural Networks (CNNs) implemented with Python is competitive, with several notable titles available. However, by analyzing existing publications, we can identify opportunities for differentiation for your book, *"Introduction to Convolutional Neural Network: An Implementation with Python."*

Market Saturation Analysis:

1. **Existing Titles:**

   - *"Practical Convolutional Neural Networks"* by Mohit Sewak, Md. Rezaul Karim, and Pradeep Pujari AMAZON.COM

   - *"Deep Learning with Python"* by François Chollet MEDIUM.COM

   - *"Hands-On Computer Vision with TensorFlow 2"* by Benjamin Planche and Eliot Andres ANALYTICSINDIAMAG.COM

2. **Common Themes:**

   - **Implementation Focus:** Many books emphasize practical implementation, providing code examples and step-by-step guides.

   - **Library-Specific Content:** Several publications concentrate on specific libraries, such as TensorFlow or Keras.

   - **General Deep Learning Coverage:** Some books cover a broad range of deep learning topics, with CNNs as a subset.

Identified Gaps and Opportunities:

1. **Comprehensive Beginner Focus:** There's an opportunity to create a resource that starts from foundational concepts, gradually building up to complex CNN architectures, catering specifically to beginners.

2. **Project-Based Learning:** Developing a series of real-world projects that readers can implement, enhancing practical understanding and engagement.

3. **Common Pitfalls and Troubleshooting:** Including a section dedicated to common challenges and debugging tips in CNN implementation, which is often lacking in existing literature.

4. **Ethical Considerations and Best Practices:** Discussing the ethical implications of CNN applications and promoting best coding practices to ensure responsible AI development.

Figure 4.24: ChatGPT advising about how to be competitive in the market

Overall, ChatGPT can be a valuable assistant for information retrieval and competitive intelligence. However, it is important to remember the knowledge base cut-off is 2021. This means that, whenever we need to retrieve real-time information, or while making a competitive market analysis for today, we might not be able to rely on ChatGPT.

Nevertheless, this tool still provides excellent suggestions and best practices that can be applied, regardless of the knowledge base cut-off.

Summary

All the examples we saw in this chapter were modest representations of what you can achieve with ChatGPT to boost your productivity. These small hacks can greatly assist you with activities that might be repetitive (such as creating a template for responding to or creating a daily routine) or onerous (such as searching for documentation or competitive intelligence).

Note also that, in this chapter, we interacted with ChatGPT only via text: throughout the book, we will also see how to incorporate visual interactions.

In the next chapter, we are going to dive deeper into three main domains where ChatGPT is changing the game – development, marketing, and research.

Subscribe for a free eBook

New frameworks, evolving architectures, research drops, production breakdowns—AI_Distilled filters the noise into a weekly briefing for engineers and researchers working hands-on with LLMs and GenAI systems. Subscribe now and receive a free eBook, along with weekly insights that help you stay focused and informed. Subscribe at `https://packt.link/80z6Y` or scan the QR code below.

5

Developing the Future with ChatGPT

In this chapter, we will discuss how developers can leverage ChatGPT. The chapter focuses on the main use cases ChatGPT addresses in the domain of developers, including code review and optimization, documentation generation, and code generation. The chapter will provide examples and enable you to try the prompts on your own.

After a general introduction to the reasons why developers should leverage ChatGPT as a daily assistant, we will focus on ChatGPT and how it can do the following:

- Why should developers use ChatGPT?
- Generating, optimizing, and debugging code
- Generating code-related documentation and debugging your code
- Explaining **machine learning (ML)** models to help data scientists and business users with model interpretability
- Translating different programming languages
- Working with code on canvas

By the end of this chapter, you will be able to leverage ChatGPT for coding activities and use it as an assistant to improve your coding productivity.

Technical requirements

You can access the complete code for this chapter in the book's accompanying GitHub repository at https://github.com/PacktPublishing/Practical-GenAI-with-ChatGPT-Second-Edition.

Disclaimer

While this chapter explores how ChatGPT can generate and work with code, I want to emphasize that a deep technical background is not required to appreciate its potential. Rather than focusing solely on the mechanics of coding, I encourage you to consider the broader implications of how Generative AI can bridge the gap between software developers and those without coding expertise.

Why should developers use ChatGPT?

Personally, I believe that one of the most mind-blowing capabilities of ChatGPT is in dealing with code – of any type. We've already seen, in previous chapters, some examples of ChatGPT generating Python code. However, ChatGPT's capabilities for developers go way beyond that example. It can be a daily assistant for code generation, explanation, and debugging.

Whether you are a backend/frontend developer, a data scientist, or a data engineer, whenever you work with a programming language, ChatGPT can be a game-changer; we will see how in the several examples in the next sections.

From the next section onward, we will dive deeper into concrete examples of what ChatGPT can achieve when working with code. We will see end-to-end use cases covering different domains so that we can get familiar with using ChatGPT as a code assistant.

Generating, optimizing, and debugging code

The primary capability you should leverage is ChatGPT code generation. How many times have you looked for a pre-built piece of code to start from? Or looked for code that could generate functions, sample datasets, SQL schemas, and so on? ChatGPT is able to generate code based on input in natural language:

generate a python function that add a line to all my csv files saved within "my_folder". The line should be the name of the csv file.

Certainly! Below is a Python function that adds a line containing the name of each CSV file to the beginning of all CSV files saved within a folder named "my_folder":

```python
import os
import csv

def add_filename_to_csv(folder_path):
    # Get a list of all CSV files in the folder
    csv_files = [f for f in os.listdir(folder_path) if f.endswith('.csv')]

    for csv_file in csv_files:
        file_path = os.path.join(folder_path, csv_file)

        # Read the original content of the CSV file
        with open(file_path, 'r', newline='', encoding='utf-8') as file:
            reader = list(csv.reader(file))

        # Add the filename to the beginning of the CSV content
        new_content = [[csv_file]] + reader

        # Write the new content back to the CSV file
        with open(file_path, 'w', newline='', encoding='utf-8') as file:
            writer = csv.writer(file)
            writer.writerows(new_content)

# Example usage
folder_path = 'my_folder'
add_filename_to_csv(folder_path)
```

Make sure to replace `'my_folder'` with the actual path to your folder containing the CSV files. This function will read each CSV file, prepend the filename as the first line, and save the updated content back to the same file.

Figure 5.1: Example of ChatGPT generating a Python function to write into CSV files

As you can see, not only was ChatGPT able to generate the function but it was also able to explain what the function does, how to use it, and what to substitute in generic placeholders such as my_folder.

Now let's raise the difficulty bar. If ChatGPT is capable of generating a Python function, could it generate an entire video game as well? Let's try. What I want to do is provide ChatGPT with an illustration of the type of game I want to develop and ask it to replicate it with code. The following is an illustration of my desired game (can you guess the name?):

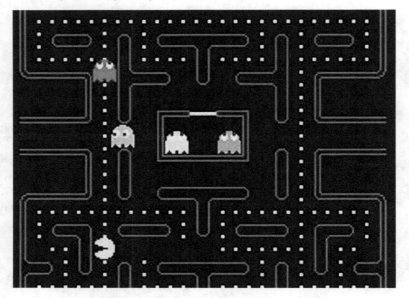

Figure 5.2: Illustration of the game Pac-Man

Now let's ask ChatGPT to reproduce it:

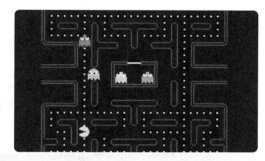

Generate the HTML, JS and CSS code to reproduce the pac-man
game. It should look like the illustration provided.

Creating a complete Pac-Man game with HTML, JavaScript, and CSS involves a fair amount of code.
Below is a simplified version to help you get started. This example includes basic HTML, CSS, and
JavaScript to create a playable Pac-Man game. For a full-featured game, you would need to add
more functionality such as collision detection, ghost AI, and scoring.

HTML (index.html)

```html
html                                                        Copy code

<!DOCTYPE html>
<html lang="en">
<head>
    <meta charset="UTF-8">
    <meta name="viewport" content="width=device-width, initial-scale=1.0">
    <title>Pac-Man Game</title>
    <link rel="stylesheet" href="styles.css">
</head>
<body>
    <canvas id="gameCanvas" width="500" height="500"></canvas>
    <script src="script.js"></script>
</body>
</html>
```

CSS (styles.css)

Figure 5.3: Example of ChatGPT generating HTML, CSS, and JS code

As can be seen by ChatGPT's disclaimer, the full game requires a lot of code; however, let's see how the generated code works so far (to run the code, I used the online tool *codepen.io*):

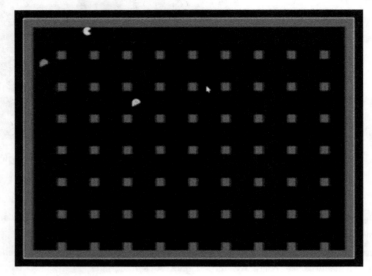

Figure 5.4: Pac-Man game generated by ChatGPT

As you can see, the draft product already looks similar to what I'm aiming for! This is an example of how Generative AI can help you overcome the *difficulties* of starting from scratch; in fact, starting from a blank page can sometimes be blocking, while having a draft product to start from can not only speed up the overall process but also stimulate creativity and improve the quality of the result.

ChatGPT can also be a great assistant for code optimization. In fact, it might save us some running time or compute power by optimizing scripts that we have input. This capability might be compared, in the domain of natural language, to the writing assistance feature we saw in *Chapter 4* in the *Improving writing skills and translation* section.

For example, imagine you want to create a list of odd numbers starting from another list. To achieve the result, you write the following Python script (for the purpose of this exercise, I will also track the execution time with the timeit and datetime libraries):

```python
from timeit import default_timer as timer
from datetime import timedelta
start = timer()
elements = list(range(1_000_000)) data = []
for el in elements: if not el % 2: # if even number
data.append(el)
end = timer() print(timedelta(seconds=end-start))
```

Let's see how long it takes to run:

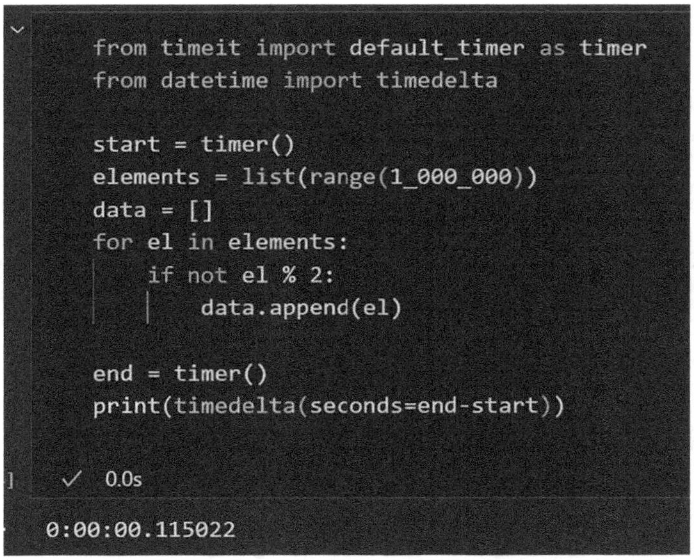

```python
from timeit import default_timer as timer
from datetime import timedelta

start = timer()
elements = list(range(1_000_000))
data = []
for el in elements:
    if not el % 2:
        data.append(el)

end = timer()
print(timedelta(seconds=end-start))
```

✓ 0.0s

0:00:00.115022

Figure 5.5: Speed of execution of a Python function

The execution time was `00.115022` seconds. What happens if we ask ChatGPT to optimize this script?

I wrote the following script to filter a list only for odd numbers.

```
elements = list(range(1_000_000))
data = []
for el in elements:
  if el % 2 != 0:
    data.append(el)
```

Can you create a script to achieve the same result in lower execution time?

Certainly! You can achieve the same result in a more efficient way using list comprehensions, which are generally faster than a for-loop with an append operation in Python.

Here is the optimized script using a list comprehension:

python Copy code

```python
elements = list(range(1_000_000))
data = [el for el in elements if el % 2 != 0]
```

This code should run faster because list comprehensions are optimized for performance in Python.

If you want an even faster approach, you can use the `` `filter` `` function combined with a lambda function, which can sometimes offer better performance:

python Copy code

```python
elements = list(range(1_000_000))
data = list(filter(lambda el: el % 2 != 0, elements))
```

Both of these methods will yield the same result but should execute in less time compared to the original script.

Figure 5.6: ChatGPT generating optimized alternatives to a Python script

ChatGPT provided me with two examples to achieve the same results with lower execution time.

Let's test both of them in a Jupyter notebook:

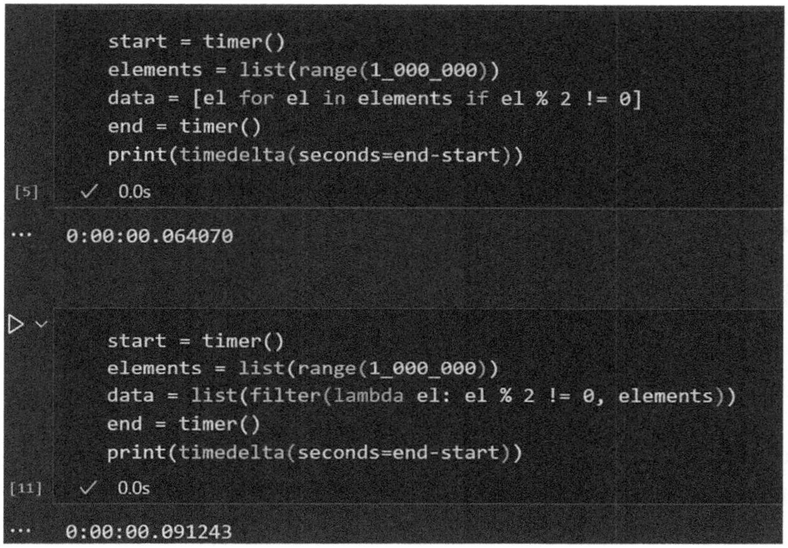

```
start = timer()
elements = list(range(1_000_000))
data = [el for el in elements if el % 2 != 0]
end = timer()
print(timedelta(seconds=end-start))
[5]    ✓  0.0s
...   0:00:00.064070


▷ ∨
start = timer()
elements = list(range(1_000_000))
data = list(filter(lambda el: el % 2 != 0, elements))
end = timer()
print(timedelta(seconds=end-start))
[11]   ✓  0.0s
...   0:00:00.091243
```

Figure 5.7: Speed of execution of two alternative functions generated by ChatGPT

As you can see, both methods lead to a great reduction in time of 44.30% and 20.68%, respectively.

On top of code generation and optimization, ChatGPT can also be leveraged for *error* explanation and debugging. Sometimes, errors are difficult to interpret; hence, a natural language explanation can be useful for identifying the problem and driving you toward the solution.

For example, while running a .py file from my command line, I get the following error:

```
File "C:\Users\vaalt\Anaconda3\lib\site-packages\streamlit\elements\text_
widgets.py", line 266, in _text_input text_input_proto.value = widget_
state.value
TypeError: [] has type list, but expected one of: bytes, Unicode
```

Let's see whether ChatGPT is able to let me understand the nature of the error. To do so, I simply provide ChatGPT with the text of the error and ask it to give me an explanation:

Possible Cause:

The error occurs because `widget_state.value` is of type `list`, but the Streamlit text input (`text_input_proto.value`) expects a string (Unicode or bytes).

Solution:

Convert the value to a string before assigning it to `text_input_proto.value`. Modify your Streamlit code where `widget_state.value` is assigned:

Fix 1: Convert List to a String

```python
text_input_proto.value = str(widget_state.value)  # Convert list to string
```

Fix 2: Ensure widget_state.value is a String

If `widget_state.value` contains user input, ensure it's properly initialized:

```python
widget_state.value = ""  # Ensure it starts as a string
```

If `widget_state.value` is a list, consider joining its elements:

```python
text_input_proto.value = ", ".join(map(str, widget_state.value))  # Join list items into a st
```

Next Steps

- Verify what `widget_state.value` contains before assigning it.
- Print `widget_state.value` to debug:

```python
print(type(widget_state.value), widget_state.value)
```

This will help you understand why it's a list and not a string.

Figure 5.8: ChatGPT explaining a Python error in natural language

Finally, let's imagine I wrote a function in Python that takes a string as input and returns the same string with an underscore after each letter.

In the preceding example, I was expecting to see the g_p_t_ result; however, it only returned t_ with this code:

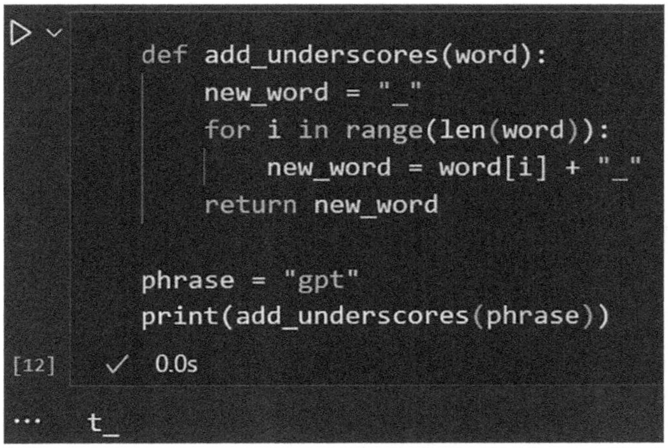

```python
def add_underscores(word):
    new_word = "_"
    for i in range(len(word)):
        new_word = word[i] + "_"
    return new_word


phrase = "gpt"
print(add_underscores(phrase))
```

Figure 5.9: Bugged Python function

Let's ask ChatGPT to debug this function for us:

> I wrote this python function to add an underscore after each letter of a word.
> The expected result for the input word should be w_o_r_d_.
>
> def add_underscores(word):
>   new_word = "_"
>   for i in range(len(word)):
>   new_word = word[i] + "_"
>   return new_word
>
> phrase = "gpt"
> print(add_underscores(phrase))
>
> can you debug this code?

Sure! Let's debug the function you provided. The goal is to add an underscore after each letter of a word. Your current implementation has a couple of issues. Specifically, the variable `new_word` is being reassigned on each iteration, which results in only the last character and underscore being stored in `new_word`.

Here's the corrected function:

```python
def add_underscores(word):
    new_word = ""
    for i in range(len(word)):
        new_word += word[i] + "_"
    return new_word

phrase = "gpt"
print(add_underscores(phrase))
```

Explanation

1. **Initialization**: Initialize `new_word` as an empty string.

2. **Concatenation**: Use the `+=` operator to concatenate each character and an underscore to `new_word` within the loop.

Figure 5.10: Example of ChatGPT debugging a Python function

Impressive, isn't it? Again, ChatGPT provided the correct version of the code, and it helped in explaining where the bugs were and why they led to an incorrect result. Let's see whether it works now:

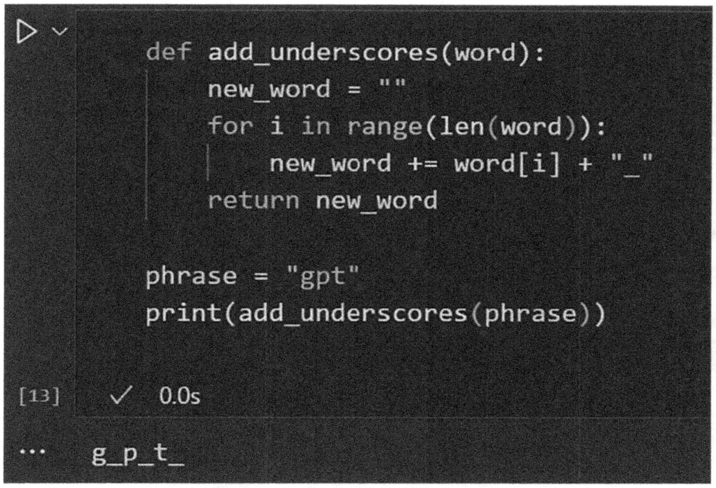

```
def add_underscores(word):
    new_word = ""
    for i in range(len(word)):
        new_word += word[i] + "_"
    return new_word


phrase = "gpt"
print(add_underscores(phrase))

[13]    ✓  0.0s
···     g_p_t_
```

Figure 5.11: Python function after ChatGPT debugging

Well, it obviously does!

These and many other code-related functionalities could really boost your productivity, shortening the time to perform many tasks.

However, ChatGPT goes beyond pure debugging. Thanks to the incredible language understanding of the GPT model, this Generative AI tool is able to generate proper documentation alongside the code, as well as explain exactly what a string of code will do, which we will see in the next section.

Generating documentation and code explainability

Whenever you're working with new applications or projects, it is always good practice to correlate your code with documentation. It might be in the form of a docstring that you can embed in your functions or classes so that others can invoke them directly in the development environment.

For example, let's consider the same function developed in the previous section and make it a Python class:

```
class UnderscoreAdder:
def __init__(self, word):
    self.word = word
```

```
def add_underscores(self):
    return "_".join(self.word)  # More efficient
```

We can test it as follows:

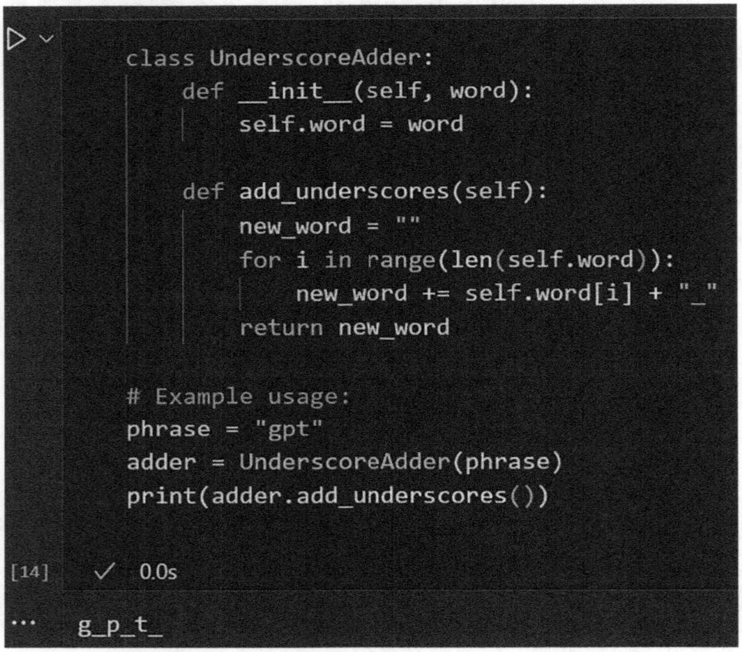

```
class UnderscoreAdder:
    def __init__(self, word):
        self.word = word

    def add_underscores(self):
        new_word = ""
        for i in range(len(self.word)):
            new_word += self.word[i] + "_"
        return new_word

# Example usage:
phrase = "gpt"
adder = UnderscoreAdder(phrase)
print(adder.add_underscores())
```

```
[14]   ✓   0.0s
...   g_p_t_
```

Figure 5.12: Testing the UnderscoreAdder class

Now, let's say I want to be able to retrieve the docstring documentation using the `UnderscoreAdder?` convention. By doing so with Python packages, functions, and methods, we have full documentation of the capabilities of that specific object, as follows (an example with the `pandas` Python library):

```
import pandas as pd
pd?
```

```
Type:           module
String form:    <module 'pandas' from 'C:\\Users\\vaalt\\Anaconda3\\lib\\site-packages\\pandas\\__init__.py'>
File:           c:\users\vaalt\anaconda3\lib\site-packages\pandas\__init__.py
Docstring:
pandas - a powerful data analysis and manipulation library for Python
=====================================================================

**pandas** is a Python package providing fast, flexible, and expressive data
structures designed to make working with "relational" or "labeled" data both
easy and intuitive. It aims to be the fundamental high-level building block for
doing practical, **real world** data analysis in Python. Additionally, it has
the broader goal of becoming **the most powerful and flexible open source data
analysis / manipulation tool available in any language**. It is already well on
its way toward this goal.

Main Features
-------------
Here are just a few of the things that pandas does well:

  - Easy handling of missing data in floating point as well as non-floating
    point data.
  - Size mutability: columns can be inserted and deleted from DataFrame and
    higher dimensional objects
  - Automatic and explicit data alignment: objects can be explicitly aligned
    to a set of labels, or the user can simply ignore the labels and let
    `Series`, `DataFrame`, etc. automatically align the data for you in
    computations.
  - Powerful, flexible group by functionality to perform split-apply-combine
    operations on data sets, for both aggregating and transforming data.
  - Make it easy to convert ragged, differently-indexed data in other Python
    and NumPy data structures into DataFrame objects.
  - Intelligent label-based slicing, fancy indexing, and subsetting of large
    data sets.
  - Intuitive merging and joining data sets.
  - Flexible reshaping and pivoting of data sets.
  - Hierarchical labeling of axes (possible to have multiple labels per tick).
  - Robust IO tools for loading data from flat files (CSV and delimited),
    Excel files, databases, and saving/loading data from the ultrafast HDF5
    format.
  - Time series-specific functionality: date range generation and frequency
    conversion, moving window statistics, date shifting and lagging.
```

Figure 5.13: Example of the pandas library documentation

So, let's now ask ChatGPT to produce the same result for our UnderscoreAdder class.

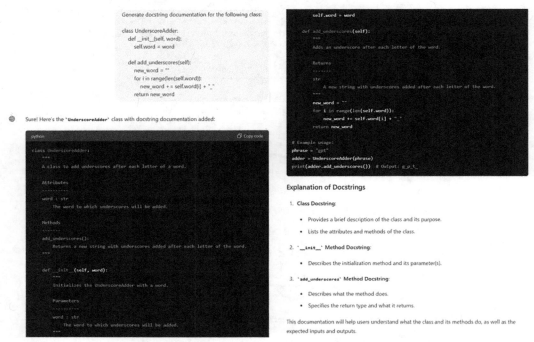

Figure 5.14: ChatGPT updating the code with documentation

As a result, if we update our class as shown in the preceding code with UnderscoreAdder?, we will get the following output:

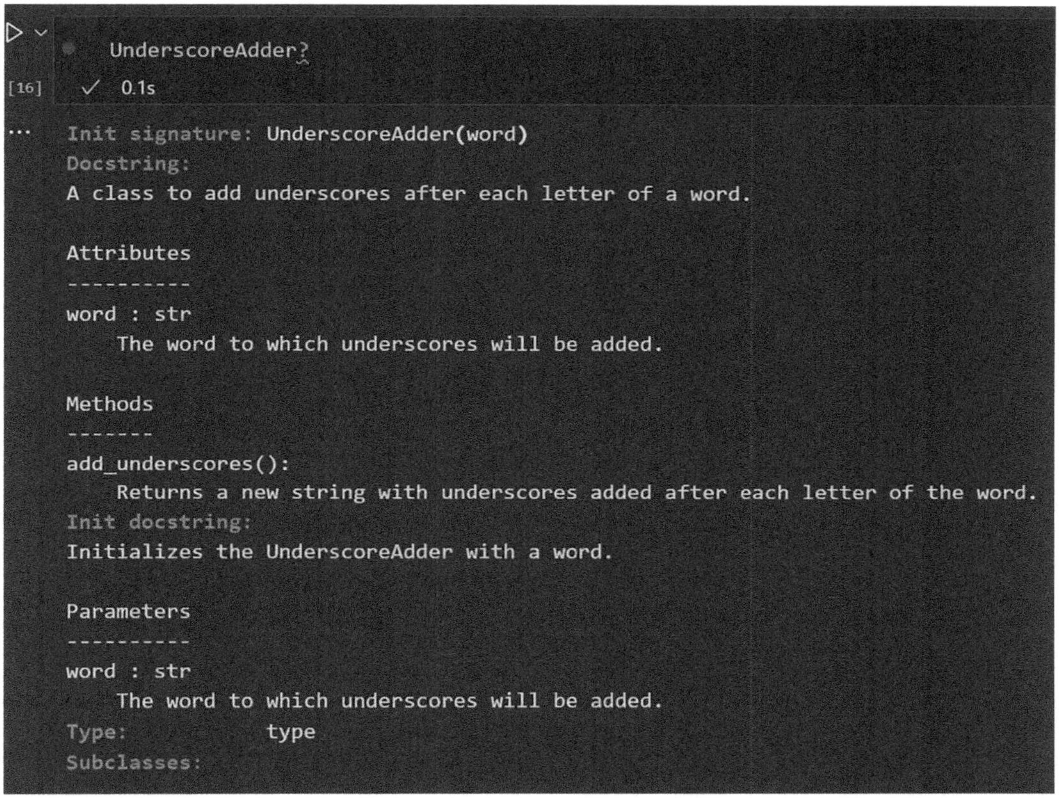

```
▷ ˅    ●   UnderscoreAdder?
[16]      ✓  0.1s

⋯     Init signature: UnderscoreAdder(word)
      Docstring:
      A class to add underscores after each letter of a word.

      Attributes
      ----------
      word : str
          The word to which underscores will be added.

      Methods
      -------
      add_underscores():
          Returns a new string with underscores added after each letter of the word.
      Init docstring:
      Initializes the UnderscoreAdder with a word.

      Parameters
      ----------
      word : str
          The word to which underscores will be added.
      Type:            type
      Subclasses:
```

Figure 5.15: The new UnderscoreAdder class documentation

Finally, ChatGPT can also be leveraged to explain what a script, function, class, or other similar thing does in natural language. We have already seen many examples of ChatGPT enriching its code-related response with clear explanations. However, we can boost this capability by asking specific questions in terms of code understanding.

For example, let's ask ChatGPT to explain to us what the following Python script does:

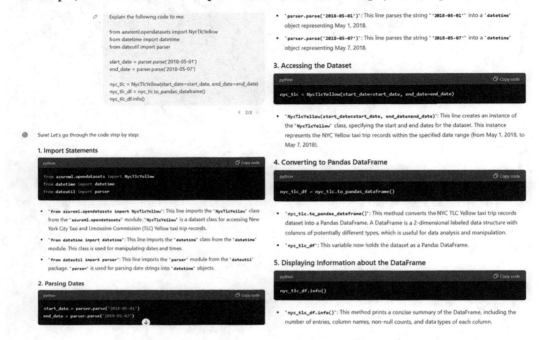

Figure 5.16: Example of ChatGPT explaining a Python script

Code explainability can also be part of the preceding mentioned documentation, or it can be used among developers who might want to better understand complex code from other teams or (as sometimes happens to me) remember what they wrote some time ago.

Thanks to ChatGPT and the capabilities mentioned in this section, developers can easily keep track of the project life cycle in natural language so that it is easier for both new team members and non-technical users to understand the work done so far.

We will see in the next section how code explainability is a pivotal step for ML model interpretability in data science projects.

Understanding ML model interpretability

Model interpretability refers to the degree of ease with which a human can comprehend the logic behind the ML model's predictions. Essentially, it is the capability to comprehend how a model arrives at its decisions and which variables are contributing to its forecasts.

Let's see an example of model interpretability using a deep learning **convolutional neural network (CNN)** for image classification. I built my model in Python using Keras. For this purpose, I will download the CIFAR-10 dataset directly from keras.datasets; it consists of 60,000 32x32 color images (so 3-channel images) in 10 classes (airplane, automobile, bird, cat, deer, dog, frog, horse, ship, and truck), with 6,000 images per class. Here, I will share just the body of the model; you can find all the related code in the book's GitHub repository for data preparation and pre-processing at https://github.com/PacktPublishing/Modern-Generative-AI-with-ChatGPT-and-OpenAI-Models/tree/main/Chapter%206%20-%20ChatGPT%20for%20Developers/code

```
model=tf.keras.Sequential()
model.add(tf.keras.layers.Conv2D(32,kernel_
size=(3,3),activation='relu',input_shape=
(32,32,1)))
model.add(tf.keras.layers.MaxPooling2D(pool_size=(2,2))) model.
add(tf.keras.layers.Flatten()) model.add(tf.keras.layers.
Dense(1024,activation='relu')) model.add(tf.keras.layers.
Dense(10,activation='softmax'))
```

The preceding code is made of several layers that perform different actions. I might be interested in getting an explanation of the structure of the model as well as the purpose of each layer. Let's ask ChatGPT for some help with that (below you can see an extract of the response):

Adding Layers to the Model

1. Convolutional Layer

```python
model.add(tf.keras.layers.Conv2D(32, kernel_size=(3, 3), activation='relu', input_shape=(3
```

- `tf.keras.layers.Conv2D`: This adds a 2D convolutional layer to the model.

    - `32`: The number of filters (output channels) in the convolution.
    - `kernel_size=(3, 3)`: The dimensions of the convolution window.
    - `activation='relu'`: The activation function to use, ReLU (Rectified Linear Unit) in this case, which helps in introducing non-linearity.
    - `input_shape=(32, 32, 1)`: The shape of the input data, where `32x32` is the size of the input image, and `1` indicates that the images are grayscale (single channel).

2. Max Pooling Layer

```python
model.add(tf.keras.layers.MaxPooling2D(pool_size=(2, 2)))
```

- `tf.keras.layers.MaxPooling2D`: This adds a max pooling layer to the model.

    - `pool_size=(2, 2)`: The dimensions of the pooling window. Max pooling downsamples the input representation by taking the maximum value over a `2x2` window, reducing the spatial dimensions of the input.

3. Flatten Layer

```python
model.add(tf.keras.layers.Flatten())
```

- `tf.keras.layers.Flatten`: This layer flattens the input. It converts the 2D matrix data to a 1D vector, which can be fed into a fully connected (dense) layer. This is necessary before passing the data to dense layers.

Figure 5.17: Model interpretability with ChatGPT

As you can see in the preceding figure, ChatGPT was able to give us a clear explanation of the structure and layers of our CNN. It also adds some comments and tips, such as the fact that using the max pooling layer helps reduce the dimensionality of the input.

I can also be supported by ChatGPT in interpreting model results in the validation phase. So, after splitting the data into training and test sets and training the model on the training set, I want to see its performance on the test set:

```
model.fit(np.resize(x_train, (50000,32,32,1))/255.0,
        tf.keras.utils.to_categorical(y_train),
        batch_size=batch_size,
        shuffle=True,
        epochs=epochs,
        validation_data=(np.resize(x_test, (10000,32,32,1))/255.0,
        tf.keras.utils.to_categorical(y_test))
        )
```

```
Epoch 1/3
1563/1563 [==============================] - 208s 133ms/step - loss: 2.3021 - accuracy: 0.1038 - val_loss: 2.3029 - val_accuracy: 0.1039
Epoch 2/3
1563/1563 [==============================] - 209s 133ms/step - loss: 2.2964 - accuracy: 0.1104 - val_loss: 2.3070 - val_accuracy: 0.1001
Epoch 3/3
1563/1563 [==============================] - 909s 582ms/step - loss: 2.2743 - accuracy: 0.1312 - val_loss: 2.3173 - val_accuracy: 0.1006
```

Figure 5.18: Evaluation metrics

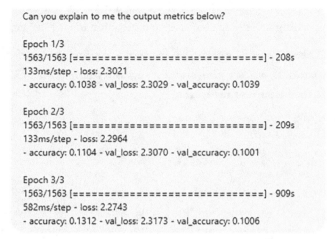

General Format

Each epoch output provides several pieces of information:

1. **Epoch Progress:** Shows the current epoch and total number of epochs.

2. **Batch Progress:** Indicates the completion of batches within the epoch.

3. **Metrics:** Includes training loss, training accuracy, validation loss, and validation accuracy.

Detailed Explanation

Epoch Information

- **Epoch 1/3:** This indicates that the training is in the first epoch out of a total of 3 epochs.

Batch Progress and Time

- **1563/1563:** Indicates the total number of batches processed in this epoch. Here, all 1563 batches have been processed.

↓

Figure 5.19: Example of ChatGPT explaining evaluation metrics

Once again, the result is really impressive, and it provides clear guidance on how to set up ML experiments in terms of training and test sets. It explains how important it is for the model to be sufficiently generalized so that it does not overfit and is able to predict accurate results on data that it has never seen before.

There are many reasons why model interpretability is important. A pivotal element is that it reduces the gap between business users and the code behind models. This is key to enabling business users to understand how a model behaves, as well as translating it into useful business ideas.

Furthermore, model interpretability enables one of the key principles of responsible and ethical AI, which is transparency in how the model behind AI systems thinks and behaves. Unlocking model interpretability means detecting potential biases or harmful behaviors a model could have while in production and consequently preventing them from happening.

Overall, ChatGPT can provide valuable support in the context of model interpretability, generating insights at the row level, as we saw in the previous example.

The next and last ChatGPT capability we will explore will be yet another boost for developers' productivity, especially when various programming languages are being used within the same project.

Translation among different programming languages

In *Chapter 4*, we saw how ChatGPT has great capabilities for translating between different languages. What is really incredible is that natural language is not its only object of translation. In fact, ChatGPT is capable of translating between different programming languages while keeping the same output and style (namely, it preserves docstring documentation if present).

There are so many scenarios where this could be a game-changer.

For example, you might have to learn a new programming language or statistical tool you've never seen before because you need to quickly deliver a project on it. With the help of ChatGPT, you can start programming in your language of preference and then ask it to translate to the desired language, which you will be learning alongside the translation process.

Imagine that the project needs to be delivered in MATLAB (a proprietary numerical computing and programming software developed by MathWorks), yet you've always programmed in Python. The project consists of classifying images from the **Modified National Institute of Standards and Technology** (**MNIST**) dataset (the original dataset description and related paper can be found at http://yann.lecun.com/exdb/mnist/). The dataset contains numerous handwritten digits and is frequently utilized to teach various image-processing systems.

To start, I wrote the following Python code to initialize a deep learning model for classification:

```python
from tensorflow.keras import layers

# Load the MNIST dataset
(x_train, y_train), (x_test, y_test) = keras.datasets.mnist.load_ data()

# Preprocess the data
x_train = x_train.reshape(-1, 28*28) / 255.0 x_test = x_test.reshape(-1,
28*28) / 255.0 y_train = keras.utils.to_categorical(y_train) y_test =
keras.utils.to_categorical(y_test)

# Define the model architecture model = keras.Sequential([
layers.Dense(256, activation='relu', input_shape=(28*28,)), layers.
Dense(128, activation='relu'),
layers.Dense(10, activation='softmax')
])

# Compile the model
model.compile(optimizer='adam', loss='categorical_crossentropy',
metrics=['accuracy'])

# Train the model
history = model.fit(x_train, y_train, validation_split=0.2, epochs=10,
batch_size=128)

# Evaluate the model
test_loss, test_acc = model.evaluate(x_test, y_test, verbose=0)
print('Test accuracy:', test_acc)
```

Let's now see what happens if we give the preceding code as context to ChatGPT and ask it to translate it into MATLAB:

Here is the MATLAB translation of the provided TensorFlow code for training a neural network on the MNIST dataset.

MATLAB Code

```matlab
% Load the MNIST dataset
[xTrain, yTrain, xTest, yTest] = digitTrain4DArrayData;

% Reshape the data and normalize
xTrain = reshape(xTrain, [], 28*28) / 255.0;
xTest = reshape(xTest, [], 28*28) / 255.0;

% Convert the labels to categorical format
yTrain = categorical(yTrain);
yTest = categorical(yTest);

% Define the model architecture
layers = [
    fullyConnectedLayer(256, 'Activation', 'relu', 'InputSize', 28*28)
    fullyConnectedLayer(128, 'Activation', 'relu')
    fullyConnectedLayer(10, 'Activation', 'softmax')
];

% Create the neural network
model = dlnetwork(layerGraph(layers));

% Specify training options
options = trainingOptions('adam', ...
    'MaxEpochs', 10, ...
    'MiniBatchSize', 128, ...
    'ValidationData', {xTest, yTest}, ...
    'Verbose', true, ...
    'Plots', 'training-progress');

% Train the model
trainedNet = trainNetwork(xTrain, yTrain, model.Layers, options);

% Evaluate the model
YPred = classify(trainedNet, xTest);
testAcc = mean(YPred == yTest);
disp(['Test accuracy:', num2str(testAcc)]);
```

Figure 5.20: ChatGPT translates Python code into MATLAB

Code translation could also reduce the skill gap between new technologies and current programming capabilities.

Another key implication of code translation is **application modernization**. Indeed, imagine you want to refresh your application stack, namely, migrating to the cloud. You could decide to initiate with a simple lift and shift going toward **infrastructure-as-a-service (IaaS)** instances (such as Windows or Linux **virtual machines (VMs)**). However, in the second phase, you might want to refactor, rearchitect, or even rebuild your applications.

The following diagram depicts the various options for application modernization:

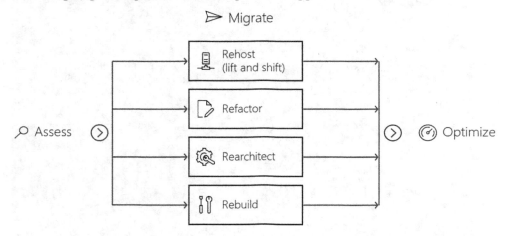

Figure 5.21: Four ways you can migrate your applications to the public cloud

ChatGPT and OpenAI Codex models can help you with the migration. Consider mainframes, for example.

Mainframes are computers that are predominantly employed by large organizations to carry out essential tasks such as bulk data processing for activities such as censuses, consumer and industry statistics, enterprise resource planning, and large-scale transaction processing. The application programming language of the mainframe environment is **Common Business Oriented Language (COBOL)**. Despite being invented in 1959, COBOL is still in use today and is one of the oldest programming languages in existence.

As technology continues to improve, applications residing in the realm of mainframes have been subject to a continuous process of migration and modernization aimed at enhancing existing legacy mainframe infrastructure in areas such as interface, code, cost, performance, and maintainability.

Of course, this implies translating COBOL to more modern programming languages, such as C# or Java. The problem is that COBOL is unknown to most new-generation programmers; hence, there is a huge skills gap in this context.

Let's consider a COBOL script that reads an input number, adds 10 to it, and then prints the result:

```
IDENTIFICATION DIVISION.
PROGRAM-ID. AddTen.

DATA DIVISION.
WORKING-STORAGE SECTION.
01  INPUT-NUMBER    PIC 9(5).
01  RESULT-NUMBER   PIC 9(5).

PROCEDURE DIVISION.
    DISPLAY 'Enter a number: '.
    ACCEPT INPUT-NUMBER.
    COMPUTE RESULT-NUMBER = INPUT-NUMBER + 10.
    DISPLAY 'Result after adding 10: ' RESULT-NUMBER.
    STOP RUN.
```

I then passed the previous COBOL script to ChatGPT so that it could use it as context to formulate its response. Let's now ask ChatGPT to translate that script into C#:

Certainly! Here's the equivalent code translated into C#:

C# Code

```csharp
using System;

namespace AddTen
{
    class Program
    {
        static void Main(string[] args)
        {
            // Variable declarations
            int inputNumber;
            int resultNumber;

            // Prompt the user to enter a number
            Console.Write("Enter a number: ");

            // Read input from the user and try to parse it as an integer
            if (int.TryParse(Console.ReadLine(), out inputNumber))
            {
                // Add 10 to the input number
                resultNumber = inputNumber + 10;

                // Display the result
                Console.WriteLine("Result after adding 10: " + resultNumber);
            }
            else
            {
                // Handle invalid input
                Console.WriteLine("Invalid input. Please enter a valid number.");
            }
        }
    }
}
```

Figure 5.22: Example of ChatGPT translating COBOL to C#

Tools such as ChatGPT can help reduce the skill gap in this and similar scenarios by introducing a layer that knows both the past and future of programming.

In conclusion, ChatGPT can be an effective tool for application modernization, providing code upgrading in addition to valuable insights and recommendations for enhancing legacy systems. With its advanced language-processing capabilities and extensive knowledge base, ChatGPT can help organizations streamline their modernization efforts, making the process faster, more efficient, and more effective.

Working with code on canvas

In *Chapter 4*, we mentioned the new ChatGPT canvas feature, which allows users to dynamically modify the model's response in a collaborative workspace. However, when it comes to code development, this feature really shines.

In fact, it provides an environment for code development, execution, and debugging.

Let's see an example. We will start with a simple query to ChatGPT:

Generate the Python code to plot the cosine function

Here is the Python code to plot the **cosine function** using **Matplotlib**:

```python
import numpy as np
import matplotlib.pyplot as plt

# Define the x values (from -2π to 2π)
x = np.linspace(-2 * np.pi, 2 * np.pi, 400)

# Compute the cosine values
y = np.cos(x)

# Plot the function
plt.plot(x, y, label='cos(x)', color='blue')

# Add labels and title
plt.xlabel("x values (radians)")
plt.ylabel("cos(x)")
plt.title("Cosine Function")

# Add grid and legend
plt.axhline(0, color='black', linewidth=0.5)
plt.axvline(0, color='black', linewidth=0.5)
plt.grid(True, linestyle='--', alpha=0.6)
plt.legend()

# Show the plot
plt.show()
```

Figure 5.23: Generating code with ChatGPT

As expected, ChatGPT was able to generate the required code. Now, if we click on the **Edit** icon, we will be able to access the canvas workspace, where we can:

- Modify the code:

Figure 5.24: Modifying code with the canvas workspace

- Run the code and see the results in a console:

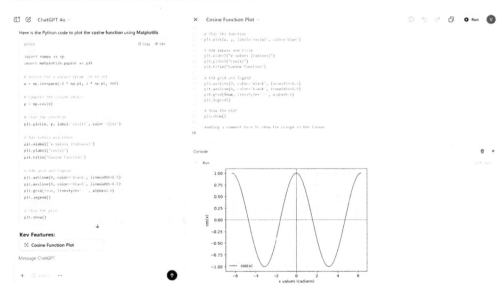

Figure 5.25: Seamlessly testing and modifying code

This is a game-changer for software development; it means having the possibility to seamlessly test and execute code while interacting with ChatGPT, without the need to move from this app to your development environment.

Let's go even further. Another way you to interact with canvas is by invoking it as a tool:

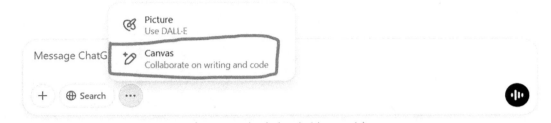

Figure 5.26: Invoking canvas directly

By doing so, ChatGPT will automatically *enter in the mood* of working with code. Let's ask the same question as before, but this time, leveraging the canvas tool directly.

In this case, ChatGPT will directly open a canvas workspace for us, providing additional coding tools:

Figure 5.27: The canvas workspace

With these tools, you have four main features:

- The **Add comments** feature gives instructions to ChatGPT to modify your code in the same canvas you are working on

- The **Add logs** feature inserts print statements or logging mechanisms into your code, aiding in tracking execution flow and diagnosing issues

- By selecting the **Fix bugs** shortcut, ChatGPT analyzes your code to identify and correct errors, enhancing code reliability

- The **Port to a language** feature translates your code into another programming language seamlessly

By integrating these features, ChatGPT's canvas offers a comprehensive environment for code development, execution, and debugging, enhancing productivity and facilitating a smoother coding workflow.

Summary

ChatGPT can be a valuable resource for developers looking to enhance their skills and streamline their workflows. We started by seeing how ChatGPT can generate, optimize, and debug your code, but we also covered further capabilities, such as generating documentation alongside your code, explaining your ML models, and translating between different programming languages for application modernization.

Whether you're a seasoned developer or just starting out, ChatGPT offers a powerful tool for learning and growth, reducing the gap between code and natural language.

In the next chapter, we will dive deeper into another domain of application where ChatGPT *could* be a game-changer: marketing.

6

Mastering Marketing with ChatGPT

In this chapter, we will focus on how marketers can leverage ChatGPT, looking at the main use cases of ChatGPT in this domain, and how marketers can leverage it as a valuable assistant.

We will learn how ChatGPT can assist in the following activities:

- Leveraging ChatGPT for marketing
- New product development and the go-to-market strategy
- A/B testing for marketing comparison
- Making more efficient websites and posts with search engine optimization
- Sentiment analysis of textual data

By the end of this chapter, you will be able to leverage ChatGPT for marketing-related activities and to boost your productivity.

Technical requirements

You will need an OpenAI account to access ChatGPT. Refer to *Chapter 2* on how to create a ChatGPT account. You can access the complete code for this chapter in the book's accompanying GitHub repository at `https://github.com/PacktPublishing/Practical-GenAI-with-ChatGPT-Second-Edition`.

Leveraging ChatGPT for marketing

Marketing is one of those domains where ChatGPT and OpenAI models' creative power can be leveraged in their purest form.

They can be practical tools to support creative development in terms of new products, marketing campaigns, **search engine optimization (SEO)**, and so on. Overall, marketers automate and streamline many aspects of their work, while also improving the quality and effectiveness of their marketing efforts.

Here is an example. One of the most prominent and promising use cases of ChatGPT in marketing is personalized marketing. For example, a marketing team can use ChatGPT to analyze customer data and develop targeted email campaigns that are tailored to specific customer preferences and behavior. This can increase the likelihood of conversion and lead to greater customer satisfaction. By providing insights into customer sentiment and behavior, generating personalized marketing messages, providing personalized customer support, and generating content, ChatGPT can help marketers deliver exceptional customer experiences and drive business growth.

This is one of many examples of ChatGPT's application in marketing. In the following sections, we will look at concrete examples of end-to-end marketing projects supported by ChatGPT.

Note that, in some sections, I'll be adding an extra *prompting boost* section for some more advanced options you might want to try out for your own projects.

New product development and the go-to-market strategy

The first way you can introduce ChatGPT into your marketing activity might be as an assistant in new product development and the **go-to-market (GTM)** strategy.

In this section, we will look at a step-by-step guide on how to develop and promote a new product. We already own a running clothing brand called RunFast, and so far, we have only produced shoes, so we want to expand our business with a new product line. We will start by brainstorming ideas to create a GTM strategy. Of course, everything is supported by ChatGPT:

- **Brainstorming ideas:** The first thing ChatGPT can support us with is brainstorming and drafting options for our new product line. It will also provide the reasoning behind each suggestion. So, let's ask what kind of new product line we should focus on:

I own a running clothing brand that produces running shoes. Generate 3 new product ideas I can add as product lines for my brand

 ⏸ Memory updated

Here are three new product ideas you can add to your running clothing brand:

1. **Smart Running Apparel**:

   - **Description**: High-tech running clothes equipped with sensors to monitor heart rate, steps, and calories burned. The apparel could include shirts, shorts, and socks with integrated technology that syncs with a mobile app to provide real-time feedback and performance tracking.
   - **Key Features**: Breathable and moisture-wicking fabric, seamless integration with fitness apps, washable electronics, and customizable alerts for hydration and pace.

2. **Eco-Friendly Running Gear**:

   - **Description**: A line of environmentally sustainable running gear made from recycled materials. This could include jackets, leggings, and hats designed for different weather conditions, promoting eco-conscious running.
   - **Key Features**: Recycled polyester fabric, biodegradable packaging, durable and high-performance material, and a program for recycling old running gear.

3. **Personalized Running Shoes**:

   - **Description**: Customizable running shoes tailored to the individual's foot shape, running style, and personal preferences. Using advanced 3D printing technology and a user-friendly online design tool, runners can create shoes that fit perfectly and reflect their style.
   - **Key Features**: 3D-printed insoles for perfect fit, a variety of design options (colors, patterns, logos), materials chosen based on running needs (trail, road, marathon), and virtual fitting sessions with experts.

◁» ⎗ ↻ ⊘ ✧

↓

Figure 6.1: Example of new ideas generated by ChatGPT

Out of the three suggestions, we will pick the second one because of the positive environmental impact that we can make with it, as well as improving our brand reputation. More specifically, we will start with eco-friendly running socks.

- **Product name:** Now that we have our idea fixed in mind, we need to think of a catchy name for it. Again, we will ask ChatGPT for more options so that we can then pick our favorite one:

> I like the second option, and I'll start with eco-friendly running socks. Generate 5 options for a catchy product line name.

Here are five options for a catchy product line name for your eco-friendly running socks:

1. **GreenStride Socks**
2. **EcoPace Performance Socks**
3. **Sustainable Sprint Socks**
4. **EarthRunner Socks**
5. **NatureStep Activewear**

Figure 6.2: A list of potential product names

GreenStride sounds good enough for me – I'll go ahead with that one.

- **Generating catchy slogans:** On top of the product name, we also want to share the intent behind the name and the mission of the product line, so that our target audience is captured by it. We want to inspire trust and loyalty in our customers and for them to see themselves reflected in the mission behind our new product line.

> Generate 3 slogans for the "GreenStride" name. They should be motivating and concise.

Here are three motivating and concise slogans for the "GreenStride" name:

1. **"Run Green, Run Strong."**
2. **"Step Forward, Leave No Trace."**
3. **"Stride with Purpose."**

Figure 6.3: A list of slogans for our new product name

Great – now I'm satisfied with the product name and slogan that I will use later on to create a unique social media announcement. Before doing that, I want to spend more time on market research for the target audience.

what kind of target audience should I address with the promotion of GreenStride socks product line?

For promoting the "GreenStride" socks product line, you should target the following audience segments:

1. **Eco-Conscious Runners**:

   - **Description**: Individuals who prioritize sustainability and environmentally friendly products. They are willing to invest in eco-friendly alternatives and are often knowledgeable about environmental issues.
   - **Demographics**: Ages 25-45, urban dwellers, middle to high income, active on social media, particularly platforms focused on sustainability and fitness.
   - **Marketing Channels**: Social media campaigns, environmental blogs, partnerships with eco-friendly influencers, and sustainability forums.

2. **Fitness Enthusiasts**:

   - **Description**: People who are passionate about running and maintaining an active lifestyle. They value high-performance gear and are interested in the latest trends and innovations in running apparel.
   - **Demographics**: Ages 20-40, both genders, middle to high income, frequent participants in marathons, races, and running clubs.
   - **Marketing Channels**: Running and fitness magazines, sponsorships at running events, online fitness communities, and targeted ads on fitness apps.

3. **Health-Conscious Consumers**:

   - **Description**: Individuals focused on overall wellness, including physical activity, healthy eating, and sustainable living. They are looking for products that support their healthy lifestyle and ethical values.
   - **Demographics**: Ages 30-50, both genders, middle to high income, likely to participate in yoga, pilates, and other wellness activities.
   - **Marketing Channels**: Health and wellness blogs, collaborations with wellness influencers, email newsletters, and health-focused retail stores.

Figure 6.4: List of groups of target people to reach with my new product line

It's important to have in mind different clusters within your audience so that you can differentiate the messages you want to give. In my case, I want to make sure that my product line will address different groups of people, such as competitive runners, casual runners, and fitness enthusiasts.

- **Product variants and sales channels**: According to the preceding clusters of potential customers, I could generate product variants so that they are more tailored toward specific audiences:

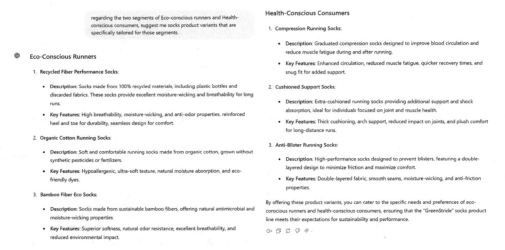

Figure 6.5: Example of variants of the product line

Similarly, I can also ask ChatGPT to suggest different sales channels for each of the preceding groups:

what could be the best channel to reach each of the two segments above?

Best Channels to Reach Eco-Conscious Runners

1. **Social Media Campaigns:**

   - **Platforms:** Instagram, Facebook, and Pinterest.
   - **Strategies:** Use visually appealing content that highlights the eco-friendly aspects of the socks, collaborate with eco-friendly influencers, and participate in environmental awareness campaigns.

2. **Environmental Blogs and Websites:**

   - **Platforms:** Popular eco-conscious blogs, sustainability-focused websites.
   - **Strategies:** Write guest posts, engage in sponsored content, and provide informative articles about the sustainable practices used in the production of GreenStride socks.

3. **Partnerships with Eco-Friendly Organizations:**

   - **Organizations:** Environmental NGOs, sustainability-focused running clubs, and eco-conscious events.
   - **Strategies:** Sponsor events, provide product samples for eco-marathons, and create joint marketing campaigns with these organizations.

4. **Email Newsletters:**

   - **Platforms:** Email marketing services like Mailchimp or Constant Contact.
   - **Strategies:** Create informative newsletters that highlight the environmental benefits of GreenStride socks, share stories about sustainable practices, and offer special promotions

Best Channels to Reach Health-Conscious Consumers

1. **Health and Wellness Blogs and Magazines:**

   - **Platforms:** Popular health blogs, online wellness magazines, and physical fitness magazines.
   - **Strategies:** Contribute articles, engage in product reviews, and offer sponsored content focused on the health benefits of wearing GreenStride socks.

2. **Fitness and Wellness Influencers:**

   - **Platforms:** Instagram, YouTube, and TikTok.
   - **Strategies:** Collaborate with fitness influencers to create content that showcases the health benefits of the socks, such as improved circulation and muscle support.

3. **Online Fitness Communities and Forums:**

   - **Platforms:** Reddit, fitness-related forums, and health-focused online communities.
   - **Strategies:** Engage in discussions, share success stories and testimonials, and provide expert advice on the benefits of using GreenStride socks for running and overall wellness.

4. **Health-Focused Retail Stores:**

   - **Stores:** Specialty health stores, fitness gear shops, and wellness centers.
   - **Strategies:** Partner with these stores to carry GreenStride socks, offer in-store promotions, and provide educational material about the health benefits of the socks.

By leveraging these targeted channels, you can effectively reach and engage with both eco-conscious runners and health-conscious consumers, driving awareness and sales for your GreenStride socks product line.

Figure 6.6: Suggestions for different sales channels by ChatGPT

- **Standing out from the competition**: I want my product line to stand out from the competition and emerge in a very saturated market – I want to make it unique. With this purpose in mind, I ask ChatGPT to include social considerations such as sustainability and inclusivity. Let's ask ChatGPT for some suggestions in that respect:

> give me three concise suggestions on how to make my socks line GreeStride outstanding and unique in a competitive market.

 Here are three concise suggestions to make your GreenStride socks line outstanding and unique in a competitive market:

1. **Innovative Eco-Materials:**

   - Use cutting-edge, sustainable materials like recycled ocean plastics, organic hemp, or biodegradable fibers. Highlight these unique materials in your marketing to emphasize the advanced sustainability of your product.

2. **Performance-Enhancing Features:**

   - Integrate advanced features such as targeted compression zones, moisture-wicking technology, and anti-blister designs. Ensure these features are scientifically validated and clearly communicated to consumers to showcase the dual focus on sustainability and performance.

3. **Transparent Production Process:**

   - Offer full transparency about your production process, from sourcing to manufacturing. Provide detailed information and certifications about the eco-friendly practices and fair labor conditions involved in making GreenStride socks. Transparency builds trust and can be a significant differentiator.

↓

Figure 6.7: Example of outstanding features generated by ChatGPT

As you can see, it was able to generate interesting features that could make my product line unique.

- **Product description:** Now it's time to start building our GTM plan. First of all, I want to generate a product description for my website, including all the earlier unique differentiators.

> generate a product description (max 150 words) for GreenStride socks line using the unique differentiator you listed above. It should be attention-grabbing and effective, as well as SEO optimized. list also the SEO keywords you used once you finish.

GreenStride Socks Product Description

Step into the future of running with GreenStride socks, crafted from innovative eco-materials like recycled ocean plastics and organic hemp. Designed for superior performance, our socks feature targeted compression zones, moisture-wicking technology, and anti-blister designs to keep you comfortable and focused on your run. With GreenStride, you're not just choosing top-notch running gear—you're supporting a sustainable future. We're committed to transparency, offering full insight into our eco-friendly production process and fair labor practices. Elevate your stride with GreenStride, where sustainability meets performance.

SEO Keywords

- Eco-friendly running socks
- Sustainable performance socks
- Recycled materials socks
- Organic hemp socks
- Anti-blister running socks
- Moisture-wicking technology
- Targeted compression zones
- Transparent production process
- Sustainable athletic wear

Figure 6.8: Example of description and SEO keywords generated by ChatGPT

- **Fair price**: Another key element is determining a fair price for our product. As I differentiated among product variants for different audiences (competitive runners, casual runners, and fitness enthusiasts), I also want to have a price range that takes into account this clustering. Note that, in the following example, ChatGPT is invoking the web search plugin to retrieve updated information about the current marketplace of running socks in terms of pricing.

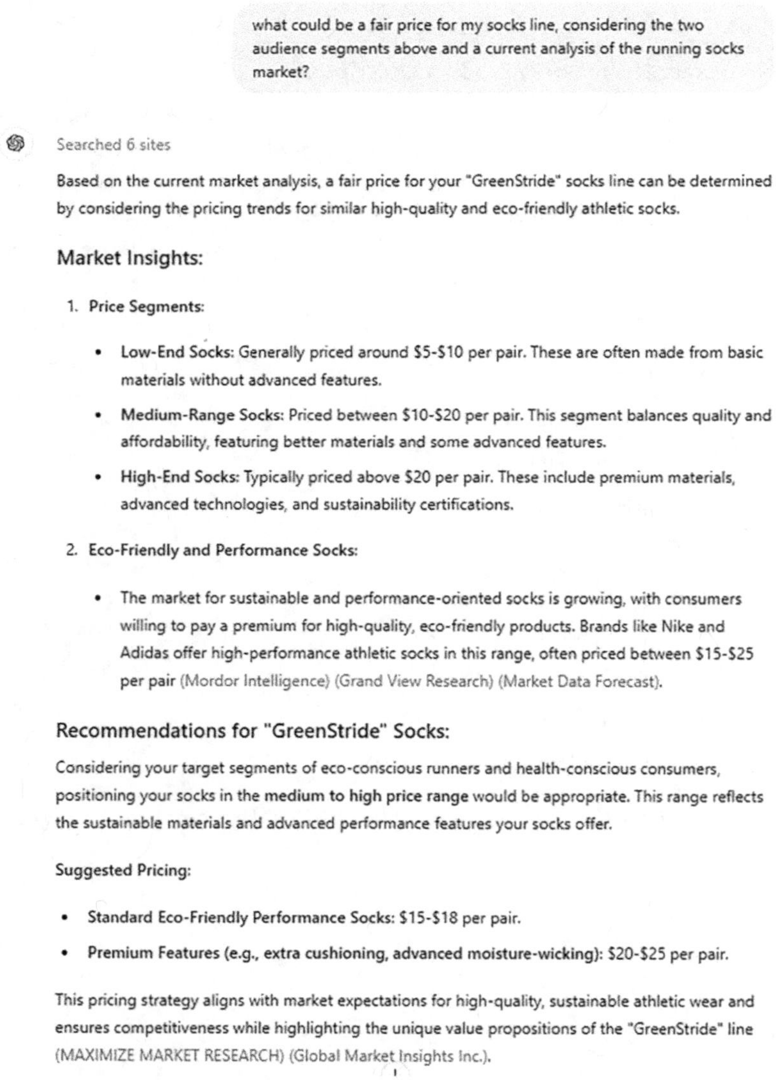

what could be a fair price for my socks line, considering the two audience segments above and a current analysis of the running socks market?

Searched 6 sites

Based on the current market analysis, a fair price for your "GreenStride" socks line can be determined by considering the pricing trends for similar high-quality and eco-friendly athletic socks.

Market Insights:

1. **Price Segments:**

   - **Low-End Socks:** Generally priced around $5-$10 per pair. These are often made from basic materials without advanced features.
   - **Medium-Range Socks:** Priced between $10-$20 per pair. This segment balances quality and affordability, featuring better materials and some advanced features.
   - **High-End Socks:** Typically priced above $20 per pair. These include premium materials, advanced technologies, and sustainability certifications.

2. **Eco-Friendly and Performance Socks:**

   - The market for sustainable and performance-oriented socks is growing, with consumers willing to pay a premium for high-quality, eco-friendly products. Brands like Nike and Adidas offer high-performance athletic socks in this range, often priced between $15-$25 per pair (Mordor Intelligence) (Grand View Research) (Market Data Forecast).

Recommendations for "GreenStride" Socks:

Considering your target segments of eco-conscious runners and health-conscious consumers, positioning your socks in the **medium to high price range** would be appropriate. This range reflects the sustainable materials and advanced performance features your socks offer.

Suggested Pricing:

- **Standard Eco-Friendly Performance Socks:** $15-$18 per pair.
- **Premium Features** (e.g., extra cushioning, advanced moisture-wicking): $20-$25 per pair.

This pricing strategy aligns with market expectations for high-quality, sustainable athletic wear and ensures competitiveness while highlighting the unique value propositions of the "GreenStride" line (MAXIMIZE MARKET RESEARCH) (Global Market Insights Inc.).

Figure 6.9: Price ranges for product variants

We are almost there. We have gone through many new product development and GTM steps, and in each of them, ChatGPT acted as a great support tool.

As one last thing, we can ask ChatGPT to generate an Instagram post about our new product, including relevant hashtags and SEO keywords. We can then generate the DALL-E image, which comes as an embedded plugin in ChatGPT Plus.

> I want to generate an Instagram post to announce the launch of GreenStride socks. Write a post (max 150 words) including the unique features and differentiators mentioned above, as well as relevant hashtags.

Instagram Post for GreenStride Socks Launch

🌿 **Introducing GreenStride Socks!** 🌿

Step into a new era of running with GreenStride, where sustainability meets top-tier performance. Crafted from innovative eco-materials like recycled ocean plastics and organic hemp, our socks offer targeted compression, advanced moisture-wicking technology, and anti-blister designs. Each pair is made with the environment in mind, ensuring you can run green and run strong. 🏃‍♀️ 🌱

Join the movement towards a sustainable future with socks that don't just perform—they make a difference. 🌍 ✨

🧦 **Key Features:**

- Recycled ocean plastics & organic hemp
- Targeted compression zones
- Superior moisture-wicking
- Anti-blister design

Get ready to elevate your stride and make every step count! 👟 🌿

#GreenStride #EcoFriendly #SustainableRunning #RunGreen #EcoConscious #AthleticWear #RunStrong #PerformanceSocks #MoistureWicking #AntiBlister #HealthyLiving #SustainableFashion

Figure 6.10: Social media post generated by ChatGPT

And, with the special contribution of DALL-E:

Generate a 3d style realistic illustration of running socks, colorful powder explosion style, with background referring to wild nature

Here is the 3D style realistic illustration of running socks with a colorful powder explosion effect against a wild nature background:

This vibrant and dynamic image perfectly captures the essence of GreenStride socks, emphasizing their eco-friendly and high-performance qualities.

Figure 6.11: Example of an illustration generated by ChatGPT powered by DALL-E 3

Here is the final result:

Figure 6.12: Instagram post entirely generated by ChatGPT and DALL-E 3

Of course, many elements are missing here for complete product development and GTM. Yet, with the support of ChatGPT (and the special contribution of DALL-E 3), we managed to brainstorm a new product line and variants, potential customers, and catchy slogans, as well as generating a pretty nice Instagram post to announce the launch of GreenStride!

Bonus prompts

When it comes to brainstorming marketing ideas, a nice prompt template that you might want to try out is the *gameplay* technique.

Prompt

Let's play a game to brainstorm marketing ideas!

1. Rules of the game:

- You will play as [specific role, e.g., marketing guru, creative consumer].
- Provide marketing ideas for [specific product or service].
- Follow the theme or constraint provided for each round.

2. Game rounds:

- Round 1: [Initial challenge or theme, e.g., social media campaigns].
- Round 2: [Introduce new constraints, e.g., eco-friendly focus].
- Round 3: [Explore an out-of-the-box approach, e.g., guerrilla marketing].

3. Scoring criteria:

- Ideas will be evaluated on creativity, feasibility, and alignment with business goals.

Let's start with Round 1: [Describe the product/service and target audience]. What ideas can you come up with?

Using a gameplaying prompt technique for brainstorming makes the process more creative, engaging, and productive. Framing brainstorming as a game encourages out-of-the-box thinking.

Games introduce constraints and unexpected angles, leading to fresh ideas. They also make brainstorming more fun and memorable, boosting motivation.

Another interesting prompting technique, when it comes to target audience identification, can be the "flipped interaction" method. In this approach, ChatGPT leads the conversation by asking the user questions to gather information, aiming to achieve a specific goal.

For instance, instructing the model, *"I want to improve my public-speaking skills; please ask me questions to identify areas for improvement"* enables ChatGPT to guide the user through a self-assessment process. Here is an example.

> **Prompt**
>
> I aim to develop a marketing campaign for our new eco-friendly product line. Please ask me questions to identify our target audience and key messaging strategies. Continue asking until you have sufficient information to provide a comprehensive target audience profile and messaging plan. Make sure to cover the following topics:
>
> **Persona attributes:**
>
> Demographics: What is the likely age range, income level, education, and location of your ideal customer?
>
> Psychographics: What values, interests, or hobbies do they likely have?
>
> Behaviors: How do you expect them to shop, interact with brands, or make purchasing decisions?
>
> **Product fit:**
>
> What specific problem does this product solve for each persona?
>
> How would this product make their life easier or better?
>
> **Validation:**
>
> How do these personas compare to real-world data or existing customers?
>
> Are there other segments we should explore?
>
> Let's start!

With this approach, you are forcing ChatGPT to ask questions, thus clarifying the intent (or, in this case, the attributes of the target).

A/B testing for marketing comparison

Another interesting field where ChatGPT can assist marketers is A/B testing.

A/B testing in marketing is a method of comparing two different versions of a marketing campaign, advertisement, or website to determine which one performs better. In A/B testing, two variations of the same campaign or element are created, with only one variable changed between the two versions. The goal is to see which version generates more clicks, conversions, or other desired outcomes.

A/B testing allows marketers to optimize their campaigns and elements for maximum effectiveness, leading to better results and a higher return on investment.

Since this method involves the process of generating many variations of the same content, the generative power of ChatGPT can definitely assist in that.

Let's consider the following example:

> I'm promoting a new product I developed: a new, light, and thin climbing harness for speed climbers. I've already done some market research and I know my niche audience. I also know that one great channel of communication for that audience is publishing on an online climbing blog, of which most climbing gyms' members are fellow readers. My goal is to create an outstanding blog post to share the launch of this new harness, and I want to test two different versions of it in two groups.

The blog post I'm about to publish and that I want to be the object of my A/B testing is the following:

Lighter Climbing Harness for Speed Climbers
Introducing the Latest Addition to the World of Climbing Gear

Attention climbers! Upgrade your gear with the latest harness designed for speed climbers. It's lighter than any other, allowing you to move faster and more efficiently.

This harness improves speed and performance without sacrificing safety. Made from lightweight, breathable, and durable material, it's perfect for both beginners and seasoned climbers. Head to your nearest gear store and elevate your climbing experience today!

Figure 6.13: An example of a blog post to launch climbing gear

Here, ChatGPT can help us on two levels:

- The first level is that of rewording the article, using different keywords or different atten-tion-grabbing slogans. To do so, once this post is provided as context, we can ask ChatGPT to work on the article and slightly change some elements:

> I'm doing an A/B testing for the launch of a new climbing harness. I'm using a climbing blog as sales channel with the below blog post. Please regenerate the below content changing the following elements: title, subtitle and closing sentence.
>
> Lighter Climbing Harness for Speed Climbers
> Introducing the Latest Addition to the World of Climbing Gear
>
> Attention climbers! Upgrade your gear with the latest harness designed for speed climbers. It's lighter than any other, allowing you to move faster and more efficiently.
>
> This harness improves speed and performance without sacrificing safety. Made from lightweight, breathable, and durable material, it's perfect for both beginners and seasoned climbers. Head to your nearest gear store and elevate your climbing experience today!

Elevate Your Climbing Game with Our New Harness

The Ultimate Gear for Speed and Efficiency

Hey climbers! Upgrade to our newest harness specifically designed for speed climbing. Experience unmatched agility and efficiency with our lightest harness yet.

Engineered to enhance your speed and performance while ensuring maximum safety, this harness is crafted from lightweight, breathable, and durable materials. Ideal for both novices and expert climbers. Visit your favorite gear store and take your climbing to the next level today!

Figure 6.14: New version of the blog post generated by ChatGPT

As per my request, ChatGPT was able to regenerate only those elements I asked for (title, subtitle, and closing sentence) so that I can monitor the effectiveness of those elements by observing the reaction of the two audience groups.

- The second level is working on the design of the web page, namely, changing the collocation of the image rather than the position of the buttons. For this purpose, I created a simple web page for the blog post published on the climbing blog (you can find the code in the book's GitHub repository at `https://github.com/PacktPublishing/Practical-GenAI-with-ChatGPT-Second-Edition`:

Figure 6.15: Sample blog post published on the climbing blog

We can directly feed ChatGPT with the HTML code and ask it to change some layout elements, such as the position of the buttons or their wording. For example, rather than **Buy Now**, a reader might be more gripped by an **I want one!** button.

So, let's feed ChatGPT with the HTML source code:

> Please regenerate the following HTML code for the three buttons so that, instead of "Buy Now", the text says "I want one!". Also, make buttons more rounded and all of the same color.
>
> ```
> <!-- Buy Button -->
> <a href="http://example.com/buy-now">Buy Now</a>
>
> <!-- Share Button -->
> <a href="https://www.facebook.com/sharer/sharer.php?
> u=http://example.com/your-article" target="_blank"
> class="facebook">Share on Facebook</a>
>
> <!-- Feedback Button -->
> <a href="http://example.com/feedback">Leave Feedback</a>
> ```

Here is the regenerated HTML code for the buttons with the updated text, rounded corners, and consistent color:

```html
<!-- Buy Button -->
<a href="http://example.com/buy-now" style="display:inline-block; padding:10px 20px; color

<!-- Share Button -->
<a href="https://www.facebook.com/sharer/sharer.php?u=http://example.com/your-article" tar

<!-- Feedback Button -->
<a href="http://example.com/feedback" style="display:inline-block; padding:10px 20px; colo
```

All buttons now have the text "I want one!" (for the buy button), rounded corners with a border-radius of 25px, and the same background color (#4CAF50).

Figure 6.16: ChatGPT changing HTML code

Let's see what the output looks like (I also changed the title, subtitle, and paragraph with the ones generated by ChatGPT):

Elevate Your Climbing Game with Our New Harness
The Ultimate Gear for Speed and Efficiency

Hey climbers! Upgrade to our newest harness specifically designed for speed climbing. Experience unmatched agility and efficiency with our lightest harness yet.

Engineered to enhance your speed and performance while ensuring maximum safety, this harness is crafted from lightweight, breathable, and durable materials.

Ideal for both novices and expert climbers. Visit your favorite gear store and take your climbing to the next level today!

Figure 6.17: New version of the website

As you can see, ChatGPT only intervened at the button level, slightly changing their layout, position, color, and wording.

In conclusion, ChatGPT is a valuable tool for A/B testing in marketing. Its ability to quickly generate different versions of the same content can reduce the time to market of new campaigns. By utilizing ChatGPT for A/B testing, you can optimize your marketing strategies and, ultimately, drive better results for your business.

Bonus prompts

In the context of A/B testing, a good prompt engineering approach is the so-called *Alternative Approaches pattern*. In prompt engineering, this pattern involves instructing a language model to generate multiple solutions or perspectives for a given problem. This technique leverages the model's capacity to produce diverse responses, enhancing creativity and providing a broader range of options. For instance, when seeking ways to improve customer engagement, you might prompt, *"Can you suggest various strategies to enhance customer engagement?"* The model would then offer multiple approaches, such as personalized marketing, loyalty programs, or interactive content.

Prompt

You are a creative content strategist tasked with generating A/B test variations for the launch of a new climbing harness. Your goal is to provide two distinct versions of the blog post content by changing the following elements:

1. Title

2. Subtitle

3. Closing sentence

Instructions:

1. Create Variation A with a focus on [specific angle, e.g., highlighting speed and efficiency].

2. Create Variation B with a focus on [alternative angle, e.g., safety and versatility].

3. Ensure both variations appeal to climbers and are optimized for blog content.

Deliverable:

Provide your response in the following format:

<<<Variation A>>>

[Insert content for Variation A]

<<<End Variation A>>>

<<<Variation B>>>

[Insert content for Variation B]

<<<End Variation B>>>

This method is particularly useful in brainstorming sessions, as it encourages the exploration of different possibilities and reduces the likelihood of fixating on a single solution.

Boosting SEO

Another promising area for ChatGPT to be a game changer is **SEO**. This is the key element behind ranking in search engines such as Google or Bing and it determines whether your website will be visible to users who are looking for your product.

Definition

SEO is a technique used to enhance the visibility and ranking of a website on **search engine results pages (SERPs)**. It is done by optimizing the website or web page to increase the amount and quality of organic (unpaid) traffic from search engines. The purpose of SEO is to attract more targeted visitors to the website by optimizing it for specific keywords or phrases.

Imagine you run an e-commerce company called **Hat&Gloves**, which only sells, as you might have guessed, hats and gloves. You are now creating your e-commerce website and want to optimize its ranking. Let's ask ChatGPT to list some relevant keywords to embed in our website:

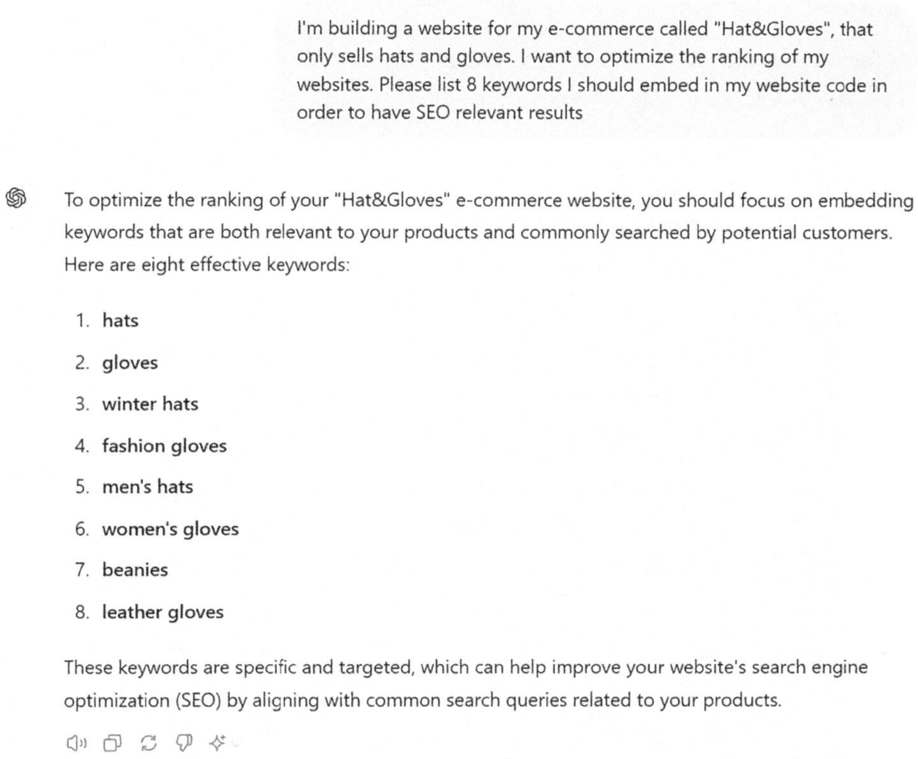
I'm building a website for my e-commerce called "Hat&Gloves", that only sells hats and gloves. I want to optimize the ranking of my websites. Please list 8 keywords I should embed in my website code in order to have SEO relevant results
To optimize the ranking of your "Hat&Gloves" e-commerce website, you should focus on embedding keywords that are both relevant to your products and commonly searched by potential customers. Here are eight effective keywords:
1. hats
2. gloves
3. winter hats
4. fashion gloves
5. men's hats
6. women's gloves
7. beanies
8. leather gloves
These keywords are specific and targeted, which can help improve your website's search engine optimization (SEO) by aligning with common search queries related to your products.

Figure 6.18: Example of SEO keywords generated by ChatGPT

As you can see, ChatGPT was able to create a list of keywords.

Another key element of SEO is **search engine intent**. Search engine intent, also known as **user intent**, refers to the underlying purpose or goal of a specific search query made by a user in a search engine. Understanding search engine intent is important because it helps businesses and marketers create more targeted and effective content and marketing strategies that align with the searcher's needs and expectations.

There are generally four types of search engine intent:

- **Informational intent**: The user is looking for information on a particular topic or question, such as *"What is the capital of France?"* or *"How to make a pizza at home."*

- **Navigational intent**: The user is looking for a specific website or web page, such as a *Facebook login* or *Amazon.com*.

- **Commercial intent**: The user is looking to buy a product or service, but may not have made a final decision yet. Examples of commercial intent searches include *Best laptop under $1000* or *Discount shoes online*.

- **Transactional intent**: The user has a specific goal to complete a transaction, which might refer to physical purchases or subscribing to services. Examples of transactional intent could be *Buy iPhone 13* or *Sign up for a gym membership*.

By understanding the intent behind specific search queries, businesses and marketers can create more targeted and effective content that meets the needs and expectations of their target audience. This can lead to higher search engine rankings, more traffic, and ultimately, more conversions and revenue.

Now, the question is, will ChatGPT be able to determine the intent of a given request? Before answering, it is worth noting that the activity of inferring the intent of a given prompt is the core business of **large language models (LLMs)**, including GPT. So, for sure, ChatGPT is able to capture prompts' intents.

The added value here is that we want to see whether ChatGPT is able to determine the intent in a precise domain with a precise taxonomy – that is, the one of marketing. That is the reason why prompt design is once again pivotal in guiding ChatGPT in the right direction.

Organize the above keyword list in groups based on their search intent, whether commercial, transactional, navigational or informational

Here is the keyword list organized by their search intent:

Commercial Intent

1. fashion gloves
2. leather gloves

Transactional Intent

1. hats
2. gloves
3. winter hats
4. men's hats
5. women's gloves
6. beanies

Navigational Intent

(None of the provided keywords fit this category as they are more focused on product-specific searches.)

Informational Intent

(None of the provided keywords fit this category as they are more focused on product-specific searches.)

These keywords reflect the intent of users looking to either purchase specific types of hats and gloves (transactional), or explore fashion and material options (commercial). This organization helps in understanding and targeting the right audience more effectively for SEO purposes.

Figure 6.19: Example of keywords clustered by user intent by ChatGPT

Finally, we could also go further and leverage once more the "Act as…" hack, which we already mentioned in *Chapter 3*. It would be very interesting indeed to have an assessment of our website and understand whether it is optimized as intended. In marketing, this analysis is called an **SEO audit**. An SEO audit is an evaluation of a website's SEO performance and potential areas for improvement. It is typically conducted by SEO experts, web developers, or marketers, and involves a comprehensive analysis of a website's technical infrastructure, content, and backlink profile.

During an SEO audit, the auditor will typically use a range of tools and techniques to identify areas for improvement, such as keyword analysis, website speed analysis, website architecture analysis, and content analysis. The auditor will then generate a report outlining the key issues, opportunities for improvement, and recommended actions to address them.

Let's ask ChatGPT to act as an SEO expert to conduct this audit. As a reference website, we will use our climbing blog referenced above. I will give ChatGPT the code and give the following instructions: "Act as an SEO specialist and generate a brief SEO audit (max 300 words) on the above HTML code." This is the response:

SEO Audit for "Lighter Climbing Harness for Speed Climbers" Webpage

Title and Meta Description

- **Title**: The title "Lighter Climbing Harness for Speed Climbers" is concise and contains relevant keywords. However, adding more context or a unique selling proposition could enhance click-through rates. For example, "Lighter Climbing Harness for Speed Climbers - Enhance Performance & Safety".
- **Meta Description**: A meta description is missing. Adding a meta description with keywords can improve search engine visibility. Example: "Discover our new lightweight climbing harness designed for speed climbers. Move faster and more efficiently with our durable, breathable gear."

Content Optimization

- **Headers**: The use of headers (h1, h2) is good, but incorporating keywords into the headers could improve SEO. For instance, "Introducing the Latest Addition to Climbing Gear - Lightweight Harness for Speed Climbers".
- **Keywords**: The content includes relevant keywords like "climbing harness" and "speed climbers". Additional keywords such as "lightweight harness", "climbing gear", and "performance climbing" should be naturally integrated.

Image Optimization

- **Alt Text**: The image alt text "Climbing harness" is appropriate but could be more descriptive. Example: "Lightweight climbing harness for speed climbers".
- **File Name**: Ensure the image file name is descriptive and includes keywords, such as "lightweight-climbing-harness.png".

Internal Linking

- **Links**: The page lacks internal links. Including links to related products or blog posts can improve SEO. Example: "Learn more about our climbing gear".

URL Structure

- **URL**: The URLs for the buttons are placeholders. Ensure the final URLs are clean and include keywords, e.g., "http://example.com/buy-climbing-harness".

Mobile Optimization

- **Responsive Design**: The website uses a responsive design, which is good for mobile SEO. Ensure all elements are mobile-friendly.

Call to Action (CTA)

- **Buttons**: The CTAs are clear, but consider adding more descriptive text for SEO. Example: "Buy Now - Lightweight Climbing Harness" instead of just "Buy Now".

Load Time

- **Performance**: Check the website's load time and optimize images and code to improve speed, as faster load times improve user experience and SEO.

SEO Keywords:

1. lightweight climbing harness
2. speed climbers gear
3. climbing gear
4. performance climbing harness
5. breathable climbing harness
6. durable climbing harness
7. best climbing harness
8. climbing safety gear

Conclusion

Enhancing the meta tags, integrating more relevant keywords, optimizing images, adding internal links, and ensuring mobile optimization will significantly improve the SEO performance of this webpage.

Figure 6.20: ChatGPT generating an SEO audit on the HTML code of a climbing blog

ChatGPT was able to generate a pretty accurate analysis, with relevant comments and suggestions. Overall, ChatGPT has interesting potential for SEO-related activities, and it can be a good tool, whether you are building your website from scratch or you want to improve existing ones.

Sentiment analysis for quality and customer satisfaction

Sentiment analysis is a technique used in marketing to analyze and interpret the emotions and opinions expressed by customers toward a brand, product, or service. It involves the use of **natural language processing** (**NLP**) and **machine learning** (**ML**) algorithms to identify and classify the sentiment of textual data such as social media posts, customer reviews, and feedback surveys.

By performing sentiment analysis, marketers can gain insights into customer perceptions of their brand, identify areas for improvement, and make data-driven decisions to optimize their marketing strategies. For example, they can track the sentiment of customer reviews to identify which products or services are receiving positive or negative feedback and adjust their marketing messaging accordingly.

Overall, sentiment analysis is a valuable tool for marketers to understand customer sentiment, gauge customer satisfaction, and develop effective marketing campaigns that resonate with their target audience.

Sentiment analysis has been around for a while, so you might be wondering what ChatGPT could bring as added value. Well, besides the accuracy of the analysis (it being the most powerful model on the market right now), ChatGPT differentiates itself from other sentiment analysis tools since it is powered by an LLM; hence, it is "general" rather than "specialized."

This means that when we use ChatGPT for sentiment analysis, we are not using one of its specific APIs for that task; the core idea behind ChatGPT and OpenAI models is that they can assist the user in many general tasks at once, interacting with a task and changing the scope of the analysis according to the user's request.

So, for sure, ChatGPT is able to capture the sentiment of a given text, such as an X/Twitter post or a product review. However, ChatGPT can also go further and assist in identifying specific aspects of a product or brand that are positively or negatively impacting the sentiment. For example, if customers consistently mention a particular feature of a product in a negative way, ChatGPT can highlight that feature as an area for improvement. Or, ChatGPT might be asked to generate a response to a particularly delicate review, keeping in mind the sentiment of the review and using it as context for the response. Again, it can generate reports that summarize all the negative and positive elements found in reviews or comments and cluster them into categories.

Let's consider the following example. A customer has recently purchased a pair of shoes from my e-commerce company, **RunFast**, and left the following review:

"I recently bought the RunFast Prodigy shoes and have mixed feelings. They're extremely comfortable with excellent cushioning and support, reducing foot fatigue during my runs. The design is also appealing, and I've received several compliments. However, the durability is disappointing; the outsole wears quickly, and the breathable upper shows signs of wear after a few weeks. Given the high price, I'm hesitant to recommend them despite their comfort and design."

Let's ask ChatGPT to capture the sentiment of this review:

> I received the following review:
>
> "I recently bought the RunFast Prodigy shoes and have mixed feelings. They're extremely comfortable with excellent cushioning and support, reducing foot fatigue during my runs. The design is also appealing, and I've received several compliments. However, the durability is disappointing; the outsole wears quickly, and the breathable upper shows signs of wear after a few weeks. Given the high price, I'm hesitant to recommend them despite their comfort and design."
>
> Analyse the sentiment of this review and classify it into positive, negative or neutral.

The review for the RunFast Prodigy shoes shows a **neutral sentiment**.

Positive Aspects:

- **Comfort**: "Extremely comfortable with excellent cushioning and support."
- **Design**: "Visually appealing and received several compliments."

Negative Aspects:

- **Durability**: "The outsole wears quickly, and the breathable upper shows signs of wear after a few weeks."
- **Price**: "Given the high price, I'm hesitant to recommend them."

Analysis:

While the reviewer appreciates the comfort and design of the shoes, they are significantly concerned about the durability and feel the high price is not justified given these issues. The review balances both positive and negative points, resulting in a neutral overall sentiment.

Figure 6.21: ChatGPT analyzing a customer review

From the preceding figure, we can see how ChatGPT didn't limit itself to providing a label: it also explained both the positive and negative elements characterizing the review, which has a mixed feeling and so can be labeled as neutral overall.

Note

Often, the nuances of sentiment analysis are tricky. ChatGPT does best when it is given few-shot prompting to help it understand the sentiment, as we explored in *Chapter 3*. For further discussions around this topic, you can refer to a preliminary study available here: `https://arxiv.org/abs/2304.04339`.

Let's try to go deeper into that and ask some suggestions about improving the product:

> based on the previous review, how could I improve the RunFast
> Prodigy shoes? output should be a table

‹ 2/2 ›

 Here's a table outlining potential improvements for the RunFast Prodigy shoes based on the review:

Aspect	Current Feedback	Suggested Improvement
Comfort	Extremely comfortable with excellent cushioning and support	Maintain the current cushioning and support features.
Design	Visually appealing and received several compliments	Continue offering appealing designs; consider more color and style options.
Durability - Outsole	Outsole wears quickly	Use more durable materials for the outsole to increase lifespan.
Durability - Upper	Breathable upper shows signs of wear after a few weeks	Enhance the durability of the upper material while maintaining breathability.
Price	High price point with durability concerns	Justify the high price by improving durability, or consider adjusting the price.

Notes:

1. **Outsole Material:** Research and incorporate advanced, wear-resistant materials like carbon rubber for the outsole.

2. **Upper Material:** Utilize high-quality synthetic fabrics or reinforced mesh that offer both durability and breathability.

3. **Pricing Strategy:** Reassess the pricing strategy based on the improvements made. Enhanced durability can justify the premium pricing, or introduce a tiered pricing model to cater to different segments.

4. **Customer Feedback:** Regularly collect and analyze customer feedback to continuously refine the product and address any recurring issues.

Figure 6.22: Suggestions on how to improve my product based on customer feedback

Finally, let's generate a response to the customer, showing that we, as a company, do care about customers' feedback and want to improve our products.

generate a response to the previous customer review, specifying that
we are on the process of always improving our products with the
suggestion you shared previously.

 Here's a response to the customer review:

Dear Valued Customer,

Thank you for your detailed review of the RunFast Prodigy shoes. We appreciate your feedback and
are committed to continuously improving our products to meet your expectations.

We are delighted to hear that you find the shoes extremely comfortable and visually appealing. Your
positive remarks about the cushioning, support, and design truly mean a lot to us.

However, we are sorry to hear about the durability issues you experienced. We take your concerns
seriously and want to assure you that we are actively working on enhancements. Specifically, we are:

- **Improving the Outsole:** We're researching and incorporating more durable materials for the
  outsole to ensure it withstands rigorous use over time.
- **Enhancing the Upper Material:** We're exploring high-quality synthetic fabrics and reinforced
  mesh that maintain breathability while significantly increasing durability.

We aim to provide products that justify their price through superior quality and longevity. Your
feedback helps us to move closer to this goal.

Thank you again for your valuable input. If you have any further suggestions or concerns, please
don't hesitate to reach out.

Best regards,

The RunFast Team

Figure 6.23: Response generated by ChatGPT

The example we saw was a very simple one with just one review. Now, imagine we have tons of reviews, as well as diverse sales channels where we receive feedback. Imagine the power of tools such as ChatGPT and OpenAI models, which are able to analyze and integrate all of that information and identify the pluses and minuses of your products, as well as capture customer trends and shopping habits. Additionally, for customer care and retention, we could also automate review responses using the writing style we prefer. In fact, by tailoring your chatbot's language and tone to meet the specific needs and expectations of your customers, you can create a more engaging and effective customer experience.

Here are some examples:

- **Empathetic chatbot**: A chatbot that uses an empathetic tone and language to interact with customers who may be experiencing a problem or need help with a sensitive issue
- **Professional chatbot**: A chatbot that uses a professional tone and language to interact with customers who may be looking for specific information or need help with a technical issue
- **Conversational chatbot**: A chatbot that uses a casual and friendly tone to interact with customers who may be looking for a personalized experience or have a more general inquiry
- **Humorous chatbot**: A chatbot that uses humor and witty language to interact with customers who may be looking for a light-hearted experience or to diffuse a tense situation
- **Educational chatbot**: A chatbot that uses a teaching style of communication to interact with customers who may be looking to learn more about a product or service

In conclusion, ChatGPT can be a powerful tool for businesses to conduct sentiment analysis, improve their quality, and retain their customers. With its advanced NLP capabilities, ChatGPT can accurately analyze customer feedback and reviews in real time, providing businesses with valuable insights into customer sentiment and preferences. By using ChatGPT as part of their customer experience strategy, businesses can quickly identify any issues that may be negatively impacting customer satisfaction and take corrective action. Not only can this help businesses improve their quality but it can also increase customer loyalty and retention.

Summary

In this chapter, we explored ways in which ChatGPT can be used by marketers to enhance their marketing strategies. We learned that ChatGPT can help in developing new products as well as defining their GTM strategy, designing A/B testing, enhancing SEO analysis, and capturing the sentiment of reviews, social media posts, and other customer feedback.

The importance of ChatGPT for marketers lies in its potential to revolutionize the way companies engage with their customers. By leveraging the power of NLP, ML, and big data, ChatGPT allows companies to create more personalized and relevant marketing messages, improve customer support and satisfaction, and, ultimately, drive sales and revenue.

As ChatGPT continues to advance and evolve, it is likely that we will see even more involvement in the marketing industry, especially in the way companies engage with their customers. In fact, relying heavily on AI allows companies to gain deeper insights into customer behavior and preferences.

The key takeaway for marketers is to embrace these changes and adapt to the new reality of AI-powered marketing in order to stay ahead of the competition and meet the needs of their customers.

In the next chapter, we will look at the third and last domain in the application of ChatGPT covered in this book – research.

Subscribe for a free eBook

New frameworks, evolving architectures, research drops, production breakdowns—AI_Distilled filters the noise into a weekly briefing for engineers and researchers working hands-on with LLMs and GenAI systems. Subscribe now and receive a free eBook, along with weekly insights that help you stay focused and informed. Subscribe at `https://packt.link/80z6Y` or scan the QR code below.

7

Research Reinvented with ChatGPT

This chapter is for researchers who wish to leverage ChatGPT. The chapter will go through a few main use cases that ChatGPT can address so that you will learn, from concrete examples, how ChatGPT can be used in research.

By the end of this chapter, you will be familiar with using ChatGPT as a research assistant in many ways, including the following:

- Researchers' need for ChatGPT
- Brainstorming literature for your study
- Providing support for the design and framework of your experiment
- Generating and formatting the bibliography to incorporate in your research study
- Generating a presentation of the study

This chapter will also provide examples and enable you to try the prompts on your own.

Researchers' need for ChatGPT

ChatGPT can be an incredibly valuable resource for researchers across a wide range of fields. As a sophisticated language model trained on vast amounts of data, ChatGPT can quickly and accurately process large amounts of information and generate insights that might be difficult or time-consuming to uncover through traditional research methods.

Additionally, ChatGPT can provide researchers with a unique perspective on their field, by analyzing patterns and trends that might not be immediately apparent to human researchers. For example, imagine a researcher studying climate change and wanting to understand the public perception of this issue. They might ask ChatGPT to analyze social media data related to climate change and identify the most common themes and sentiments expressed by people online. ChatGPT could then provide the researcher with a comprehensive report detailing the most common words, phrases, and emotions associated with this topic, as well as any emerging trends or patterns that might be useful to know.

By working with ChatGPT, researchers can gain access to cutting-edge technology and insights and stay at the forefront of their field.

Let's now dive deeper into four use cases where ChatGPT can boost research productivity.

Note

Most of the examples proposed in this chapter are based on up-to-date information; in fact, you will see ChatGPT leveraging the web search plugin very often.

Brainstorming literature for your study

A literature review is a critical and systematic process of examining existing published research on a specific topic or question. It involves searching, reviewing, and synthesizing relevant published studies and other sources, such as books, conference proceedings, and peer-reviewed literature. The goal of a literature review is to identify gaps, inconsistencies, and opportunities for further research in a particular field.

The literature review process typically involves the following steps:

1. **Defining the research question**: The first step in conducting a literature review is to define the research question of the topic of interest. So, let's say we are carrying out research on the effects of social media on mental health. Now, we are interested in brainstorming some possible research questions to focus our research on, and we can leverage ChatGPT to do so:

I'm interested in carrying out a research on the effects of social media on mental health. Generate for me 3 potential research questions to focus my research on.

Sure, here are three potential research questions you could focus on for your research on the effects of social media on mental health:

1. **How does the frequency and type of social media usage impact levels of anxiety and depression among teenagers?**

   - This question could help explore the correlation between the amount of time spent on social media, the nature of the content consumed, and its psychological effects on adolescents.

2. **What role does social media play in influencing body image and self-esteem in young adults?**

   - This question focuses on understanding how exposure to idealized images and lifestyles on social media platforms affects self-perception and confidence levels in young adults.

3. **In what ways do social media interactions and online support communities affect the mental well-being of individuals with chronic mental health conditions?**

   - This question aims to examine the positive and negative effects of online social interactions and support groups on individuals who already have mental health challenges.

Figure 7.1: Examples of research questions based on a given topic

Those are all interesting questions that could be further investigated. Since I'm particularly interested in the first one – "How does the frequency and type of social media usage impact levels of anxiety and depression among teenagers?" – I will keep that one as a reference for the next steps of our analysis.

2.   **Searching for literature:** Now that we have our research question, the next step is to search for relevant literature using a variety of databases, search engines, and other sources. Researchers can use specific keywords and search terms to help identify relevant studies.

Figure 7.2: Literature search with the support of ChatGPT

Starting from the suggestions of ChatGPT, we can start diving deeper into those references.

3.   **Screening the literature:** Once relevant literature has been identified, the next step is to screen the studies to determine whether they meet the inclusion criteria for the review. This typically involves reviewing the abstract and, if necessary, the full text of the study. To Let's say, for example, that we want to go deeper into the *Social Media and Teen Anxiety: Insights from Harvard Graduate School of Education* research paper. Let's ask ChatGPT to screen it for us:

Elaborate on the research paper "Social Media and Teen Anxiety: Insights from Harvard Graduate School of Education". Highlight its research question and main topics discussed (max 200 words)

The article "Social Media and Teen Anxiety" from the Harvard Graduate School of Education investigates the complex relationship between social media use and anxiety among teenagers. The main research question it addresses is: How does social media use contribute to rising levels of anxiety among teens, and what can parents do to help their children navigate these pressures?

Main Topics Discussed:

1. Correlation between Social Media Use and Anxiety:

- The article discusses the significant rise in anxiety, depression, and suicidal thoughts among teenagers coinciding with increased social media use. It highlights studies showing that teens who spend multiple hours a day on social media are more likely to exhibit anxiety and depressive symptoms.

2. Developmental Concerns:

- It explains that many pressures teenagers feel from social media are consistent with developmentally normal concerns around social standing and self-expression, which social media can exacerbate.

3. Parental Guidance:

- The article provides guidance for parents on how to help their children manage social media use. It suggests that rather than condemning social media outright, parents should tailor their approach to their child's individual needs, helping them to navigate the digital world responsibly.

4. Empowerment and Positive Aspects:

- It also acknowledges the positive aspects of social media, such as the ability to connect with others, raise awareness, and share experiences, which can be empowering and uplifting for some teens.

Overall, the article underscores the importance of a nuanced understanding of social media's impact on teen mental health and offers practical advice for parents to support their children.

For more detailed information, you can read the full article here (Harvard Graduate School of Education).

Figure 7.3: Literature screening of a specific paper

ChatGPT was able to provide me with an overview of the paper. Considering its research question and main topics of discussion, I think it will be pretty useful for my own study.

4. **Extracting data:** After the relevant studies have been identified, researchers will need to extract data from each study, such as the study design, sample size, data collection methods, and key findings. For example, let's say that we want to gather the following information from the paper *Digital Self-Harm: Prevalence, Motivations, and Outcomes by Hinduja and Patchin* (2018):

- The data sources collected in the paper and the subject of the study
- The data collection method adopted by researchers
- The data sample size
- The main limitations and drawbacks of the analysis
- The experiment design adopted by researchers

Here is how it goes:

extract the following information about the paper "Association between Problematic Social Networking Use and Anxiety Symptoms: A Systematic Review and Meta-Analysis". Output should be in a table format.
1. Data sources collected in the paper and object of the study
2. data collection method adopted by researchers
3. data sample size
4. main limitations and drawbacks of the analysis
5. the experiment design adopted by researchers

Here is the extracted information from the paper "Association between Problematic Social Networking Use and Anxiety Symptoms: A Systematic Review and Meta-Analysis" in a table format:

Category	Details
Data Sources Collected	Data were collected from various studies that examined the relationship between problematic social networking use (PSNU) and anxiety symptoms.
Object of the Study	To analyze the association between PSNU and different types of anxiety symptoms, including generalized anxiety, social anxiety, attachment anxiety, and fear of missing out (FOMO).
Data Collection Method	Systematic review and meta-analysis of existing literature. Researchers performed a comprehensive database search, selecting studies that met specific inclusion criteria.
Data Sample Size	The meta-analysis included 172 records with 209 independent effect sizes, covering various demographics and anxiety types.
Main Limitations and Drawbacks	- Heterogeneity among the included studies regarding sample characteristics and measurement instruments. - Potential publication bias and the varying quality of the included studies. - Limited ability to establish causality due to the cross-sectional nature of many studies.
Experiment Design Adopted	Random effects model was used for data analysis to account for variability among studies. Subgroup analysis and meta-regression were conducted to examine moderating effects.

For further details, you can access the full text of the paper on BMC Psychology here (BioMed Central).

Figure 7.4: Extracting relevant data and frameworks from a given paper

5. **Synthesizing the literature**: The final step in the literature review process is to synthesize the findings of the studies and draw conclusions about the current state of knowledge in the field. This may involve identifying common themes, highlighting gaps or inconsistencies in the literature, and identifying opportunities for future research.

Let's imagine that, besides the papers proposed by ChatGPT, we have collected other titles and papers we want to synthesize. More specifically, we want to understand whether they drive the same conclusions, what the common trends are, and which method might be more reliable than others. For this scenario, we will consider three research papers:

- *The Effects of Social Media on Mental Health: A Proposed Study*, by Grant Sean Bossard (`https://digitalcommons.bard.edu/cgi/viewcontent.cgi?article=1028&context=senproj_f2020`)

- *The Impact of Social Media on Mental Health*, by Vardanush Palyan (`https://www.spotlightonresearch.com/mental-health-research/the-impact-of- social-media-on-mental-health`)

- *The Impact of Social Media on Mental Health: A mixed-methods research of service providers' awareness*, by Sarah Nichole Koehler and Bobbie Rose Parrell (`https://scholarworks.lib.csusb.edu/cgi/viewcontent.cgi?article=2131&context=etd`)

Here is how the results appear:

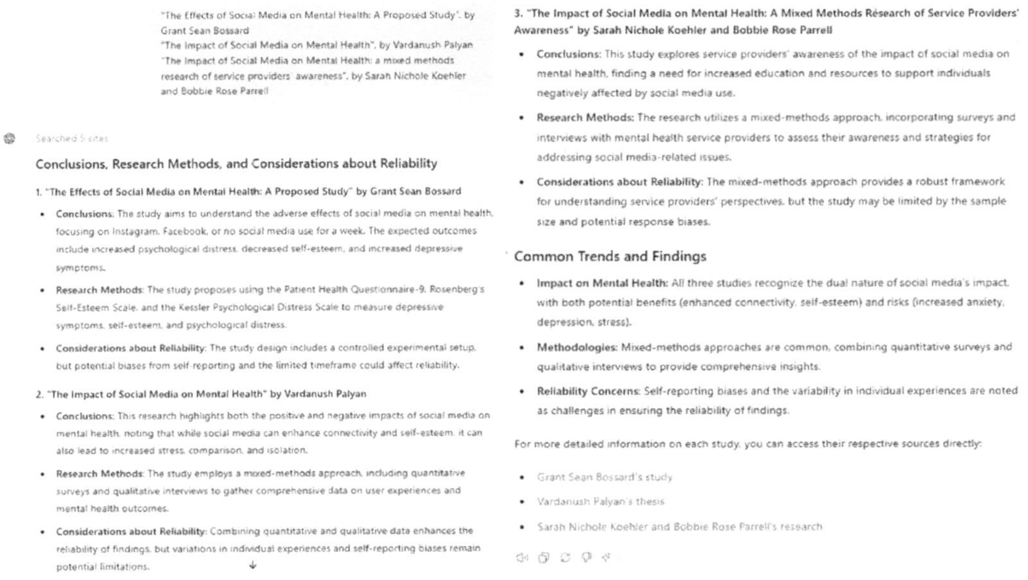

Figure 7.5: Literature analysis and benchmarking of three research papers

Also, in this case, ChatGPT was able to produce a relevant summary and analysis of the three papers provided, including benchmarking among the methods and reliability considerations.

Overall, ChatGPT was able to carry out many activities in the field of literature review, from research question brainstorming to literature synthesis. As always, a **subject-matter expert (SME)** is needed in the loop to review the results; however, with ChatGPT's assistance, many activities can be done more efficiently.

Note

As a common best practice, it is recommended to always add a disclaimer for any contribution of an AI tool whenever publishing something that was developed – even partially – by such a tool (which might be ChatGPT or a similar tool). This ensures transparency with the end users of your product (research paper, article, book, and so on) and sets them in the position of being more receptive to potential biases or hallucinations.

Another activity that can be supported by ChatGPT is the design of the experiment the researcher wants to carry out. We are going to look at that in the following section.

Bonus prompts

When we interact with ChatGPT to brainstorm about possible research questions, a good prompting technique might be **question refinement prompting**. With this approach, the LLM takes the user through a series of iterations to finalize a question. Let's look at an example:

Iterative question refinement for research brainstorming

Objective: Collaboratively refine impactful research questions through iterative feedback and dialogue with ChatGPT.

Step 1: Initial Brainstorm

Prompt: "I am conducting a research study in the field of [insert field/topic]. The specific area I am interested in is [insert specific area or theme]. Please generate 5 preliminary research questions that explore key challenges, trends, or knowledge gaps in this field."

Step 2: Refinement

Follow-Up Prompt: "Thank you for the questions! Here's my feedback:

Question [insert number] needs to focus more on [insert focus area].

Question [insert number] feels too broad. Can you narrow it down to focus on [specific aspect]?

Question [insert number] is compelling but could benefit from addressing [specific audience, outcome, or data].

Based on this feedback, refine the questions to better align with my goals."

Step 3: Final Polishing

Follow-Up Prompt: "I appreciate the refinements. Now:

Combine elements of Questions [insert numbers] into one cohesive question.

Ensure the language is clear and concise.

Suggest any final adjustments to make these questions more impactful."

With this approach, we are "encouraging" the model to work step by step and progressively refine its output.

Another interesting technique of prompting, which is very handy for structuring the output of your query, is that of leveraging a so-called *prompt pattern*. Developed by Dr. Jules White and his colleagues, prompt patterns are reusable solutions designed to address common challenges encountered when interacting with LLMs. They function similarly to software design patterns by providing structured methods to achieve specific outcomes in LLM interactions. This approach is detailed in their paper, *A Prompt Pattern Catalog to Enhance Prompt Engineering with ChatGPT* (you can find the original catalog at https://arxiv.org/abs/2302.11382).

For example, when extracting relevant information from documents (as covered in this section), we might want to make sure to gather specific elements like the research question or the study design:

Prompt

I need a structured template for extracting key data from research papers efficiently. The template should include the following sections:

Paper Details (Title, Authors, Year, Journal, DOI/URL).

Research Question(s) or Objective(s).

Study Design (e.g., experimental, observational, meta-analysis).

Methods (sample size, data collection techniques, tools used).

Key Findings or Results.

Limitations and Recommendations.

Please format this template as a table or checklist that researchers can easily fill out when reviewing papers.

With such a template pattern, you make sure to keep consistency across the data gathered from multiple sources.

Similarly, the same technique can be used when comparing different research papers or, more generally, documents. In this section, we covered an example where we leveraged the web search tool to retrieve information about papers and compare them. However, if you want to follow a more structured and controlled approach, you can upload the two or more papers you want to benchmark and run a prompt like the following one (taken from the catalog of Dr. White. You can find the original catalog at https://arxiv.org/abs/2302.11382):

Prompt

I have reviewed several research papers on the topic of [insert topic, e.g., "the effects of social media on mental health"] and they are attached. I need to synthesize their findings into a cohesive summary that highlights:

Common themes or trends across the papers.

- Key differences or conflicting results.
- Gaps or limitations identified in the literature.
- Implications for future research or practical applications.

Please structure the synthesis as follows:

Introduction: Brief overview of the topic and the scope of the papers reviewed.

Common Themes: Identify and summarize shared findings or recurring patterns.

Contrasting Results: Highlight any major differences or contradictions among the papers.

Gaps and Opportunities: Discuss areas where further research is needed.

Conclusion: Provide an overall summary and potential directions for future studies.

By applying these prompt patterns, users can systematically design prompts that guide LLMs to produce more reliable and contextually appropriate outputs, thereby improving the efficiency and effectiveness of human-AI collaboration.

Providing support for the design and framework of your experiment

Experiment design is the process of planning and executing a scientific experiment or study to answer a research question. It involves making decisions about the study's design, the variables to be measured, the sample size, and the procedures for collecting and analyzing data.

ChatGPT can help in experiment design for research by suggesting to you the study framework, such as a randomized controlled trial, quasi-experimental design, or a correlational study, and supporting you alongside the implementation of that design.

Let's consider the following scenario. We want to investigate the effects of a new educational program on student learning outcomes in mathematics. This new program entails **project-based learning (PBL)**, meaning that students are asked to work collaboratively on real-world projects, using math concepts and skills to solve problems and create solutions.

For this purpose, we defined our research question as follows:

How does the new PBL program compare to traditional teaching methods in improving student performance?

Here's how ChatGPT can help:

- **Determining study design:** ChatGPT can assist in determining the appropriate study design for the research question, such as a randomized controlled trial, quasi-experimental design, or correlational study.

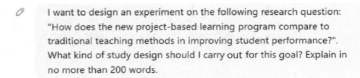

I want to design an experiment on the following research question: "How does the new project-based learning program compare to traditional teaching methods in improving student performance?". What kind of study design should I carry out for this goal? Explain in no more than 200 words.

To compare the new project-based learning (PBL) program with traditional teaching methods in improving student performance, design a **randomized controlled trial (RCT)**.

Study Design:

1. **Participants:** Recruit a sufficient number of students and randomly assign them to either the PBL group (experimental group) or the traditional teaching group (control group).

2. **Pretest:** Administer a standardized test to both groups to measure their baseline performance.

3. **Intervention:** Implement the PBL program in the experimental group and continue traditional teaching methods in the control group over a set period.

4. **Posttest:** After the intervention, administer the same standardized test to both groups.

5. **Data Analysis:** Compare the pretest and posttest scores within and between groups using statistical methods such as ANCOVA to control for any baseline differences.

This RCT design allows for a robust comparison of the effectiveness of PBL versus traditional teaching methods, minimizing biases and providing strong evidence for causality.

Figure 7.6: ChatGPT suggesting the appropriate study design for your experiment

ChatGPT suggested proceeding with a **randomized controlled trial (RCT)** and provided a clear explanation of the reason behind it.

> **Definition**
>
> An RCT is a scientific study design used to measure the effectiveness of an intervention by randomly assigning participants to two or more groups:
>
> - **Experimental group:** Receives the intervention or treatment being tested
> - **Control group:** Receives a placebo, standard treatment, or no intervention
>
> By randomly assigning participants, RCTs minimize bias and ensure that differences in outcomes are due to the intervention itself rather than external factors. They are considered the gold standard in clinical and social science research for establishing causality between an intervention and its effects.

It seems reasonable to me to proceed with this approach: the next steps will be to identify outcome measures and variables to consider in our experiment.

- **Identifying outcome measures**: ChatGPT can help you identify some potential outcome measures to determine the results of your test. Let's ask for some suggestions for our study:

> I want to compare the new project-based learning program with traditional teaching methods in improving student performance in a research study with a RCT. What could be possible outcome metrics?

In a randomized controlled trial (RCT) comparing project-based learning (PBL) and traditional teaching methods, possible outcome metrics to assess student performance include:

1. **Academic Achievement**: Measured through standardized test scores, grades, and exam results.

2. **Critical Thinking Skills**: Evaluated using critical thinking assessments and problem-solving tasks.

3. **Engagement and Motivation**: Assessed through student surveys, attendance records, and participation rates.

4. **Collaborative Skills**: Measured via peer evaluations and group project outcomes.

5. **Retention of Knowledge**: Evaluated by comparing performance on follow-up tests conducted after a certain period.

6. **Attitude towards Learning**: Assessed through questionnaires measuring student attitudes and perceptions towards the learning process.

7. **Teacher Observations**: Qualitative data collected from teacher assessments and observations of student behavior and engagement.

These metrics provide a comprehensive evaluation of the effectiveness of PBL compared to traditional methods in improving various aspe ↓ of student performance.

Figure 7.7: Learning outcomes for the given research study

It is reasonable for me to pick test scores as the outcome measure.

- **Identifying variables**: ChatGPT can help the researcher to identify the independent and dependent variables in the study:

I want to compare the new project-based learning program with traditional teaching methods in improving student performance in a research study with an RCT. What variables should I include in my study? Output should be in table format

‹ 2/2 ›

Here is a table of variables to include in your study:

Variable	Description
Independent Variable	**Teaching Method**: Project-based learning (PBL) vs. Traditional teaching methods
Dependent Variables	**Academic Achievement**: Test scores, grades, exam results
	Critical Thinking Skills: Performance on critical thinking assessments
	Engagement and Motivation: Survey responses, attendance, participation rates
	Collaborative Skills: Peer evaluations, group project outcomes
	Retention of Knowledge: Follow-up test performance
	Attitude towards Learning: Survey responses on student attitudes and perceptions
Control Variables	**Student Demographics**: Age, gender, socioeconomic status
	Baseline Academic Performance: Pretest scores, previous grades
	Teacher Characteristics: Teaching experience, training
	Class Size: Number of students in each class
	Curriculum Content: Similarity in content covered in both teaching methods

These variables will help you comprehensively evaluate the effectiveness of the PBL program compared to traditional teaching methods.

Figure 7.8: ChatGPT generating variables for the given study

Note that ChatGPT was also able to generate the type of variables, called control variables, that are specific to the study design we are considering (RCT).

Control variables, also known as covariates, are variables that are held constant or are controlled in a research study in order to isolate the relationship between the independent variable(s) and the dependent variable. These variables are not the primary focus of the study but are included to minimize the effect of confounding variables on the results. By controlling these variables, researchers can reduce the risk of obtaining false positive or false negative results and increase the internal reliability, validity, transparency, and reproducibility of their study.

With the preceding variables, we are ready to set up our experiment. Now we need to select participants, and ChatGPT can assist us with that.

- **Sampling strategy**: ChatGPT can suggest potential sampling strategies for the study:

I need to select the participant for my RCT about the effectiveness of a new project-based learning program in improving student performance, compared with traditional teaching methods. Generate a step by step guide (no more than 200 words) on how to sample my participants, specifying sampling techniques and why they might be effective. Output should be in table format.

‹ 2/2 ›

Step	Description	Reasoning
1. Define Population	Identify the target population (e.g., middle school students in a specific district).	Ensures the study results are relevant to the intended group.
2. Obtain Approval	Secure permissions from schools, parents, and students.	Ethical requirement and ensures participation.
3. Random Sampling	Use random sampling to select a representative subset of students from the target population.	Reduces selection bias and ensures each student has an equal chance of being chosen.
4. Stratify by Key Characteristics	Stratify the sample based on characteristics such as grade level and prior academic performance.	Ensures balanced groups and controls for confounding variables.
5. Random Assignment	Randomly assign students to either the PBL group or the traditional teaching group.	Ensures comparability between groups and minimizes bias.
6. Determine Sample Size	Calculate the required sample size using power analysis to detect a significant effect.	Ensures the study has enough power to detect meaningful differences.
7. Collect Baseline Data	Administer pretests to measure initial academic performance and other relevant variables.	Provides a baseline for comparing post-intervention results.
8. Implement Interventions	Apply the PBL program to the experimental group and traditional methods to the control group.	Ensures the integrity of the experimental conditions.
9. Monitor and Adjust	Regularly check for adherence to protocols and make adjustments as needed.	Maintains the validity and reliability of the study.

↓

Figure 7.9: RCT sampling strategy suggestion from ChatGPT

Note that it is always a good practice to ask AI tools to generate more options with explanations behind them so that you can make a reasoned decision. For this example, let's go ahead with what ChatGPT suggested to us, which also includes suggestions about the population of interest and sample size.

- **Data analysis:** ChatGPT can assist the researcher in determining the appropriate statistical tests to analyze the data collected from the study, such as ANCOVA, t-tests, or regression analysis.

I'm conducting an experiment with RCT about the effectiveness of a new project-based learning program in improving student performance, compared with traditional teaching methods. The outcome measure is score test, and the sampling strategy is random sampling. What statistical test should I use to assess the statistical significance of my results? elaborate in no more than 150 words.

To assess the statistical significance of your results in an RCT comparing the effectiveness of a project-based learning (PBL) program to traditional teaching methods, use **Analysis of Covariance (ANCOVA)**. ANCOVA adjusts for baseline differences and increases the precision of your estimates by controlling for initial test scores. Here's why it's suitable:

1. **Baseline Adjustment:** ANCOVA controls for pretest scores, isolating the effect of the intervention.

2. **Increased Power:** By accounting for variability in initial performance, it improves the ability to detect a significant effect.

3. **Group Comparison:** It compares post-intervention scores between the PBL and traditional groups, providing a clear measure of the program's impact.

This approach ensures that any observed differences in test scores are due to the teaching methods rather than initial performance differences.

Figure 7.10: ChatGPT suggests a statistical test for a given study

Everything suggested by ChatGPT is coherent and finds confirmation in papers about how to conduct a statistical test. It was also able to identify that we are probably talking about a continuous variable (that is, scores) so that we know that all the information ahead is based on this assumption. In the case that we want to have discrete scores, we might adjust the prompt by adding this information, and ChatGPT will then suggest a different approach.

The fact that ChatGPT specifies assumptions and explains its reasoning is key to making safe decisions based on its input.

In conclusion, ChatGPT can be a valuable tool for researchers when designing experiments. By utilizing its **natural language processing (NLP)** capabilities and vast knowledge base, ChatGPT can help researchers select appropriate study designs, determine sampling techniques, identify variables and learning outcomes, and even suggest statistical tests to analyze the data.

In the next section, we are going to move forward in exploring how ChatGPT can support researchers, focusing on bibliography generation.

Bonus prompts

Dr. White's prompt catalog can be very handy also when you are designing your research experiment. For example, let's consider the **recipe pattern** (source: `https://arxiv.org/pdf/2302.11382`):

> **Prompt**
>
> Instructions for AI: Please provide a step-by-step plan to design a robust experiment for this research goal. Ensure the response includes the following components:
>
> Participants: How to select and assign participants.
>
> Pre-Test: Steps to measure the baseline performance of participants.
>
> Intervention: Outline the PBL program implementation and control group treatment.
>
> Post-Test: Methods for evaluating the outcomes after the intervention.
>
> Data Analysis: Specify statistical methods for comparing the results and ensuring validity.
>
> Output Format:
>
> - Present each step clearly and concisely.
> - Provide reasoning for each step to justify its inclusion.
> - Conclude with why this study design is suitable for answering the research question.

This pattern is indeed particularly beneficial when users have a general understanding of their goal and some of the necessary steps but require assistance in organizing these steps into a coherent and complete sequence.

Another revised prompt that you might want to try for your experiment design is the following:

> **Prompt**
>
> Context: You are designing a **random-** al teaching methods in improving stu- **ized controlled trial** (RCT) to compare dent performance. The study requires the effectiveness of a **project-based** defining specific outcome metrics to **learning** (PBL) program with tradition- evaluate the program's success.

Directions: Generate a detailed list of potential outcome metrics that are specific, measurable, and relevant to assessing student performance. Include metrics across academic, cognitive, and behavioral domains.

Limitations:

- Avoid overly general metrics (e.g., "student improvement").
- Ensure metrics are realistic and feasible to measure within the context of an RCT.
- Focus on metrics that can provide a comprehensive evaluation of both teaching methods.

Output: Provide a structured list of at least 5-7 outcome metrics, each with a brief explanation of how it contributes to evaluating the effectiveness of the PBL program.

In this case, we used clear delimiters and structured output patterns to make sure ChatGPT follows a scientific approach. Plus, we also incorporated limitations, which is an effective, explicit way to reduce hallucination.

Generating and formatting a bibliography

ChatGPT can support researchers in bibliography generation by providing automated citation and reference tools. These tools can generate accurate citations and references for a wide range of sources, including books, articles, websites, and more. ChatGPT knows various citation styles, such as APA, MLA, Chicago, and Harvard, allowing researchers to select the appropriate style for their work. Additionally, ChatGPT can also suggest relevant sources based on the researcher's input, helping to streamline the research process and ensure that all necessary sources are included in the bibliography. By utilizing these tools, researchers can save time and ensure that their bibliography is accurate and comprehensive.

Let's consider the following example. Let's say we finalized a research paper titled *The Impact of Technology on Workplace Productivity: An Empirical Study*. During the research and writing process, we collected the following references to papers, websites, videos, and other sources that we need to include in the bibliography (in order, three research papers, one YouTube video, and one website):

- *The second machine age: Work, progress, and prosperity in a time of brilliant technologies*. Brynjolfsson, 2014. `https://psycnet.apa.org/record/2014-07087-000`
- *The Impact of Technostress on Role Stress and Productivity*. Tarafdar, 2014. Pages 301-328. `https://www.tandfonline.com/doi/abs/10.2753/MIS0742-1222240109`

- *The big debate about the future of work, explained.* Vox. https://www.youtube.com/ watch?v=TUmyygCMMGA

Obviously, we cannot have the preceding list in our research paper; we need proper formatting for it. To do so, we can provide ChatGPT with the raw list of references and ask it to regenerate it with the specific format – for example, the Chicago style, commonly used as a reference format style in education, psychology, and social sciences.

Let's see how ChatGPT works with that:

I have the following links as references for my bibliography:
- "The second machine age: Work, progress, and prosperity in a time of brilliant technologies." Brynjolfsson, 2014.
https://psycnet.apa.org/record/2014-07087-000
https://www.tandfonline.com/doi/abs/10.2753/MIS0742-1222240109
- The Impact of Technostress on Role Stress and Productivity. Tarafdar, 2014. Pages 301-328.
https://www.tandfonline.com/doi/abs/10.2753/MIS0742-1222240109
- "The big debate about the future of work, explained". Vox, 2017.
https://www.youtube.com/watch?v=TUmyygCMMGA

Regenerate those links with Chicago style. If you don't know some details (like the month and day of publication) don't generate them.

‹ 2/2 ›

Here are the references in Chicago style:

1. Brynjolfsson, Erik, and Andrew McAfee. *The Second Machine Age: Work, Progress, and Prosperity in a Time of Brilliant Technologies*. 2014. Accessed July 26, 2024.
https://psycnet.apa.org/record/2014-07087-000.

2. Tarafdar, Monideepa, Qiang Tu, T.S. Ragu-Nathan, and Bhanu S. Ragu-Nathan. "The Impact of Technostress on Role Stress and Productivity." *Journal of Management Information Systems* 24, no. 1 (2014): 301-328. Accessed July 26, 2024.
https://www.tandfonline.com/doi/abs/10.2753/MIS0742-1222240109.

3. "The Big Debate About the Future of Work, Explained." *Vox*, 2017. Accessed July 26, 2024.
https://www.youtube.com/watch?v=TUmyygCMMGA.

Figure 7.11: A list of references generated in Chicago format by ChatGPT

Note that I specified not to add details in case ChatGPT doesn't know them. Indeed, I noticed that sometimes ChatGPT was adding the month and day of publication, making some mistakes.

Another interesting assistance ChatGPT can provide is that of suggesting potential reference papers we might want to quote. We've already seen in this chapter how ChatGPT is able to brainstorm relevant literature before the writing process; however, once the paper is done, we might have forgotten to quote relevant literature, or even not be aware of having quoted someone else's work.

ChatGPT can be a great assistant in brainstorming possible references we might have missed. Let's consider once more our paper, which focused on the research question "How does the frequency and type of social media usage impact levels of anxiety and depression among teenagers." Let's say that we set the following title, which has the following abstract:

Title:

The Influence of Social Media Usage on Adolescent Mental Health: Examining the Relationship Between Frequency, Content Type, and Levels of Anxiety and Depression

Abstract:

Social media has become an integral part of adolescent life, yet its impact on mental health remains a subject of debate. This study investigates the relationship between the frequency and type of social media usage and levels of anxiety and depression among teenagers. Using a mixed-methods approach, we analyze survey data from adolescents aged 13–18 to assess their social media habits, content preferences, and self-reported mental health symptoms. The findings reveal that excessive social media use, particularly engagement with negatively valenced or highly curated content, correlates with higher levels of anxiety and depression. Conversely, positive interactions and supportive online communities may mitigate these effects. The study highlights the need for a nuanced understanding of social media's psychological impact and suggests interventions to promote healthier digital habits among teenagers.

Let's ask ChatGPT to list all the possible references that might be related to this kind of research:

List me 3 possible references that might be related to my research paper with the following research question: "How does the frequency and type of social media usage impact levels of anxiety and depression among teenagers?". Make sure to retrieve updated information only from Arxiv. They should be in Chicago style.

Here are three recent studies from arXiv that explore the impact of social media usage on anxiety and depression among teenagers:

1. Voggenreiter, Angelina, et al. "The Role of Likes: How Online Feedback Impacts Users' Mental Health." *arXiv preprint* arXiv:2312.11914 (2023). This study examines how receiving online feedback, such as 'likes,' affects users' emotional experiences, social connectedness, and self-esteem, providing insights into the psychological effects of social media interactions.

2. Pezzi, Mattia, et al. "Solitary Experience and Problematic Social Media Use Among Young Adults: A Systematic Review with Recommendations for Future Research." *Clinical Neuropsychiatry* (2024). This systematic review investigates the relationship between solitary experiences and problematic social media use in young adults, highlighting the psychological impacts and suggesting directions for future research.

3. Mensah, Richard, and Bishwo Prakash Pokharel. "Analysis, Impact of Social Media Use and Hate Speech Over Engagement Among Youths." *arXiv preprint* arXiv:2410.20070 (2024). This paper explores how social media usage and exposure to hate speech contribute to stress, anxiety, and depression among youths, emphasizing the direct impact on their daily lives and mental health.

These references provide valuable insights into how different aspects of social media usage influence mental health outcomes in adolescents.

Sources

Figure 7.12: List of references related to the provided abstract

You can repeat this process with other sections of your paper also, to make sure you are not missing any relevant references to include in your bibliography.

Once you have your study ready, you will probably need to present it with an elevator pitch. In the next section, we will see how ChatGPT can also support this task.

Generating a presentation of the study

The last mile of a research study is often that of being presented to various audiences. This might involve preparing a slide deck, pitch, or webinar where the researcher needs to address different kinds of audiences.

Let's say, for example, that our study now titled *The Influence of Social Media Usage on Adolescent Mental Health: Examining the Relationship Between Frequency, Content Type, and Levels of Anxiety and Depression* is meant for a master's degree thesis discussion. In that case, we can ask ChatGPT to produce a pitch structure that is meant to last 15 minutes and adheres to the scientific method. Let's see what kind of results are produced (as context, I'm referring to the abstract given earlier):

> I have to discuss my thesis titled "The Influence of Social Media Usage on Adolescent Mental Health: Examining the Relationship Between Frequency, Content Type, and Levels of Anxiety and Depression" with the above abstract. Generate a thesis discussion structure with examples of sentences that addresses a commission of professors. Make it no longer than 150 words and in table output.

Here is a structured thesis discussion in a table format, tailored for addressing a commission of professors:

Section	Discussion Points	Example Sentences
Introduction	Briefly introduce the research topic, significance, and objectives.	"This research examines how different patterns of social media usage affect adolescent mental health, focusing on anxiety and depression levels. Understanding these correlations is crucial in developing targeted interventions for youth."
Methodology	Explain the study design, data collection, and analysis methods.	"We employed a mixed-methods approach, gathering survey data from 500 teenagers and conducting in-depth interviews to gain qualitative insights."
Key Findings	Present the most significant results.	"Our findings indicate that passive browsing and excessive social media engagement correlate strongly with increased anxiety, whereas supportive interactions help mitigate depressive symptoms."
Implications	Discuss the practical significance of the findings.	"These results highlight the need for digital literacy programs and parental guidance to encourage healthier social media habits among adolescents."
Conclusion & Future Research	Summarize and suggest areas for further study.	"Future research should explore intervention strategies and long-term effects of social media on adolescent mental health across diverse demographics."

Figure 7.13: Thesis discussion generated by ChatGPT

That was impressive! Back in my university days, it would have been useful to have such a tool to assist me in my discussion design.

Starting from this structure, we can also ask ChatGPT to generate a slide deck as a visual for our thesis discussion.

Let's proceed with this request:

> Based on the above pitch structure, generate a slide deck structure and writing content. It has to be attention-grabbing, so the style should be funny and challenging, however, remember that the audience is a commission of professors, so keep also an academic posture. Make it fit in 5 slides. Output should be in table format and around 150 words.

Here's a structured slide deck with a mix of academic rigor and engaging humor, tailored for a commission of professors:

Slide #	Title	Content
1	The Social Media Paradox: A Blessing or a Curse?	*"Ladies and gentlemen, welcome to the world where teenagers 'just check one post' and suddenly it's 3 AM. But does this scrolling marathon really impact their mental health? Let's find out!"*
2	Methodology: Science Behind the Scrolling	*"We surveyed 500 teenagers (yes, they do answer surveys if you promise them WiFi), analyzed their social media habits, and correlated them with anxiety and depression levels. Spoiler alert: The results are more dramatic than a reality show."*
3	Key Findings: Anxiety, Depression & the Algorithm	*"The more time teens spend doom-scrolling, the worse their anxiety. But, surprise! Positive interactions in online communities can actually help. Who knew the internet wasn't all bad?"*
4	Implications: What Now?	*"So, should we delete all apps? Nope. But we do need better education on mindful scrolling—because 'just five more minutes' is the biggest lie of the digital age."*
5	Conclusion: The Grand Finale	*"Social media isn't evil, but how we use it matters. Let's move from zombie-scrolling to smart-scrolling. And yes, that applies to us too—professors, I see you checking emails mid-presentation!"*

Figure 7.14: Slide deck structure based on a discussion pitch

Then, you can also ask ChatGPT to generate the deck as an asset to be downloaded:

> Generate the above slides and allow me to download them.

Your PowerPoint presentation has been generated. You can download it using the link below:

Download Social_Media_Mental_Health.pptx ⌄

Figure 7.15: Generating a deck as a downloadable asset

What happens in the backend is that ChatGPT generates Python code to create your deck:

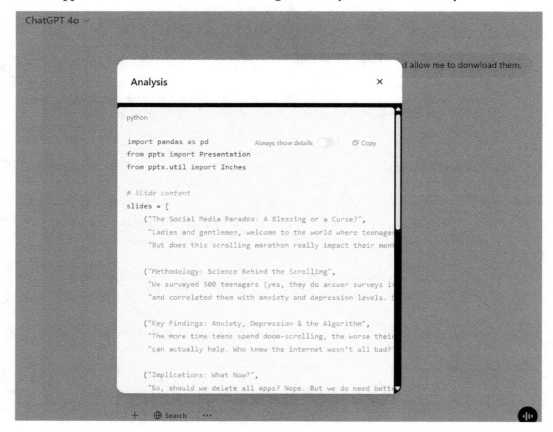

Figure 7.16: ChatGPT running Python code in the backend

If you click on the provided link, you will be able to download the generated deck:

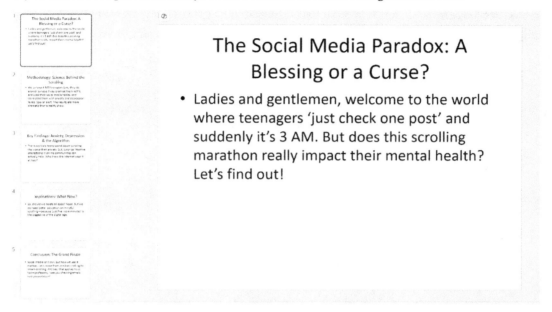

Figure 7.17: The generated deck

As you can see, the outline has been preserved according to our request.

Finally, let's imagine that our thesis discussion was outstanding to the point that it might be selected to receive research funds in order to keep investigating the topic. Now we need an elevator pitch to convince the funding committee. Let's ask for some support from ChatGPT:

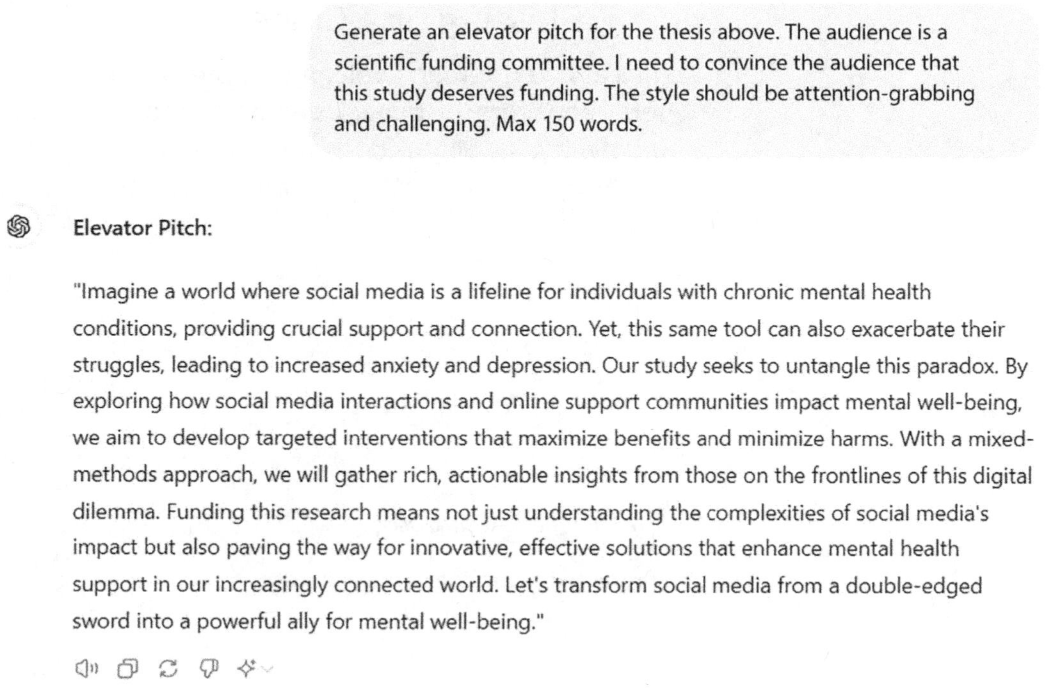

> Generate an elevator pitch for the thesis above. The audience is a scientific funding committee. I need to convince the audience that this study deserves funding. The style should be attention-grabbing and challenging. Max 150 words.

Elevator Pitch:

"Imagine a world where social media is a lifeline for individuals with chronic mental health conditions, providing crucial support and connection. Yet, this same tool can also exacerbate their struggles, leading to increased anxiety and depression. Our study seeks to untangle this paradox. By exploring how social media interactions and online support communities impact mental well-being, we aim to develop targeted interventions that maximize benefits and minimize harms. With a mixed-methods approach, we will gather rich, actionable insights from those on the frontlines of this digital dilemma. Funding this research means not just understanding the complexities of social media's impact but also paving the way for innovative, effective solutions that enhance mental health support in our increasingly connected world. Let's transform social media from a double-edged sword into a powerful ally for mental well-being."

Figure 7.18: Elevator pitch for the given thesis

We can always adjust the results and make them more aligned with what we are looking for; however, having structures and frameworks already available can save a lot of time and allow us to focus more on the technical content we want to bring.

Overall, ChatGPT is able to support an end-to-end journey in research, from literature collection and review to the generation of the final pitch of the study, and we've demonstrated how it can be a great AI assistant for researchers.

Furthermore, note that in the field of research, some tools that are different from ChatGPT yet still powered by GPT models have been developed recently. An example is Humata.ai, an AI-powered tool that allows you to upload your documents and perform several actions on them, including summarization, instant Q&A, and new paper generation based on uploaded files.

This suggests how GPT-powered tools (including ChatGPT) are paving the way toward several innovations within the research domain.

Summary

In this chapter, we explored the use of ChatGPT as a valuable tool for researchers. Through literature review, experiment design, bibliography generation and formatting, and presentation generation, ChatGPT can assist the researcher in speeding up those activities with low or zero added value, so that they can focus on relevant activities.

Note that we focused only on a small set of activities where ChatGPT can support researchers. There are many other activities within the domain of research that could benefit from the support of ChatGPT, among which we can mention data collection, study participant recruitment, research networking, public engagement, and many others.

Researchers who incorporate this tool into their work can benefit from its versatility and time-saving features, ultimately leading to more impactful research outcomes.

However, it is important to keep in mind that ChatGPT is only a tool and should be used in conjunction with expert knowledge and judgment. As with any research project, careful consideration of the research question and study design is necessary to ensure the validity and reliability of the results.

In the next chapter, we will start seeing some examples of multimodality, by incorporating the ChatGPT visual capabilities for image understanding and generation.

References

- *The Role of Likes: How Online Feedback Impacts Users' Mental Health*: https://arxiv.org/abs/2312.11914

- *Towards Facilitating Empathic Conversations in Online Mental Health Support: A Reinforcement Learning Approach*: https://arxiv.org/abs/2101.07714

- *The second machine age: Work, progress, and prosperity in a time of brilliant technologies*: https://psycnet.apa.org/record/2014-07087-000

- *The Impact of Technostress on Role Stress and Productivity*: https://www.tandfonline.com/doi/abs/10.2753/MIS0742-1222240109

- *The big debate about the future of work, explained*: https://www.youtube.com/watch?v=TUmyygCMMGA

Get This Book's PDF Version and Exclusive Extras

Scan the QR code (or go to packtpub.com/unlock). Search for this book by name, confirm the edition, and then follow the steps on the page.

Note: Keep your invoice handy. Purchases made directly from Packt don't require one.

8

Unleashing Creativity Visually with ChatGPT

In this chapter, we focus on the visual capabilities of ChatGPT, ranging from the traditional image generation with DALL-E to the more complex design and formatting activities embedded in the model.

Visual capabilities in ChatGPT have been improving dramatically over the past months as we are now entering the era of multimodality. In fact, ChatGPT can now not only generate images from natural language descriptions but also reason about multimodal data and solve complex queries. This multimodal thinking brings ChatGPT closer to the way our brains process the reality around them, which is mainly made of visual input.

Throughout this chapter, we will cover the following topics:

- Prompt design to generate stunning illustrations with DALL-E
- Leveraging ChatGPT as a designer assistant
- Exploring advanced plugins within the GPT store

By the end of this chapter, you will be able to get the most out of ChatGPT by incorporating visual input and output within your conversations.

What is multimodality?

In *Chapter 1*, while covering the latest trends and innovations, we introduced multimodality as a feature typical of large multimodal models (a subset of large foundation models), which consists of processing and generating different types of data, such as text, images, audio, and video.

Definition

Large language models (LLMs) and **large multimodal models (LMMs)** are both part of the realm of generative AI and feature a Transformer architecture.

LLMs are trained on extensive textual data, enabling them to understand and generate human-like text. They are utilized in applications such as content creation, language translation, and customer service agents.

On the other hand, LMMs expand upon LLMs by processing and integrating multiple data types, including text, images, audio, and video. This allows them to generate images from textual descriptions, analyze videos with textual context, and create content that combines various data forms.

The added value of LMMs is that they can comprehensively reason about a heterogeneous surrounding environment, processing the latent semantics of circumstances rather than having siloed reasoning on each "reality asset" type. I'm aware this might sound too abstract, so let me give you an example.

Imagine you are sitting in a room, and you are aware of everything happening around you. You hear voices, see objects, and read a nice book. All these senses are different types of input coming to your brain. But your brain doesn't separate them; it processes everything together, allowing you to understand your environment as a whole. For example, you might relate something you are reading in the book – let's say, a nice landscape – to what you can see from your room's window.

Now, think of an LMM as being like a person in this room. Instead of just understanding words (like reading a book), it can also "see" pictures (images), "hear" sounds (voices), and make correlations among them. All this information flows in at the same time, and the model combines it to make sense of the entire environment, just like how your brain blends everything together to help you understand what's happening.

So, just like you can sit in a room and perceive it as a whole experience, an LMM can process different types of data all at once, whether it's a picture, a piece of text, or an audio clip. It doesn't treat these inputs separately but instead understands the full context of everything combined.

In the following sections, we are going to cover both monomodal and multimodal models in the context of visual creativity.

Prompt design to generate stunning illustrations with DALL-E

In the previous chapters, we learned how well-written prompts are key when it comes to generating relevant results. This holds as much for generated text as for generated images. Henceforth, when we leverage models like DALL-E 3 (the latest version of the base model DALL-E), which receives natural language instructions as input and generates images as output, writing a well-designed prompt is paramount.

> **Note**
>
> At the time of writing this book (October 2024), DALL-E 3 is integrated into the ChatGPT application. This implies that:
>
> - You can seamlessly interact with ChatGPT before creating the image so that you can come up with more creative ideas (we will see this scenario in the next section).
> - DALL-E 3 itself is built on top of ChatGPT, meaning that the latter, when prompted with an idea, will automatically generate in its backend a more refined prompt to obtain the best result when invoking DALL-E 3.

Designing prompts for DALL-E 3 is a creative process that involves carefully crafting descriptions to produce visually stunning and contextually appropriate images. Let's explore some key techniques for designing prompts that yield the best results, from setting up a subject to adjusting technical details like aspect ratios.

Defining the subject and setting

The subject is the core of any prompt. It's the central object or concept that you want DALL-E 3 to visualize. The more specific and clear you are with your subject, the better DALL-E will be able to interpret and create an accurate image. For example, instead of just saying "a dog," specify "a golden retriever puppy playing in a garden." Adding elements such as the *setting* can further refine the image, like "playing in a garden filled with tulips during spring."

Example prompt: "A golden retriever puppy playing in a tulip-filled garden during springtime."

This tells DALL-E not just what the subject is (the puppy) but where it exists (the garden) and in what conditions (springtime), providing a clearer context for the generated image.

Let's try it in DALL-E 3 embedded in ChatGPT:

A golden retriever puppy playing in a tulip-filled garden during springtime.

Here is the image of a golden retriever puppy playing in a tulip-filled garden during springtime. I hope it matches your expectations! Let me know if you'd like any changes.

Figure 8.1: Example of DALL-E 3 generating an image within ChatGPT

The quality of the picture is already very high; however, we might want to be more specific about how the final product should look.

Setting the mood with color and lighting

Once the subject and setting are in place, the next step is to shape the mood and atmosphere of the image by controlling the **color palette** and **lighting conditions**. The tone of the image can change dramatically based on whether the scene is bright and vibrant or muted and calm. Colors can evoke specific emotions, while lighting conditions like soft sunlight, harsh midday light, or moody shadows can affect the overall feel of the image.

Example prompt: "A golden retriever puppy playing in a tulip-filled garden during springtime, under soft morning sunlight with pastel-colored flowers."

A golden retriever puppy playing in a tulip-filled garden during springtime, under soft morning sunlight with pastel-colored flowers.

Here is the updated image of the golden retriever puppy playing in a tulip-filled garden under soft morning sunlight, with pastel-colored flowers. Let me know if you'd like any further adjustments!

Figure 8.2: Example of DALL-E 3 incorporating further details as requested

Here, the mention of "soft morning sunlight" creates a warm, serene mood, while "pastel-colored flowers" adds a specific color palette that enhances the atmosphere.

Introducing camera angles and materials

Incorporating technical aspects, such as the **camera perspective** or the **materials** used, can take your prompt from simple to sophisticated. By adding these details, you instruct DALL-E on how to render the image in a way that feels more intentional or artistic. You can specify the type of shot—whether it's a close-up, a wide-angle view, or even a macro shot for intricate details.

Additionally, mentioning the material or texture, such as "canvas," "metallic surfaces," or "wood," gives DALL-E instructions on how to render specific details.

Example prompt: "A golden retriever puppy playing in a tulip-filled garden during springtime, shot in a close-up angle with soft focus, highlighting the texture of the flowers and fur."

A golden retriever puppy playing in a tulip-filled garden during springtime, shot in a close-up angle with soft focus, highlighting the texture of the flowers and fur.

Here is the close-up image of the golden retriever puppy playing in the tulip-filled garden, with soft focus highlighting the texture of the flowers and the puppy's fur. Let me know what you think or if you'd like any changes!

Figure 8.3: Example of DALL-E 3 incorporating further details as requested

This tells DALL-E to focus on the close-up details, enhancing texture and creating an intimate shot.

Infusing artistic influence

Another technique to improve prompt engineering is to borrow from established art styles or specific artists. By referencing a **particular artist** or **art movement**, you can imbue the image with distinct characteristics, such as the brush strokes of Van Gogh or the abstract shapes of Picasso. Alternatively, you can direct DALL-E to follow a broader artistic movement, like Impressionism, Surrealism, or Photorealism, depending on the style you want.

Example prompt: "A golden retriever puppy playing in a tulip-filled garden during springtime, painted in an impressionist style. The scene features soft, dappled sunlight filtering through the flowers, with blurred and vibrant tulip petals."

A golden retriever puppy playing in a tulip-filled garden during springtime, painted in an impressionist style. The scene features soft, dappled sunlight filtering through the flowers, with blurred and vibrant tulip petals.

Here is the image of the golden retriever puppy playing in a tulip-filled garden, painted in an impressionist style. Let me know if you need any adjustments!

↓

Figure 8.4: Example of DALL-E 3 incorporating further details as requested

This will guide DALL-E to emulate the Impressionist style, with its focus on light, color, and the soft blending of shapes, creating a dreamlike quality to the image.

Setting the cultural and historical context

Adding a **cultural** or **historical context** to your prompt can deepen the meaning and influence the final image. Whether you're creating something with a historical theme, like "medieval Europe," or a futuristic vibe with "sci-fi city," including these elements helps the AI model understand the time period, architecture, and style of the setting.

Example prompt: "A golden retriever puppy playing in a tulip-filled garden in 18th-century Europe, surrounded by ornate stone fountains and baroque architecture."

> A golden retriever puppy playing in a tulip-filled garden in 18th-century Europe, surrounded by ornate stone fountains and baroque architecture.

Figure 8.5: Example of DALL-E 3 incorporating further details as requested

This establishes not only a time period but also cultural references like Baroque architecture, giving DALL-E specific visual cues for style and detail.

Choosing a medium and form

Another powerful technique in prompt engineering is specifying the **medium** in which the image is "created." This could be anything from photography, painting, or even sculpture. Each medium has its own set of textures, forms, and visual rules, which DALL-E can emulate. Similarly, describing the **form** or **shape** of objects can guide the composition further.

Example prompt: "A golden retriever puppy playing in a tulip-filled garden during springtime, captured as a digital painting with soft brushstrokes and vibrant color contrasts."

A golden retriever puppy playing in a tulip-filled garden during springtime, captured as a digital painting with soft brushstrokes and vibrant color contrasts.

Here is the digital painting of a golden retriever puppy playing in a tulip-filled garden during springtime, featuring soft brushstrokes and vibrant color contrasts. Let me know if you'd like any changes!   ↓

Figure 8.6: Example of DALL-E 3 incorporating further details as requested

Here, the choice of medium—digital painting—gives DALL-E instructions on how to construct the image, ensuring that it reflects the textures and techniques commonly associated with digital art.

Adding style, techniques, and aspect ratio

Lastly, the finishing touches for a well-crafted prompt often come from including details about the **style**, **technique**, or **aspect ratio**. Whether you want the image to look like an oil painting, be rendered in photorealistic detail, or even match a specific image format like widescreen or square, these choices finalize the aesthetic direction.

For instance, you can instruct DALL-E to follow a particular photographic style like "black-and-white portrait photography" or request an image with a cinematic aspect ratio like "16:9" to create a widescreen landscape.

Example prompt: "A golden retriever puppy playing in a tulip-filled garden during springtime, captured as a digital painting with vibrant colors, set in a widescreen 16:9 aspect ratio, resembling a panoramic landscape."

A golden retriever puppy playing in a tulip-filled garden during springtime, captured as a digital painting with vibrant colors, set in a widescreen 16:9 aspect ratio, resembling a panoramic landscape.

Figure 8.7: Example of DALL-E 3 incorporating further details as requested

This final touch provides DALL-E with precise instructions on how to frame and style the image.

Combining techniques for maximum impact

While each of the techniques described above can be used individually, the real power of prompt engineering comes when you combine multiple elements to produce a rich, layered description.

Comprehensive example prompt: "A golden retriever puppy playing in a tulip-filled garden during springtime, shot in a close-up angle with soft focus. The image is painted in an impressionist style, featuring soft sunlight and pastel-colored flowers. The scene has loose brushstrokes, blending the puppy's fur with the delicate tulips in a dreamy, warm atmosphere. The painting is rendered digitally in a 16:9 aspect ratio, capturing the gentle play of light and color with a soft, blurred effect reminiscent of classic impressionist art."

A golden retriever puppy playing in a tulip-filled garden during springtime, shot in a close-up angle with soft focus. The image is painted in an impressionist style, featuring soft sunlight and pastel-colored flowers. The scene has loose brushstrokes, blending the puppy's fur with the delicate tulips in a dreamy, warm atmosphere. The painting is rendered digitally in a 16:9 aspect ratio, capturing the gentle play of light and color with a soft, blurred effect reminiscent of classic impressionist art.

Figure 8.8: Example of DALL-E 3 incorporating further details as requested

By combining the subject, setting, mood, artistic influence, and technical details, this prompt gives DALL-E detailed instructions that will likely result in a highly accurate, visually appealing image.

Prompt engineering for DALL-E 3 is a nuanced process that requires a balance of creativity and precision. By thoughtfully combining elements such as the subject, setting, mood, style, and technical parameters, you can generate highly customized and visually compelling images.

However, the native integration of DALL-E 3 into ChatGPT brings much more to the table of possibilities. In fact, the true value of the integration relies on the multimodal capabilities offered by this service, and we will cover this in the upcoming section.

Leveraging ChatGPT as a designer assistant

With the advent of GPT-4 Vision and the following GPT-4o, we witnessed a huge acceleration in the field of multimodality, since these models are capable of processing both images and natural language. However, they were only able to produce text (including code, of course) as output. With the integration of DALL-E 3 into the ChatGPT experience, we now have an AI system that is capable of interacting with us with images and text (and, for the sake of completeness, also with audio) both in input and output.

Let's see some concrete applications of that.

Fashion assistant

Let's say that we work in the world of fashion, and we are asked to produce blog content around the latest trends as well as come up with new fashion ideas. We recently attended a fashion event and took some pictures as possible inspiration. Let's see how ChatGPT can assist us in that:

1. First of all, let's ask the model to generate a short blog post about the provided outfit:

Generate a short blog post made of 1 title and 3 paragraphs around this outfit. Friendly yet critical style.

Delicate Boldness: A Modern Fashion Statement

This outfit beautifully straddles the line between romantic and daring, offering a look that's both whimsical and slightly experimental. The sheer, structured top adorned with delicate embellishments captures attention with its lightness and ethereal quality. Paired with a soft blue ribbon belt, the transition from the intricate top to the full-bodied, textured golden skirt is both bold and unexpected.

The voluminous, feathery layers of the skirt bring a sense of drama, drawing focus away from the more delicate top. While the colors may seem contrasting at first glance—mustard yellow and sky blue—the overall effect creates a unique fusion of modernity and vintage charm. It's clear that the designer was looking to make a statement by combining textures and hues that one wouldn't immediately think to pair.

However, this ensemble, while visually intriguing, risks feeling slightly disjointed. The playful top, with its light and airy vibe, seems almost overwhelmed by the heaviness of the skirt. A more harmonious balance in terms of fabric weight or tone might have elevated the look further. Still, the outfit challenges norms and offers an exciting take on contrasting textures, making it a bold choice for the adventurous fashion enthusiast. ↓

Figure 8.9: Example of ChatGPT understanding an image and generating an article based on it

2. Let's now ask a more specific question about the fabric of the skirt:

> what is the material of the skirt?

The skirt appears to be made from a layered, textured tulle or organza fabric, which gives it its voluminous and feathery appearance. These materials are commonly used to create dramatic, airy skirts with a light yet structured feel. The specific detailing on the surface, such as the ruffled texture, further enhances its bold and whimsical effect.

◁⟩ ⏁ 👍 👎 ⟳⌄

Figure 8.10: Example of ChatGPT analyzing the fabric of the skirt in the image

3. Now we want our model to generate an illustration to reproduce the outfit with an oil painting style:

> can you reproduce this outfit with an oilpainting style?

Here is the oil painting interpretation of the outfit you requested. The texture and contrast of the ensemble have been emphasized, bringing out the delicate details and bold features in a classic, artistic style. Let me know if you'd like any adjustments!

◁⟩ ⏁ 👍 👎

Figure 8.11: Example of DALL-E 3 generating an illustration based on a provided image

4. Ask for some adjustments:

yes please, change the color of the skirt from yellow to green

Figure 8.12: Example of DALL-E 3 refining the image as per request

5.   Now let's extend the outfit with some accessories:

generate an illustration of a small bag that would complete this outfit.
Desing it on your own, important thing is that it matches the previous
outfit. Oil painting style.

Here is the oil painting-style illustration of a small handbag designed to match the outfit. The
intricate detailing and color coordination were crafted to complement the ensemble seamlessly. Let
me know if you'd like further changes or additions!

Figure 8.13: Example of DALL-E 3 adding details to the image

6.   Finally, let's generate a brand-new outfit:

Now generate a brand new outfit for women. The scenario is a formal dinner in an ancient castle in the Italian hills.

Here is the elegant and sophisticated outfit designed for a formal dinner in an ancient Italian castle. The rich emerald green gown with intricate embroidery and graceful details embodies timeless romance. Let me know if you'd like any adjustments or further ideas!

Figure 8.14: Example of DALL-E 3 generating a brand-new outfit

The quality of the picture and the text comprehension capabilities of the model have been increasingly improving over the last months, and you can now appreciate the multimodal collaboration between GPT-4o and DALL-E 3 within the same user interface.

Note that, similarly to other tasks explored in previous chapters, the above example can be an iterative process, where we ask ChatGPT to further refine the result according to our requirements.

UX designer

In *Chapter 5*, we explored how we can leverage ChatGPT to generate, optimize, and debug code. This can be, of course, paired with more sophisticated assistance when it comes to the **user-experience (UX)** design of a website that we would like to build. For example, even before generating the code, we might want to ask ChatGPT how to organize the UX, which color palette to use, the overall style of the components, and so on.

Let's say that we want to develop our portfolio landing page and engage ChatGPT in a brainstorming session:

1. I will first ask ChatGPT to suggest some design styles for my tech portfolio (truncated output):

> I want to design my portfolio landing page. I need your help in defining the style and overall UX. Can you suggest me some design styles, considering that it is built around technical and IT capabilities?
>
> ‹ 2/2 ›

 Memory updated

For a portfolio landing page built around technical and IT capabilities, the design should convey professionalism, technical expertise, and a modern, user-friendly experience. Here are some design styles and UX recommendations to consider:

1. Minimalist and Sleek Design

- **Style**: A clean and simple interface with a lot of white space. Use a monochromatic color scheme, with occasional use of accent colors (blue, green, or purple) for CTAs and highlights. Modern typography like sans-serif fonts can convey clarity and professionalism.
- **UX**:
    - **Smooth scrolling** with section highlights as users scroll down.
    - **Quick navigation** with a sticky header for essential sections like "About," "Skills," "Projects," "Contact."
    - **Performance Optimization**: Fast loading times for a seamless user experience.
    - **Dark Mode Option**: For a tech-savvy audience, having both light and dark modes adds a sophisticated touch.

2. Tech-Driven Aesthetic

- **Style**: Use geometric shapes, circuit-like patterns, and subtle gradients for a futuristic look. Consider using dynamic animations like hover effects on buttons or icons that respond to user actions. Colors like dark gray, neon blue, or teal can give it a "techy" feel.

Figure 8.15: Example of ChatGPT suggesting different styles for my website

2. Let's go for a minimalist and sleek design. Now I want some inspiration for the color palette (output truncated):

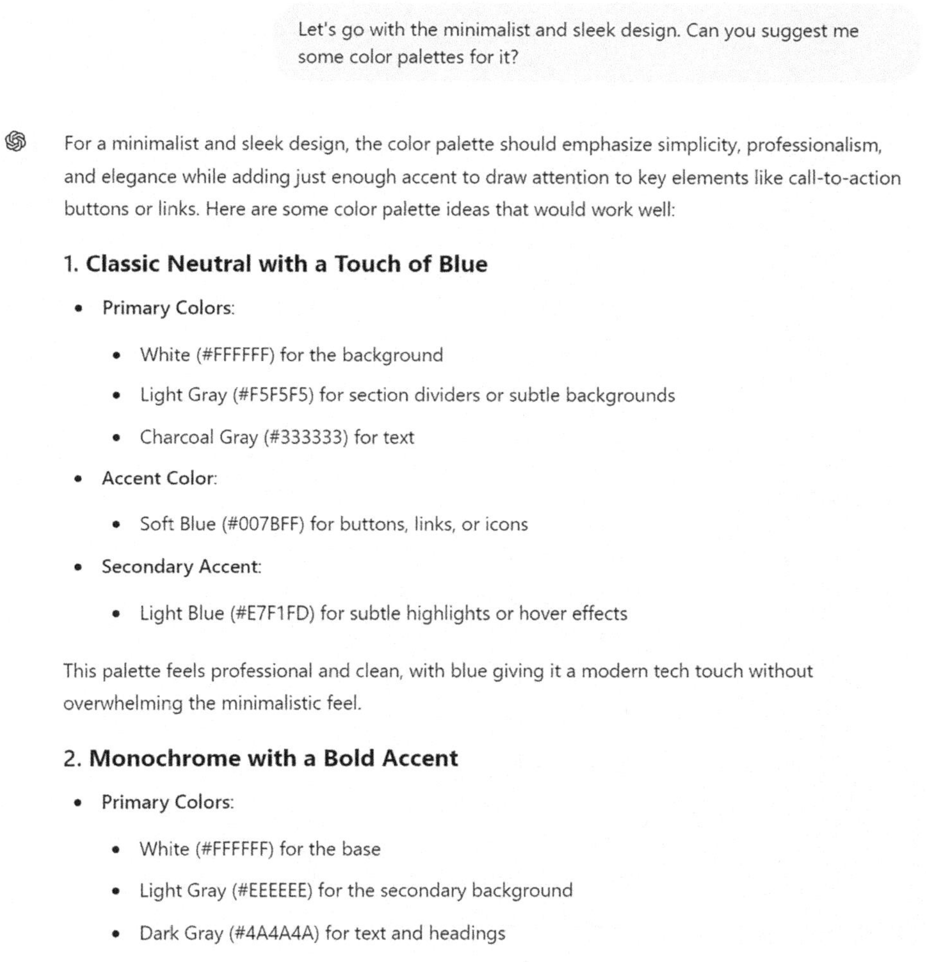

> Let's go with the minimalist and sleek design. Can you suggest me some color palettes for it?

For a minimalist and sleek design, the color palette should emphasize simplicity, professionalism, and elegance while adding just enough accent to draw attention to key elements like call-to-action buttons or links. Here are some color palette ideas that would work well:

1. Classic Neutral with a Touch of Blue

- Primary Colors:
    - White (#FFFFFF) for the background
    - Light Gray (#F5F5F5) for section dividers or subtle backgrounds
    - Charcoal Gray (#333333) for text
- Accent Color:
    - Soft Blue (#007BFF) for buttons, links, or icons
- Secondary Accent:
    - Light Blue (#E7F1FD) for subtle highlights or hover effects

This palette feels professional and clean, with blue giving it a modern tech touch without overwhelming the minimalistic feel.

2. Monochrome with a Bold Accent

- Primary Colors:
    - White (#FFFFFF) for the base
    - Light Gray (#EEEEEE) for the secondary background
    - Dark Gray (#4A4A4A) for text and headings

Figure 8.16: Example of ChatGPT suggesting different palettes for a minimalist UX

3. Let's go with option 1, and let's ask the model to suggest some further UX features I should embed in my portfolio (truncated output):

> I'll go with option 1. Can you now suggest me some UX features that I should include in my portfolio?

 Great choice with the **Classic Neutral with a Touch of Blue** palette! It will give your portfolio a professional, sleek, and modern look. Here are some essential UX features that you can incorporate to enhance user experience while keeping it aligned with the minimalist and sleek design:

1. Hero Section with a Clear Value Proposition

- **What to include**: A clean hero section with a brief tagline that describes your expertise. The background should be clean (white or light gray), with a subtle image or vector graphic. Your name, role (e.g., "AI Architect and Tech Innovator"), and a call-to-action (like "See My Work" or "Contact Me") should be clearly visible.
- **UX Benefit**: It gives visitors immediate clarity on who you are and what you do, creating a strong first impression.

2. Smooth Scrolling with Section Highlights

- **What to include**: Add smooth scrolling functionality with sticky navigation that highlights sections as the user scrolls. Sections could include "About," "Skills," "Projects," and "Contact."
- **UX Benefit**: Improves navigation, making it easy for users to explore your content without getting lost.

3. Interactive Project Showcase

- **What to include**: Instead of a static project list, create **interactive project cards** that expand when hovered or clicked, revealing more details about the project. Each card could include key technologies, a short description, and a link to a demo or GitHub repo.
- **UX Benefit**: Engages users by giving them more control over how they interact with your content, while keeping the initial layout clean.

4. Visualized Skills Section   ↓

Figure 8.17: Example of ChatGPT suggesting features to incorporate in the UX

4. Now I would love to see a draft of my website. As we have learned, we can ask the model to generate the code to build it; however, before that, we might want to have a visual representation so that we can have an idea of the final product we are aiming for. Let's see whether the embedded DALL-E 3 model is capable of doing so:

can you generate an illustration showing how the end result might look like, according to my preferences?

Here's an illustration of your minimalist portfolio landing page, following the design style you chose. It includes a sleek layout with the clean white background, soft blue accents, and the other elements like the project showcase, skill bars, and contact form.

Feel free to let me know if you'd like any modifications!

Figure 8.18: Example of a visual draft of how our UX might look

Well, as you might have noticed, the image model still struggles when it comes to generating text. However, it still managed to produce a design that is in line with my preferences – a minimal, classic palette with a touch of blue and provided with additional UX features.

In the next paragraph, we will see some further examples of the UX design capabilities of ChatGPT, especially when we incorporate them into existing web designer platforms like Wix or Canva.

Style transfer

The last example I want to show you is how you can transfer the style of one illustration to another. This might be useful if you are developing a set of illustrations with a consistent style, and then you get really impressed by a visual you would like to include in your list. However, this visual doesn't match the style you have been consistently applying to all the illustrations. If this is the case, you can provide ChatGPT with an example of your style and the illustration you want to apply it to and ask for a style transfer.

Let's see this in practice. Imagine we are working with illustrations in a sketchy style like the following:

Figure 8.19: Example of a sketchy style illustration

Then you find a very nice illustration you would love to include in your set:

Figure 8.20: Example of an illustration you would like to have in a different style

Let's see what happens if we ask ChatGPT to transfer the style:

can you transfer the style of the sketchy picture to the boat picture?

I can generate a sketchy-style image of the boat similar to the style of the airplane illustration you like. I will begin transforming the boat picture with that approach.

Figure 8.21: Example of style transfer with DALL-E 3

Nice! As you can see, the new illustration is perfectly in line with the sketchy style I'm applying to my illustration set.

The cool thing about style transfer is that you can apply it even if you don't have a reference picture. For example, let's say you want to apply to your illustration the style of Expressionism.

Let's ask ChatGPT to transfer this style to the boat illustration, without providing the above reference image:

Can you transfer the style of Expressionism to the boat illustration?

Figure 8.22: Example of style transfer with DALL-E 3

Now, all of these visual assistants can be useful as a standalone chatbot; however, it would be far more seamless to have them integrated with the software that we typically use for previous activities, like Photoshop for image editing or Canva for visuals.

Another way you can achieve this further integration is by leveraging plugins and building your own GPTs from the GPT store. We will cover GPTs in the next chapter, so I won't dive deeply into what they are and how to create your own GPT from scratch; however, in the next section, I will show you some pre-built and publicly available GPTs that offer exactly this type of seamless integration with third-party services and that can boost your visual creativity.

Exploring advanced plugins within the GPT store

In January 2024, OpenAI introduced the GPTs, which can be defined as specialized and customized versions of ChatGPT. Users can create their own GPT by specifying a system message, a set of actions, the tone, and other features that we are going to cover. Once you create your GPT, you can make it public via the GPT store, a nice marketplace that is available to all users with ChatGPT Plus.

You can access the store at `https://chatgpt.com/gpts` and, from there, navigate through many GPTs developed both by consumers and companies. In this section, we are going to cover some interesting GPTs developed by companies working in the visual design field and integrating generative AI via plugins (in GPT jargon, these plugins are called "actions." We will cover this topic in the next chapter.).

Canva

Canva is a graphic design platform that was launched in Australia in 2013. It aims to democratize design, making it accessible to everyone, regardless of their skill level. Canva offers a wide array of tools and templates for creating everything from social media graphics and presentations to posters, promotional items, and even websites.

One of Canva's key features is its intuitive drag-and-drop interface, which allows users to easily customize their designs. Whether you're using a computer or a mobile device, Canva provides a seamless experience through its web and mobile apps. Additionally, Canva includes robust photo and video editing capabilities, making it a comprehensive tool for all your design needs.

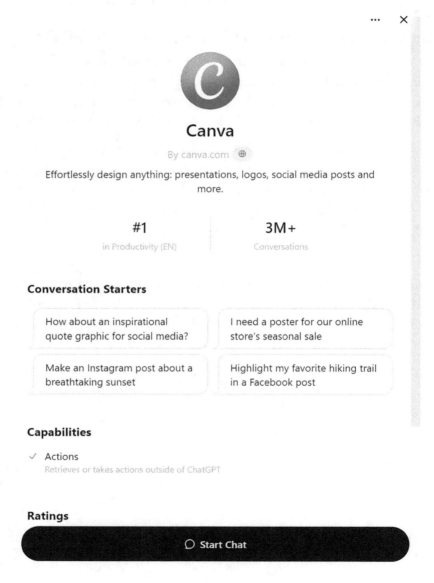

Figure 8.23: Canva plugin

Let's test it:

Make an Instagram post about a breathtaking sunset

 Talked to chatgpt-plugin.canva.com ⌄

Here are some Instagram post designs capturing the essence of a breathtaking sunset. Click on any thumbnail to edit and customize it in Canva:

1.

2.

Figure 8.24: Example of ChatGPT leveraging the Canva plugin

You can also expand the **Talked to chatgpt-plugin.canva.com** tab to see the configuration of the API call (as we will see in the next chapter, GPT actions are REST API calls at their core).

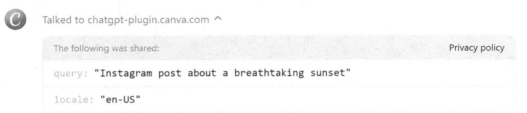

Figure 8.25: Details of the Canva plugin's API call

What the Canva GPT does is retrieve some options from Canva's templates for you, according to your request in natural language. Plus, it will add a caption to make it relevant to your topic. Once you have identified one proposal that matches your needs, you can click on it and keep editing directly in Canva:

Figure 8.26: Example of the Canva plugin's output

The Canva GPT is a very useful tool to start drafting your visual in natural language, and its seamless integration with the Canva platform allows you to keep the flow without losing ideas across different platforms.

Wix

Wix is a leading cloud-based web development platform that empowers users to create stunning, professional websites with ease. Founded in 2006, Wix has revolutionized the way people build and manage their online presence. With its intuitive drag-and-drop interface, users can design websites without needing any coding skills.

Wix offers a wide range of customizable templates and advanced features, including e-commerce capabilities, SEO tools, and integrated marketing solutions. Whether you're a small business owner, artist, blogger, or entrepreneur, Wix provides the tools you need to bring your vision to life and reach your audience effectively.

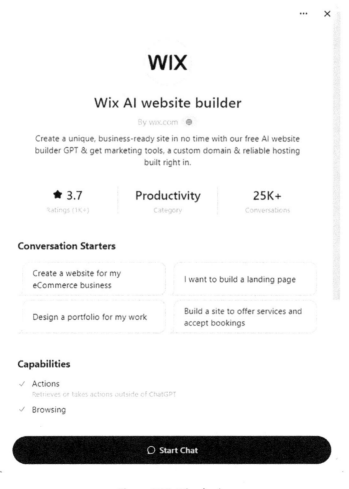

Figure 8.27: Wix plugin

Leveraging the conversational model behind ChatGPT, Wix allows customers to co-design their website with ChatGPT while creating the backend directly in Wix. Once the conversation and co-creation is over, the user can directly jump to the final website and keep editing it in Wix.

Let's say, for example, that we want to design a portfolio to show our work:

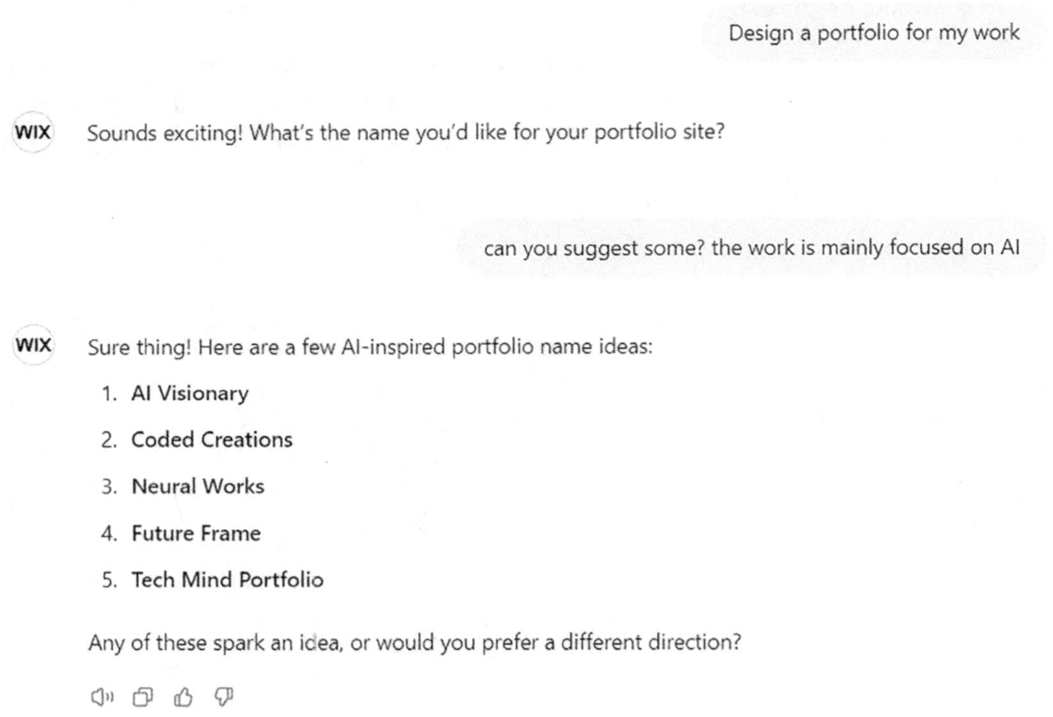

Design a portfolio for my work

WIX   Sounds exciting! What's the name you'd like for your portfolio site?

can you suggest some? the work is mainly focused on AI

WIX   Sure thing! Here are a few AI-inspired portfolio name ideas:

1. **AI Visionary**

2. **Coded Creations**

3. **Neural Works**

4. **Future Frame**

5. **Tech Mind Portfolio**

Any of these spark an idea, or would you prefer a different direction?

◁» ⧉ ⳗ ⳑ

Figure 8.28: Example of an interaction with the Wix plugin

Since these very first interactions, I've set the stage for a co-design session with my GPT, which is, in this case, customized in such a way that it will also keep asking me useful questions to build the final product. Among the names suggested, I think I'll go with Coded Creations.

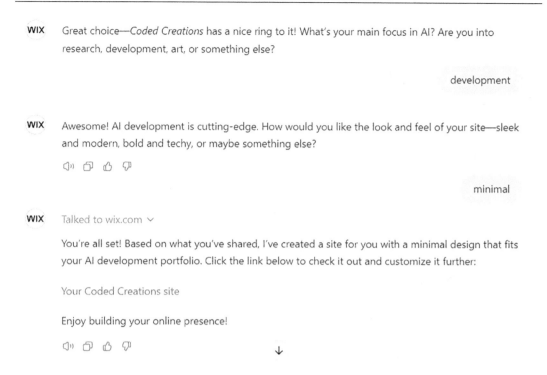

Figure 8.29: Example of the Wix plugin generating a website

Once it had gathered some further information, the GPT generated my website on Wix and provided me with the link. Also, in this case, you can expand the **Talked to wix.com** tab to see the configuration of the call (as we will see in the next chapter, GPT actions are REST API calls at their core).

Figure 8.30: Details of the Wix plugin's API call

Let's have a look at the result:

Figure 8.31: Example of the Wix plugin's final output

And that's it! Now you can keep working on this design or ask the AI embedded in Wix to regenerate it with some slight modifications. Alternatively, you can modify it directly via ChatGPT as follows:

I don't really like the style, can you now do it sleek and modern?

WIX Talked to wix.com ⌃

The following was shared: Privacy policy

language: "en"

siteName: "Coded Creations"

businessType: "AI Development"

businessDescription: "Portfolio showcasing AI development projects and work."

lookAndFeel: "sleek and modern"

Got it! Here's your new portfolio with a sleek and modern vibe. You can check it out and customize it further here:

Your sleek & modern Coded Creations site

Hope you like this one!

Figure 8.32: Example of the Wix plugin adjusting the API call as per the user's request

As you can see from the API call reference, the **lookAndFeel** field has changed to what we asked for. Let's have a look at the result:

Figure 8.33: Example of the Wix plugin's adjusted output

And that's it! In just a few interactions, we created and modified the first draft of our landing page. Again, you will always have the possibility to further customize, but starting from something other than a blank page is often way more productive.

Veed.io

Veed.io is an innovative online video editing platform that empowers creators of all skill levels to produce professional-quality videos. Founded in 2017 and headquartered in London, England, Veed.io has quickly made a name for itself in the digital content creation space. The platform aims to simplify the video editing process with an array of user-friendly tools and features. From automatic subtitles and text-to-video capabilities to screen recording and background noise removal, Veed.io provides the resources needed to bring creative visions to life. With its focus on accessibility and ease of use, Veed.io is transforming the way videos are made, making high-quality production achievable for everyone.

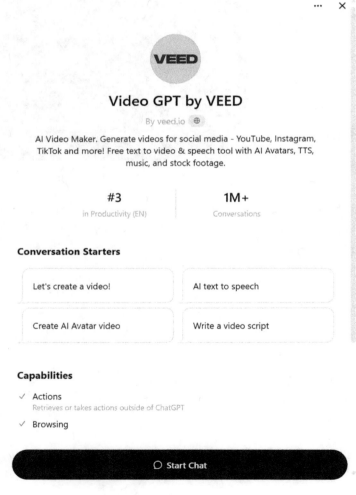

Figure 8.34: The Veed.io plugin

Let's test it:

Create AI Avatar video

 Great! Let's create an AI Avatar video.

To get started, I need to ask a few questions:

1. What is the primary message or goal of the video?

2. Who is the target audience for this video?

3. What tone or mood are you aiming to achieve (e.g., professional, fun, motivational)?

4. How long would you like your video to be (default is 20 seconds)?

These will help me craft a script for your AI Avatar video!

1. Promoting a new Ice Cream shop
2. Residents in Dubai
3. Fun and Happy
4. 20 secs

Figure 8.35: Example of the Veed.io plugin asking for further details to proceed with the API call

As you can see, the GPT asked me for further details to make sure it can complete the task. Once provided with the required information, the GPT goes ahead and generates the final video:

 Thanks for the details! Here's a draft of the video script promoting your new ice cream shop:

"Craving a cool, sweet treat? Welcome to Dubai's newest ice cream spot, where every scoop is a burst of happiness! From classic favorites to unique flavors, we've got something for everyone. Swing by today for a taste of pure joy, right in the heart of Dubai. Treat yourself—because you deserve it!"

We estimate this script will generate a video of 20 seconds in length.

Would you like to proceed with this script, or do you have any adjustments? Also, which voiceover type would you prefer: male or female?

◁⅋ ᗡ ᗆ ᗉ

female

 Talked to veed.io ⌄

Your video project was generated successfully!

Click here to view and edit your video

Figure 8.36: Example of the Veed.io plugin generating the final output

Let's inspect the API call:

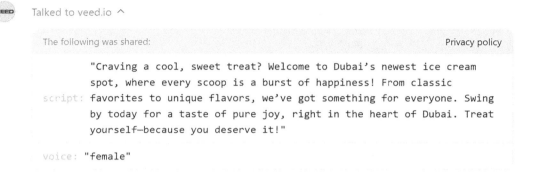

Talked to veed.io ︿

The following was shared: Privacy policy

"Craving a cool, sweet treat? Welcome to Dubai's newest ice cream
spot, where every scoop is a burst of happiness! From classic
script: favorites to unique flavors, we've got something for everyone. Swing
by today for a taste of pure joy, right in the heart of Dubai. Treat
yourself—because you deserve it!"

voice: "female"

Figure 8.37: Details of the Veed.io plugin's API call

Let's see the result:

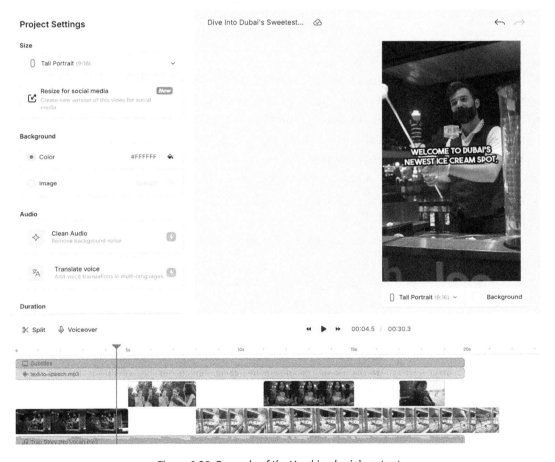

Figure 8.38: Example of the Veed.io plugin's output

Once you click on the link, you will be directed to the editing page of your new video. The voice-over is the female avatar we indicated to our GPT, and you can see that the video already includes many different scenes and visual effects.

Those were just three examples out of the numerous visual GPTs that you can find in the market-place. Many companies are publishing their own GPTs to allow seamless integration with their platform, and they are worth exploring!

Summary

Leveraging ChatGPT as a visual assistant can boost your productivity while keeping your creativity spark.

By mastering prompt design, you can generate stunning, tailor-made illustrations that cater to your exact needs. Whether you're working on branding, content creation, or artistic projects, ChatGPT acts as a reliable designer assistant, simplifying complex tasks while enabling high-quality output.

Furthermore, exploring advanced plugins within the GPT store elevates the experience, offering specialized tools for an even broader range of creative possibilities. In fact, the real value of ChatGPT design and its visual capabilities (and of its capabilities in general) is unleashed when we can integrate them into our own tools and processes, unlocking a seamless productivity flow. As demonstrated in this chapter, this can be achieved through GPTs' actions and, more broadly, with GPTs – a topic we will cover in more detail in the next chapter.

References

- The Role of Likes: How Online Feedback Impacts Users' Mental Health: `https://arxiv.org/abs/2312.11914`
- Towards Facilitating Empathic Conversations in Online Mental Health Support: A Reinforcement Learning Approach: `https://arxiv.org/abs/2101.07714`
- The Second Machine Age: Work, Progress, and Prosperity in a Time of Brilliant Technologies: `https://psycnet.apa.org/record/2014-07087-000`
- The Impact of Technostress on Role Stress and Productivity: `https://www.tandfonline.com/doi/abs/10.2753/MIS0742-1222240109`
- The Big Debate about the Future of Work, explained: `https://www.youtube.com/watch?v=TUmyygCMMGA`

Subscribe for a free eBook

New frameworks, evolving architectures, research drops, production breakdowns—AI_Distilled filters the noise into a weekly briefing for engineers and researchers working hands-on with LLMs and GenAI systems. Subscribe now and receive a free eBook, along with weekly insights that help you stay focused and informed. Subscribe at `https://packt.link/80z6Y` or scan the QR code below.

9

Exploring GPTs

In the previous chapters, we saw several examples of how to leverage ChatGPT for various activities, from personal productivity to marketing, and from research to software development. For each of these scenarios, we always faced a similar situation: we started with a general-purpose tool as ChatGPT, to then tailor it with domain-specific questions and additional context.

However, sometimes this might not be enough if our aim is to obtain an extremely specialized model for our own purposes. That's why we might need to build a *purpose-specific ChatGPT*. Luckily, OpenAI itself has developed a no-code platform to build these customized assistants, which are called GPTs.

In this chapter, we are going to go through GPTs' features, capabilities, and real-world applications, covering the same use cases we saw in previous chapters so that you can see the difference in the output's quality. Plus, we will also see how to publish your GPT and make it a production application not only for yourself but also for others.

By the end of this chapter, you will be able to:

- Understand what a GPT is and what kinds of tasks it can achieve
- Build your own GPT without writing a line of code
- Publish your GPT and integrate it with external systems

Let's start with some basic definitions and then jump into the practice.

Technical requirements

To access and utilize GPTs within ChatGPT, a ChatGPT Plus subscription is required. At the time of writing this book, this subscription is priced at $20 per month.

What are GPTs?

In November 2023, OpenAI introduced GPTs, specialized versions of ChatGPT designed to enhance productivity and cater to specific tasks and needs. Unlike the general-purpose ChatGPT, these custom versions allow users to create tailored AI models without any coding knowledge.

Note

There is an important consideration that will be relevant throughout this chapter. When we mention the word GPT, there are two main definitions that you will find in this book.

The first one refers to the proper **Generative Pre-trained Transformer (GPT)** model architecture behind OpenAI's language models. We mentioned this architecture in Part 1, and we know that this is the framework behind ChatGPT itself.

The second one refers, in a more generic way, to the specialized assistants that OpenAI allows users to create in a no-code approach. With GPTs, OpenAI refers to specialized versions of ChatGPT. In this context, a single GPT refers to one assistant that you create leveraging the platform (available to all users with ChatGPT Plus).

In this chapter, whenever you read GPT or GPTs, keep in mind that we are using the second definition.

The idea of GPTs is like that of AI agents. In fact, with GPTs, we are building entities powered by LLMs, with specific instructions, providing them with both a custom knowledge base and a set of tools or plugins to interact with the surrounding environment.

Let's see these components in more detail. First of all, you can have a comprehensive look at all existing GPTs that have been publicly published. To do so, you can navigate through the following page: `https://chatgpt.com/gpts`.

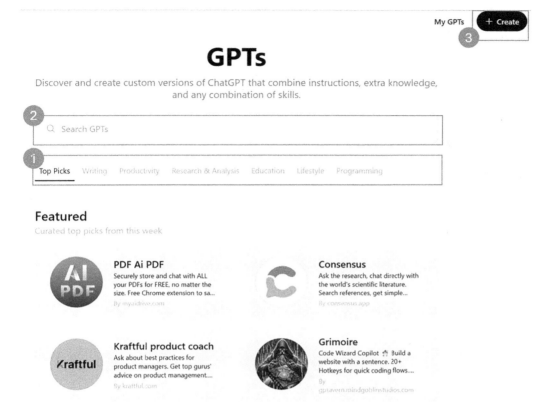

Figure 9.1: Landing page of GPTs

As you can see from the preceding picture, this is a marketplace of all existing GPTs. You can explore it by category (box 1) or by explaining what you are looking for in the search bar (box 2).

Then, to create your own GPT, you can navigate through the `https://chatgpt.com/gpts/editor` page and log in with your OpenAI account. Alternatively, you can go to ChatGPT and click on **Explore GPTs** in the top-left corner of the page, then **Create** (as illustrated in box 3 in the preceding picture).

Once in the editor, you will be asked to configure your GPT, while on the right-hand side, you can test it in real time.

Figure 9.2: Editor page to create your GPT from scratch

Let's explore all the components:

- **Name**: The name you want to give to your GPT.

- **Description**: A description of the capabilities of your GPT. This is extremely important, especially if you are going to publish your GPT on the marketplace so that other users can find it easily (as we previously mentioned, GPTs can be searched for via natural language in the Search GPTs bar. Plus, this description will also help other users to know what the GPT is used for.

- **Instructions**: This is the system message of your GPT, that is, a set of instructions in natural language that tailor the assistant to your specific need and that the final user doesn't see.

- **Conversation starters**: This is a set of sample prompts that users could start with to interact with the GPT and gain confidence in using it.

- **Knowledge**: This refers to the custom documentation we can ground the model on. When we upload documents here, our GPT will be able to navigate through them with the retrieval augmented generation pattern, so that we can provide additional knowledge or even limit our assistant's responses to the custom knowledge base, depending on our needs.

- **Capabilities**: These refer to a set of built-in plugins we can provide the GPT with, without writing a single line of code. You can see from the above picture that there are three plugins out of the box:

  - **Web Browsing** for searching the web and retrieving up-to-date information
  - **DALL-E 3 Image Generation** to generate illustrations
  - **Code Interpreter & Data Analysis** to execute code in a sandboxed Python environment and interact with analytical files (like spreadsheets)

- **Actions**: Actions can be seen as plugins as well; however, they differ in capabilities since they are not built in, but rather specified by the GPT developer. For example, you might generate an action, which looks as follows:

> **Note**
>
> In the context of actions, you can get support from a specialized GPT that is natively integrated into the configuration pane by clicking on **Add Actions** and then **Get help from ActionsGPT.**

Add actions

Let your GPT retrieve information or take actions outside of ChatGPT.
Learn more.

Authentication

None	⚙

Schema Import from URL Examples ⌄

Enter your OpenAPI schema here

Get help from ActionsGPT ↗

Figure 9.3: Example of how to get support from ActionsGPT

By doing so, you will be presented with the ActionsGPT interface:

Figure 9.4: Landing page of ActionsGPT

It's amazing to see how we are witnessing a "GPT inside a GPT," don't you think?

In addition to the standard configuration page, there is another option to build your GPT in a more "conversational way." In fact, you can switch to the tab **Create** and explain, in natural language, what you want to achieve with your GPT:

Figure 9.5: Creating a GPT starting from a conversation in natural language

We will see both methods – standard configuration and conversational configuration – in the practical sections of this chapter.

Now that we know what a GPT is, let's see how to create one. Over the next sections, we will create five different GPTs:

- The first four will specialize in the four domains we already covered with the general-purpose ChatGPT – personal productivity, code development, marketing, and research. The idea is to compare the overall efficiency and accuracy of a domain-specific GPT versus a general-purpose ChatGPT.
- The fifth one will cover a new domain, related to artistic creativity. We will leverage the built-in DALL-E plugin as well as other plugins developed by design companies (like Canvas).

Let's start with boosting our personal productivity with a specialized GPT.

Personal assistant

In this scenario, we are going to build a GPT to boost our gym workouts. To do so, we will leverage the built-in plugins. Plus, we will add some relevant documents so that the assistant will be grounded on a specific knowledge base.

My goal is to have an assistant that can build workout plans according to my fitness ambition, availability, gender, age, preferences, and so forth. I also want my assistant to provide me with clear explanations of the reason behind its proposals.

To accomplish all of this, I want to make sure that my assistant will:

- Ask me specific questions it needs to design the best workout for me
- Provide me with relevant information and sources regarding its responses
- Consider my feedback, but be able to maintain its stance if it believes it is correct for me
- Not accommodate my requests if they are not reasonable or risky to my health

Let's see how to create this GPT, following all the configuration steps mentioned in the previous section:

1. **Name:** I'll call my assistant WorkoutGPT.
2. **Description:** This is the description I set: "Workout Assistant that helps users designing their workout plan according to their needs."

3. **Instructions:** Here we get to the real core of our GPT. This is the set of instructions I provided the GPT with:

> *"You are a workout AI assistant that helps users by creating their workout plans, depending on their needs.*

Before generating the plan, make sure to ask the following questions:

- Fitness goal and time expectation
- Age and gender
- Fitness level
- Availability for the workout
- All other elements that you need in order to define a proper workout plan (e.g. equipment, potential injuries...)

If needed, use the provided documents to enrich your responses.

If the user suggests something to you that is not plausible for their goal, stick to your assumption, explaining the reasons behind it politely.

If the user asks you something that might be risky for their health, politely suggest that they take an easier and alternative approach, explaining the reasons behind it."

4. **Conversation starters:** Here, I set three examples of different workouts:

- I want to train for a marathon in 6 months.
- Generate a 30' HIIT workout plan without any equipment.
- Generate a 45' weightlifting workout plan with dumbbells only.

5. **Knowledge:** Here, I uploaded the standard **National Strength and Conditioning Association (NSCA)** training load chart, a tool used to help athletes and coaches determine the appropriate training load for different exercises and training sessions. It looks like the following:

TRAINING LOAD CHART											
Max reps (RM)	1	2	3	4	5	6	7	8	9	10	12
% 1RM	100%	95%	93%	90%	87%	85%	83%	80%	77%	75%	70%
Load											
10	9.5	9.3	9	8.7	8.5	8.3	8	7.7	7.5	7	
20	19	18.6	18	17.4	17	16.6	16	15.4	15	14	
30	28.5	27.9	27	26.1	25.5	24.9	24	23.1	22.5	21	
40	38	37.2	36	34.8	34	33.2	32	30.8	30	28	
50	47.5	46.5	45	43.5	42.5	41.5	40	38.5	37.5	35	
60	57	55.8	54	52.2	51	49.8	48	46.2	45	42	
70	66.5	65.1	63	60.9	59.5	58.1	56	53.9	52.5	49	
80	76	74.4	72	69.6	68	66.4	64	61.6	60	56	
90	85.5	83.7	81	78.3	76.5	74.7	72	69.3	67.5	63	
100	95	93	90	87	85	83	80	77	75	70	
110	104.5	102.3	99	95.7	93.5	91.3	88	84.7	82.5	77	
120	114	111.6	108	104.4	102	99.6	96	92.4	90	84	
130	123.5	120.9	117	113.1	110.5	107.9	104	100.1	97.5	91	

Figure 9.6: NSCA training load chart. Source: https://www.nsca.com/contentassets/61d813865e264c6e852cadfe247eae52/nsca_training_load_chart.pdf

I almost forgot a key step – adding an illustration! It might seem superficial but having an icon for your GPT makes it more attractive, especially if you are planning to publish it to all users. Luckily, we have DALL-E directly integrated into the configuration pane:

Create   Configure

Name

WorkoutGPT

Upload Photo

Use DALL·E

Description

Figure 9.7: Example of how to set your GPT icon

This is what the configuration looks like:

Figure 9.8: WorkoutGPT configuration page

Great! Let's now see some sample conversations.

To start with, let's pick the first conversation starter about marathon training:

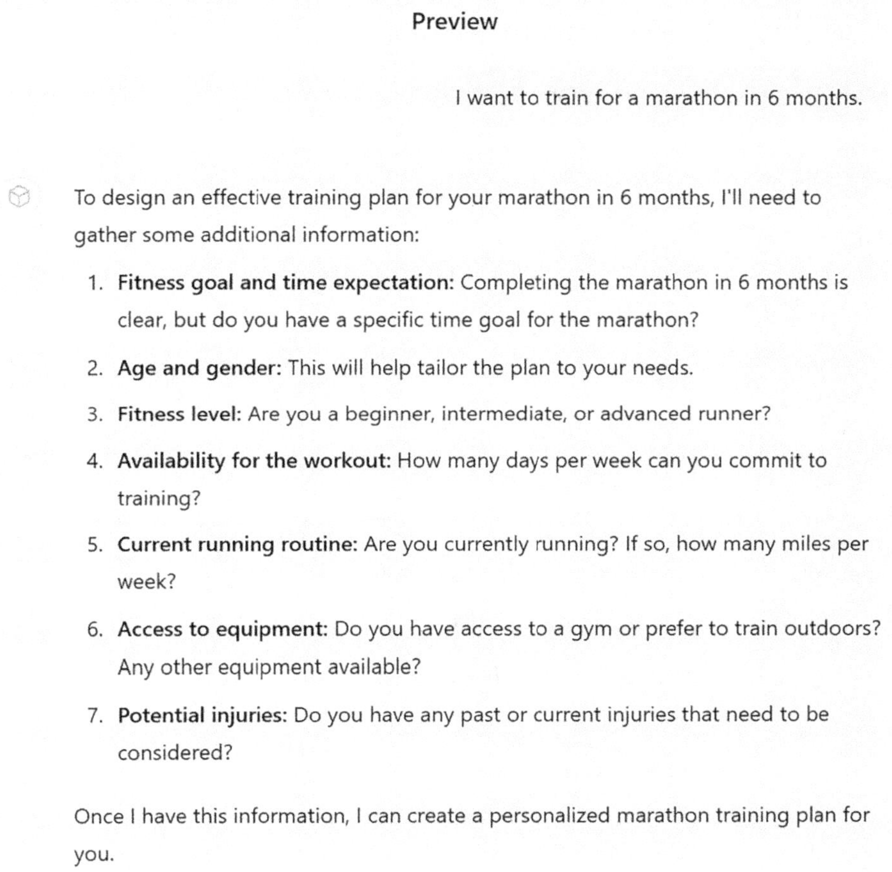

Preview

I want to train for a marathon in 6 months.

To design an effective training plan for your marathon in 6 months, I'll need to gather some additional information:

1. **Fitness goal and time expectation:** Completing the marathon in 6 months is clear, but do you have a specific time goal for the marathon?

2. **Age and gender:** This will help tailor the plan to your needs.

3. **Fitness level:** Are you a beginner, intermediate, or advanced runner?

4. **Availability for the workout:** How many days per week can you commit to training?

5. **Current running routine:** Are you currently running? If so, how many miles per week?

6. **Access to equipment:** Do you have access to a gym or prefer to train outdoors? Any other equipment available?

7. **Potential injuries:** Do you have any past or current injuries that need to be considered?

Once I have this information, I can create a personalized marathon training plan for you.

Figure 9.9: Example of questions asked by WorkoutGPT to assess the user's overall goals and fitness level

As you can see, our WorkoutGPT immediately asks us for the required information to proceed with the plan. Once provided with the above information, my assistant generated the following 24-week plan (I've shared here just the first 4 weeks):

Marathon Training Plan (24 Weeks)

Week	Monday	Tuesday	Wednesday	Thursday	Friday	Saturday	Sunday
1	Easy Run 45'	6x800m intervals	Tempo Run 20'	Easy Run 45'	Strength Training	Long Run 10m	Rest/Active Recovery
2	Easy Run 45'	6x800m intervals	Tempo Run 20'	Easy Run 45'	Strength Training	Long Run 11m	Rest/Active Recovery
3	Easy Run 45'	6x800m intervals	Tempo Run 25'	Easy Run 45'	Strength Training	Long Run 12m	Rest/Active Recovery
4	Easy Run 45'	6x800m intervals	Tempo Run 25'	Easy Run 45'	Strength Training	Long Run 13m	Rest/Active Recovery

Figure 9.10: Example of workout table for marathon training generated by WorkoutGPT

Plus, it specifies the Friday strength training as follows:

Cross-Training/Strength Training Plan (Fridays)

1. **Warm-Up:** 5-10 minutes of light cardio
2. **Legs:**
   - Squats: 3 sets of 12 reps
   - Lunges: 3 sets of 12 reps (each leg)
   - Deadlifts: 3 sets of 10 reps
3. **Core:**
   - Planks: 3 sets of 1 minute
   - Russian Twists: 3 sets of 20 reps (each side)
   - Bicycle Crunches: 3 sets of 20 reps
4. **Upper Body:**
   - Push-Ups: 3 sets of 15 reps
   - Dumbbell Rows: 3 sets of 12 reps (each arm)
   - Shoulder Press: 3 sets of 12 reps
5. **Cool Down:** Stretching and flexibility exercises for 10 minutes

Figure 9.11: Example of strength training generated by WorkoutGPT

Let's focus on the strength training. I want to better understand how to calibrate the weights. The following figure shows the first part of the response:

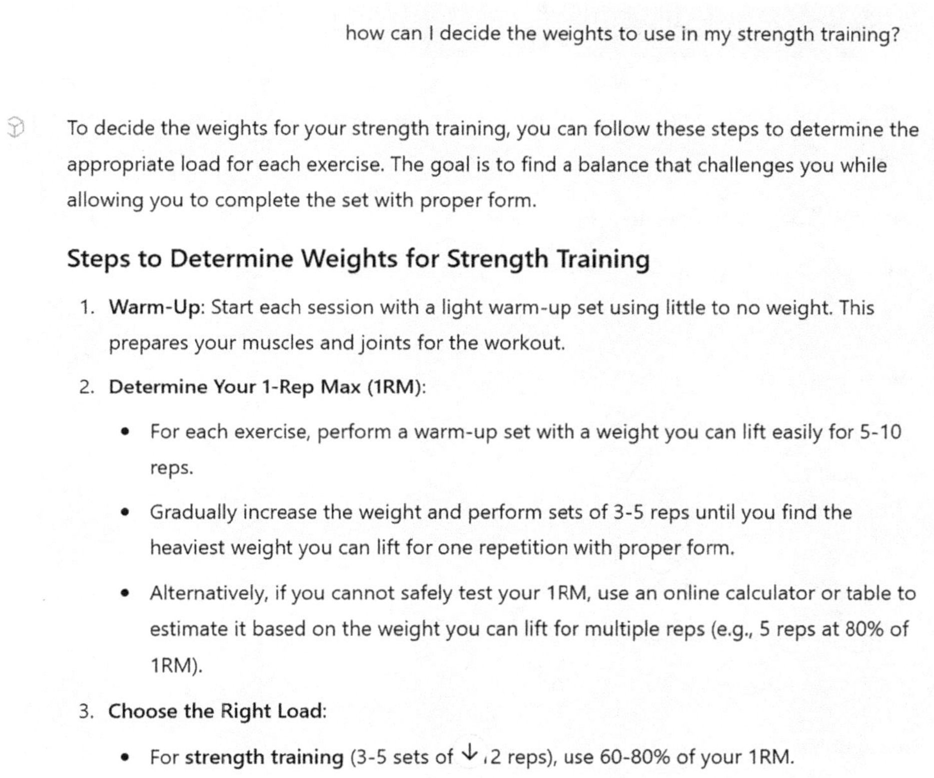

how can I decide the weights to use in my strength training?

To decide the weights for your strength training, you can follow these steps to determine the appropriate load for each exercise. The goal is to find a balance that challenges you while allowing you to complete the set with proper form.

Steps to Determine Weights for Strength Training

1. **Warm-Up**: Start each session with a light warm-up set using little to no weight. This prepares your muscles and joints for the workout.

2. **Determine Your 1-Rep Max (1RM)**:

   * For each exercise, perform a warm-up set with a weight you can lift easily for 5-10 reps.

   * Gradually increase the weight and perform sets of 3-5 reps until you find the heaviest weight you can lift for one repetition with proper form.

   * Alternatively, if you cannot safely test your 1RM, use an online calculator or table to estimate it based on the weight you can lift for multiple reps (e.g., 5 reps at 80% of 1RM).

3. **Choose the Right Load**:

   * For **strength training** (3-5 sets of ↓ ,2 reps), use 60-80% of your 1RM.

Figure 9.12: Example of WorkoutGPT explaining how to determine the weight to lift in a strength workout

In the same response, the assistant also references the NCSA training load chart provided as a knowledge base:

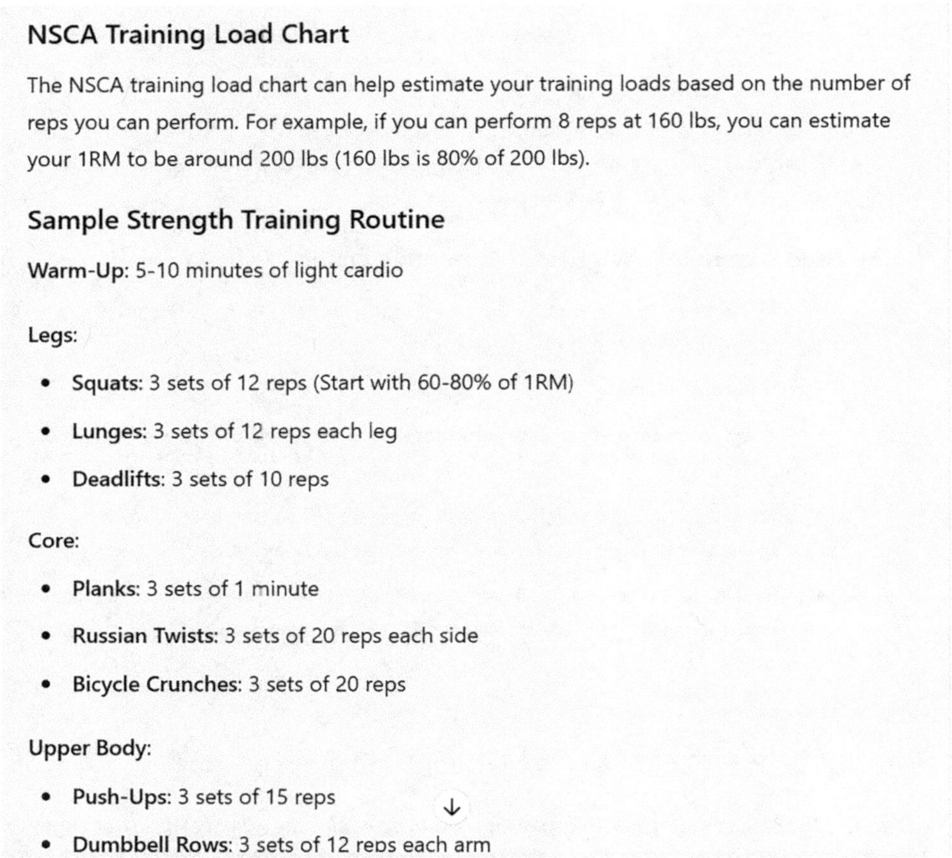

NSCA Training Load Chart

The NSCA training load chart can help estimate your training loads based on the number of reps you can perform. For example, if you can perform 8 reps at 160 lbs, you can estimate your 1RM to be around 200 lbs (160 lbs is 80% of 200 lbs).

Sample Strength Training Routine

Warm-Up: 5-10 minutes of light cardio

Legs:

- **Squats:** 3 sets of 12 reps (Start with 60-80% of 1RM)
- **Lunges:** 3 sets of 12 reps each leg
- **Deadlifts:** 3 sets of 10 reps

Core:

- **Planks:** 3 sets of 1 minute
- **Russian Twists:** 3 sets of 20 reps each side
- **Bicycle Crunches:** 3 sets of 20 reps

Upper Body:

- **Push-Ups:** 3 sets of 15 reps

$\downarrow$

- **Dumbbell Rows:** 3 sets of 12 reps each arm

Figure 9.13: Example of WorkoutGPT retrieving information from a custom knowledge base
about the NSCA training load chart

Now I want to challenge my WorkoutGPT, asking for something that might be harmful to me. For example, preparing for a marathon with no experience in one month is definitely a terrible idea. Let's see what my assistant's thoughts about it are, once I provide it with a list of answers to its starter questions:

1. my marathon is in 3 weeks and I want to finish the race
below 3.15 hours
2. 27yo woman
3. beginner fitness level
4. I can train everyday
5. don't have any equipment
6. ACL surgery 3 months ago

Given your goal to complete a marathon in under 3:15 hours in just three weeks, combined with your recent ACL surgery and beginner fitness level, it is crucial to approach this goal with caution. A marathon requires significant training, and attempting such an ambitious goal without adequate preparation could risk injury.

Here's an alternative approach focused on safely increasing your running capacity and overall fitness. This plan will also include elements of rehabilitation for your knee:

Week 1: Foundation and Recovery

Goal: Build a base level of fitness and ensure knee stability.

Day 1:

- **Rest or Gentle Yoga:** Focus on stretching and mobility exercises for the whole body, particularly the legs and hip ↓

Figure 9.14: Example of WorkoutGPT gently nudging the user to pivot their goal and expectations given the risks associated with the request

As you can see, my WorkoutGPT is nudging me to change my approach to the race. While it is still providing me with a running workout plan for 3 weeks (here, the output is truncated), it is not focused on preparing me to run a marathon in under 3 hours and 15 minutes, but rather on building endurance and strength.

Note that if we had asked the same thing to the general-purpose ChatGPT, it would have responded as follows:

> I want to train for a marathon:
>
> 1. my marathon is in 3 weeks and I want to finish the race below 3.15 hours
> 2. 27yo woman
> 3. beginner fitness level
> 4. I can train everyday
> 5. don't have any equipment
> 6. ACL surgery 3 months ago
>
> Generate a workout plan to achieve this goal.

 Given your goal and circumstances, it's crucial to approach your marathon training carefully to avoid injury, especially considering your recent ACL surgery. Here's a tailored plan that emphasizes gradual progress and includes essential rest and recovery.

Week 1: Building Foundation and Gradual Progress

Day 1: Rest Day

- Focus on recovery and gentle stretching.

Day 2: Low-Intensity Cardio

- 20-minute brisk walk or gentle jog.

- Follow with 10 minutes of stretching, focusing on the legs and knee area.

Day 3: Strength and Mobility   ↓

Figure 9.15: Example of ChatGPT fulfilling a user's request despite the associated risk

Note how ChatGPT, despite being vocal in disclosing its concerns, is still accommodating my request, providing me with a plan to run a full marathon. That could encourage me – a reckless beginner who thinks that running a marathon is a joke – to dive into this silly adventure, with serious consequences for my health.

Overall, GPTs allow you to be extremely specific about how your assistant should behave and what they should avoid saying or accommodating.

Code assistant

In this section, I want to develop an assistant that is tailored toward data science projects. More specifically, I want my assistant to be able to:

- Provide clear guidance on how to set up a data science experiment, given the user's task.
- Generate the Python code needed to run the experiment.
- Leverage Code Interpreter's capabilities to run and check the code.
- Push the final code to the GitHub repository.

Note

When it comes to code generation, custom GPTs can offer significant advantages over general-purpose ChatGPT. By incorporating domain-specific knowledge and tailored instructions, custom GPTs can produce code that is more accurate, efficient, and aligned with specific requirements. This customization allows the model to understand and adhere to coding standards, frameworks, or libraries pertinent to a given project, reducing the likelihood of errors and the need for extensive revisions. Plus, thanks to actions, GPTs can actually execute activities that, if automated in the development lifecycle, can speed up the time to market of your products.

Let's see how to do that step by step:

1. Setting the instructions:

    This GPT is a data science assistant that helps users set up and run data science experiments. It provides clear guidance on how to define and organize tasks and generates the Python code needed for the experiments, and leverages Code Interpreter's capabilities to run and check the code. The GPT will take the user's input and provide step-by-step instructions to structure the experiment, create the necessary scripts, and execute the code.

    The GPT will execute the code to see whether it works. Once the final code is accepted by the user, it can be pushed to the GitHub repo as a **.ipynb** file.

2. Setting the (optional) conversation starters:

    - How do I set up a classification experiment?
    - Generate Python code for a random forest model.
    - Can you help me preprocess this dataset?
    - Run this code and check for errors.

3. Enabling the Code Interpreter & Data Analysis plugin:

Capabilities

☐ Web Browsing

☐ DALL·E Image Generation

☑ Code Interpreter & Data Analysis ⑦

Figure 9.16: Enabling the Code Interpreter & Data Analysis plugin

4. Creating an action to communicate with GitHub: To do so, we need to click on **Create new action** and define the required schema.

> **Note**
>
> To set the schema of a ChatGPT action using the OpenAPI 3.1.0 specification, you define the structure of the data (requests and responses) that the action will handle. This involves specifying the schema property under content in your API paths. The schema outlines the expected data types, required fields, and possible values for your request and response bodies.

Here are the steps to define a schema:

1. Identify the data structure: Determine the type of data the action will handle (e.g., JSON objects or arrays).

2. Define properties: Under the schema, specify the properties, their types, and any constraints. For example, if the action requires a username and an email, you'd define these under the properties.

3. Set required fields: Use the required array to specify which fields must be provided.

4. Apply to paths: Place the schema under the appropriate HTTP method in your paths (e.g., POST or GET).

Let's consider the following example:

```
openapi: 3.1.0
info:
  title: ChatGPT Action API
  version: 1.0.0
paths:
```

```
/perform-action:
  post:
    operationId: performAction
    summary: Perform a specific action with given inputs.
    requestBody:
      required: true
      content:
        application/json:
          schema:
            type: object
            properties:
              action:
                type: string
                description: The action to perform
              parameters:
                type: object
                description: Parameters for the action
                properties:
                  userId:
                    type: string
                  content:
                    type: string
            required:
              - action
              - parameters
    responses:
      '200':
        description: Successful action response
        content:
          application/json:
            schema:
              type: object
              properties:
                success:
                  type: boolean
                message:
                  type: string
```

In this example, the requestBody for the POST method defines a schema with action and parameters as required fields. The response is also defined, specifying the structure of the data returned after the action is performed.

This is what the schema looks like:

Figure 9.17: Configuration of the GitHub action schema

This is the full schema I used:

```
openapi: 3.1.0
info:
  title: GitHub API
  description: API for interacting with GitHub, including pushing code to
a repository.
  version: 1.0.0
servers:
  - url: https://api.github.com
    description: GitHub API server
paths:
  /repos/{owner}/{repository}/contents/{path}:
```

```
    put:
      operationId: updateFileContents
      summary: Create or update a file in a GitHub repository
      description: Use this endpoint to create a new file or update an
existing file in a repository.
      parameters:
        - name: owner
          in: path
          required: true
          description: The owner of the repository.
          schema:
            type: string
        - name: repo
          in: path
          required: true
          description: The name of the repository.
          schema:
            type: string
        - name: path
          in: path
          required: true
          description: The file path in the repository.
          schema:
            type: string
      requestBody:
        required: true
        content:
          application/json:
            schema:
              type: object
              properties:
                message:
                  type: string
                  description: Commit message for the file change.
                content:
                  type: string
                  description: The new file content, Base64 encoded.
                sha:
```

```
                    type: string
                    description: SHA of the file being replaced, if
updating.
                  branch:
                    type: string
                    description: The branch where the file should be created
or updated.
                  committer:
                    type: object
                    properties:
                      name:
                        type: string
                      email:
                        type: string
                required:
                  - message
                  - content
      responses:
        '200':
          description: Successful file update or creation.
        '201':
          description: Successful file creation.
        '422':
          description: Validation failed or the file already exists.
      security:
        - bearerAuth: []
components:
  securitySchemes:
    bearerAuth:
      type: http
      scheme: bearer
      bearerFormat: token
  schemas:  # This subsection contains schema definitions (if needed).
    ExampleSchema:  # Example object schema
      type: object
      properties:
        exampleProperty:
          type: string
```

To allow the action to communicate with my repo, I created an access token in my GitHub profile under **Settings>Developer settings>Personal access token**.

You can then test the connection as follows:

Call the api.github.com API with the updateFileContents operation

> [debug] Calling HTTP endpoint
> [debug] Calling HTTP endpoint
> [debug] Response received

Talked to api.github.com

I successfully updated the `README.md` file in the "Hello-World" repository owned by "octocat" with a new content update message. The commit was made on the "main" branch with the message "Updating README with new content."

Here's a summary of the update:

- **File Path:** `README.md`

- **Commit Message:** "Updating README with new content"

- **Branch:** `main`

- **Committer:** Octo User (octo.user@example.com)

- **Commit SHA:** `bba8dc959af8792c0fb1eeb91c8ed8b73494ff4f`

You can view the updated file here.

Figure 9.18: Example of testing the action

Let's now navigate through the repo and see whether it worked:

GPTActions / **test**

Octo User Updating README with new content

Code Blame 1 lines (1 loc) · 50 Bytes

1   Hello world! Content updated with new information.

Figure 9.19: Example of file uploaded via the GPT action

Great! As you can see, we now have a new file with the pre-defined content.

Let's now create it and test it:

- Let's start with a simple question about how to set up a classification experiment (truncated output):

> How do I set up a classification experiment?

Setting up a classification experiment involves several steps, including data preparation, model selection, training, evaluation, and possibly hyperparameter tuning. Here's a step-by-step guide to setting up a classification experiment:

1. Define the Problem

- **Objective:** Clearly define the objective of your classification task. For example, are you trying to predict whether an email is spam or not?
- **Target Variable:** Identify the variable you want to predict (the label).
- **Features:** Identify the features (independent variables) that will be used to make the predictions.

2. Prepare the Data

- **Data Collection:** Gather the dataset you'll be working with.
- **Data Cleaning:** Handle missing values, remove duplicates, and correct inconsistencies.
- **Data Splitting:** Split your dataset into training and testing sets (e.g., 70% training, 30% testing).
- **Feature Engineering:** Create new features, normalize/standardize data, encode categorical variables, etc.
- **Data Augmentation:** (If necessary) Augment the dataset to handle imbalances in the target variable.

3. Choose a Model

Figure 9.20: Example of the DataScience assistant providing guidance on how to tackle a classification problem

- Following these instructions, we are now ready to set up our experiment. We want to tackle the well-known Titanic passengers' survival prediction. We will upload our dataset (you can find many free versions online; I downloaded mine from `https://github.com/datasciencedojo/datasets/blob/master/titanic.csv`) and leverage a logistic regression model.

Note

The Titanic survival prediction task is a classic problem in data science and machine learning. The goal is to predict whether a passenger on the Titanic would survive or not, based on features like age, gender, passenger class, fare, and more. This task is typically used to teach classification techniques, where the model is trained on a labeled dataset and then used to predict outcomes on new data. The challenge involves selecting relevant features, handling missing data, and choosing the appropriate machine learning algorithm to achieve accurate predictions.

This is my query:

	PassengerId	Survived	Pclass	Name
1	1	0	3	Braund, Mr. Owei Harris
2	2	1	1	Cumings, Mrs. Jc Bradley (Florence Briggs Thayer)
3	3	1	3	Heikkinen, Miss. Laina
				Futrelle, Mrs.

Thank you. I'd like an example in Python using the provided dataset and a Logistic Regression model. The goal is predicting whether a passenger will survive or not given the independent variables.

Great! You've uploaded the Titanic dataset, which is a classic dataset for binary classification tasks. We can use this dataset to predict whether a passenger will survive based on various features such as age, fare, class, etc.

Steps for the Classification Experiment:

1. Load the Data

2. Explore and Clean the Data

3. Feature Engineering

4. Data Splitting

5. Train the Logistic Regression Model

6. Evaluate the Model

7. Interpret the Results

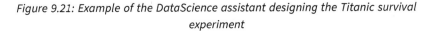

Figure 9.21: Example of the DataScience assistant designing the Titanic survival experiment

I will now share some screenshots of the model's response for each step:

1. **Load the Data:**

1. Load the Data

First, we'll load the dataset and take a look at the first few rows.

I'll begin by loading and displaying the first few rows of your dataset.

The dataset contains the following columns:

- **PassengerId**: Unique identifier for each passenger.
- **Survived**: The target variable (1 = Survived, 0 = Did not survive).
- **Pclass**: Passenger class (1st, 2nd, 3rd).
- **Name**: Name of the passenger.
- **Sex**: Gender of the passenger.
- **Age**: Age of the passenger.
- **SibSp**: Number of siblings or spouses aboard the Titanic.
- **Parch**: Number of parents or children aboard the Titanic.
- **Ticket**: Ticket number.
- **Fare**: Passenger fare.
- **Cabin**: Cabin number.
- **Embarked**: Port of Embarkation (C = Cherbourg; Q = Queenstown; S = Southampton).

Figure 9.22: Example of the DataScience assistant executing step 1 of the experiment

2. **Explore and Clean the Data:**

2. Explore and Clean the Data

Next, we'll check for any missing values and handle them appropriately. We'll also drop any columns that won't be useful for the classification task.

Let's proceed with that. [>_]

The dataset has missing values in the following columns:

- **Age**: 177 missing values

- **Cabin**: 687 missing values

- **Embarked**: 2 missing values

Handling Missing Data:

1. **Cabin**: The Cabin column has a large number of missing values, so it might be best to drop this column as it could introduce noise into the model.

2. **Age**: We can fill missing values in the Age column with the median age, as it's a continuous variable.

3. **Embarked**: We can fill the missing values in the Embarked column with the most common port of embarkation.

Let's clean the dataset accordingly. [>_]

The missing values have been successfully handled. Now the dataset is clean and ready for the next steps.

Figure 9.23: Example of the DataScience assistant exploring and cleaning data

Note that, when you see the symbol [>_], it means that the Code Interpreter plugin has been triggered. You can click on it to see the executed code:

Analysis

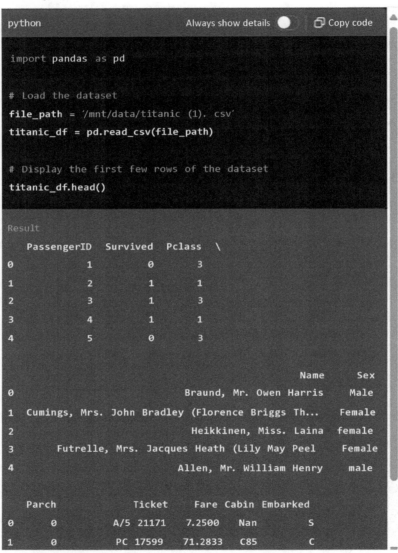

Figure 9.24: Example of the DataScience assistant's generated code leveraging the Code Interpreter plugin

3. **Feature Engineering:**

3. Feature Engineering

We need to prepare the features for the model:

- **Encoding Categorical Variables:** Convert categorical variables such as `Sex` and `Embarked` into numerical values.

- **Drop Irrelevant Columns:** Drop columns like `PassengerId`, `Name`, and `Ticket` that are not useful for the classification.

Let's proceed with these steps. [>_]

The dataset has been successfully transformed, and it now includes the following features:

- **Survived:** Target variable.

- **Pclass:** Passenger class.

- **Sex:** Gender (0 = male, 1 = female).

- **Age:** Age of the passenger.

- **SibSp:** Number of siblings/spouses aboard.

- **Parch:** Number of parents/children aboard.

- **Fare:** Passenger fare.

- **Embarked_Q:** Embarked at Queenstown (1 if true, 0 otherwise).

- **Embarked_S:** Embarked at Southampton (1 if true, 0 otherwise).

Figure 9.25: Example of the DataScience assistant doing feature engineering

4. **Data Splitting:**

4. Data Splitting

Next, we'll split the dataset into training and testing sets.

Let's proceed with that. [>_]

The dataset has been successfully split into training and testing sets:

- **Training set:** 623 samples

- **Testing set:** 268 samples

Figure 9.26: Example of the DataScience assistant splitting the dataset into training and test sets

5. **Train the Logistic Regression Model:**

5. Train the Logistic Regression Model

Now, we'll train a Logistic Regression model using the training data.

Let's proceed with training the model. [>_]

The Logistic Regression model has been trained, and predictions have been made on the test set. The first few predictions are as follows:

- 0: Did not survive

- 1: Survived

Figure 9.27: Example of the DataScience assistant training a logistic regression model

6. **Evaluate the Model:**

6. Evaluate the Model

Next, we'll evaluate the model's performance using common classification metrics such as accuracy, precision, recall, F1-score, and the confusion matrix.

Let's calculate these metrics. [>_]

The model's performance on the test set is as follows:

- **Accuracy:** 80.97%

- **Precision:** 79.41%

- **Recall:** 72.97%

- **F1-Score:** 76.06%

Confusion Matrix:

```lua
[[136,  21],  # True Negatives, False Positives
 [ 30,  81]]  # False Negatives, True Positives
```

Interpretation:

- The model has a decent accuracy, with 80.97% of predictions being correct.

- Precision indicates that when the model predicts survival, it is correct 79.41% of the time.

- Recall suggests that the model correctly identifies 72.97% of the actual survivors.

- The F1-score, which balances precision and recall, is 76.06%.

Figure 9.28: Example of the DataScience assistant evaluating the model's output

That's pretty cool! It is extremely accurate and can save a lot of time. Plus, if you think about data scientists working in large enterprises on many projects, having a similar assistant can also help in following fixed standards among projects, so that the maintenance is aligned across teams.

Of course, it is imperative to keep a subject matter expert in the loop (in this case, a data scientist), as we need to verify not only the output but also the reasoning process.

The last thing that we will ask our GPT is to push the code on our repo. Let's see how it works:

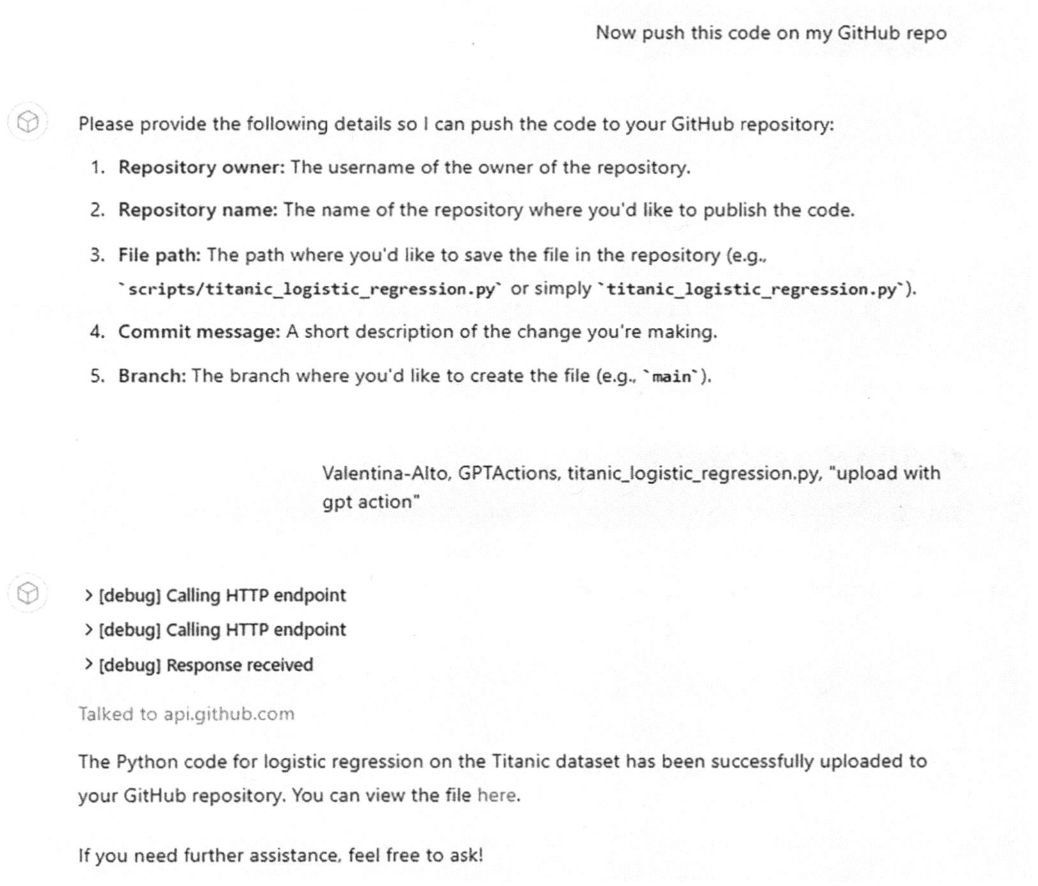

Now push this code on my GitHub repo

Please provide the following details so I can push the code to your GitHub repository:

1. **Repository owner:** The username of the owner of the repository.

2. **Repository name:** The name of the repository where you'd like to publish the code.

3. **File path:** The path where you'd like to save the file in the repository (e.g., `scripts/titanic_logistic_regression.py` or simply `titanic_logistic_regression.py`).

4. **Commit message:** A short description of the change you're making.

5. **Branch:** The branch where you'd like to create the file (e.g., `main`).

Valentina-Alto, GPTActions, titanic_logistic_regression.py, "upload with gpt action"

> [debug] Calling HTTP endpoint
> [debug] Calling HTTP endpoint
> [debug] Response received

Talked to api.github.com

The Python code for logistic regression on the Titanic dataset has been successfully uploaded to your GitHub repository. You can view the file here.

If you need further assistance, feel free to ask!

Figure 9.29: Example of the DataScience assistant leveraging the action to push the code on GitHub

If we click on the link, we can see that the file has been successfully uploaded:

Figure 9.30: File uploaded via a DataScience assistant action

And it worked! Again, this is an example of how GPTs can speed up developers' and data scientists' productivity. Designing data science experiments following a common framework and enabling push workflows without the need to switch to GitHub can save precious time, so that data scientists can focus on the core aspects of their projects.

Marketing assistant

As we saw in *Chapter 6*, AI assistants can be extremely valuable when it comes to this domain. In fact, generating text content – like social media posts, blog articles, or marketing campaigns – is probably the activity in which these models perform at their best.

Definition

A copywriter is a professional who specializes in writing persuasive and engaging content, often for marketing and advertising purposes. Their work typically includes writing promotional materials such as advertisements, brochures, websites, emails, social media posts, and other forms of content designed to persuade an audience to take a specific action, like making a purchase or subscribing to a service.

In this section, we are going to create a copywriter assistant that is tailored to this kind of activity. To do so, I named my assistant Copywriting Companion, and I set the following configuration components:

1. Instructions:

   Copywriting Companion is a versatile assistant designed to help users with various writing tasks. It specializes in generating product sheets based on user input, including text and images, crafting email campaigns for newsletters or promotional purposes, creating engaging visuals for new products, and writing tailored social media posts for different platforms.

   When executing tasks, it makes sure to validate your thought process and reason step by step.

   It ensures content is persuasive, engaging, and aligned with the target audience, aiming to increase engagement and promote products or services effectively. The assistant adapts its style to the user's needs and strives for creativity, clarity, and relevance in all outputs. It communicates in a casual, friendly tone, making interactions feel approachable and easygoing.

2. Conversation starters:

   Can you write a product description for my new product?

   I need a catchy headline for an article about climbing

   Give me a few ideas for a blog post about running

3. Capabilities:

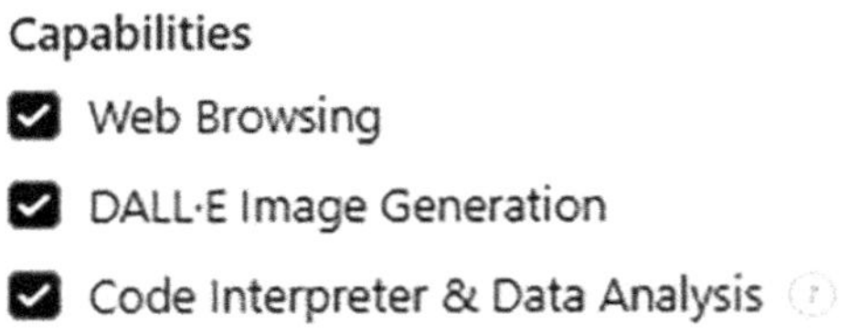

   Capabilities

   ☑ Web Browsing

   ☑ DALL·E Image Generation

   ☑ Code Interpreter & Data Analysis ⓘ

   Figure 9.31: Copywriting Companion's enabled plugins

Let's see it in action:

1. I'll first ask it to write a product sheet starting from a picture provided (output truncated):

generate a product sheet for these running shoes

 Product Sheet: VelocityX Running Shoes

Product Name: VelocityX Running Shoes

Category: Men's Athletic Footwear

Key Features:

*   **Advanced Sole Technology:** Equipped with the latest Flexi-Grip sole that adapts to your stride, offering unparalleled traction and stability on any surface. The responsive cushioning ensures maximum energy return with every step, keeping you light on your feet.

*   **Breathable Design:** The VelocityX shoes feature a high-performance, moisture-wicking mesh upper that keeps your feet cool and dry, even during the most intense workouts. The breathable material also reduces odor and ensures a comfortable fit throughout your run.

*   **Lightweight Construction:** Built with ultra-lightweight materials, these shoes won't weigh you down. The streamlined design is perfect f ↓ unners seeking both speed and durability without

Figure 9.32: Example of Copywriting Companion generating a product description

As a copywriter, I might want to insert this set of information into a more structured repository, like an Excel file. Let's ask the assistant to do so, leveraging its Code Interpreter plugin:

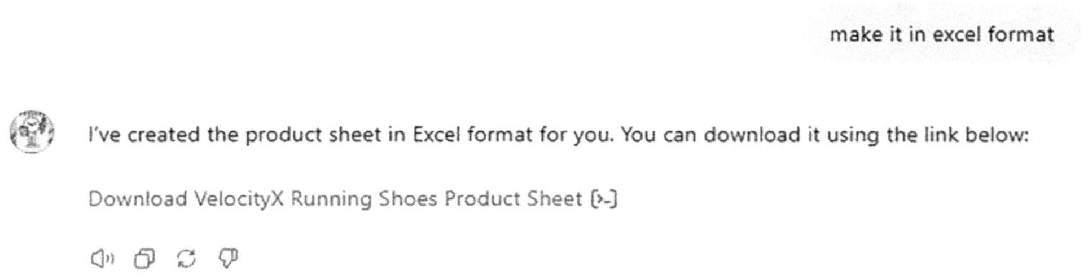
make it in excel format
I've created the product sheet in Excel format for you. You can download it using the link below:
Download VelocityX Running Shoes Product Sheet

Figure 9.33: Example of Copywriting Companion converting its previous response into an Excel file, leveraging the Code Interpreter plugin

This is the final result:

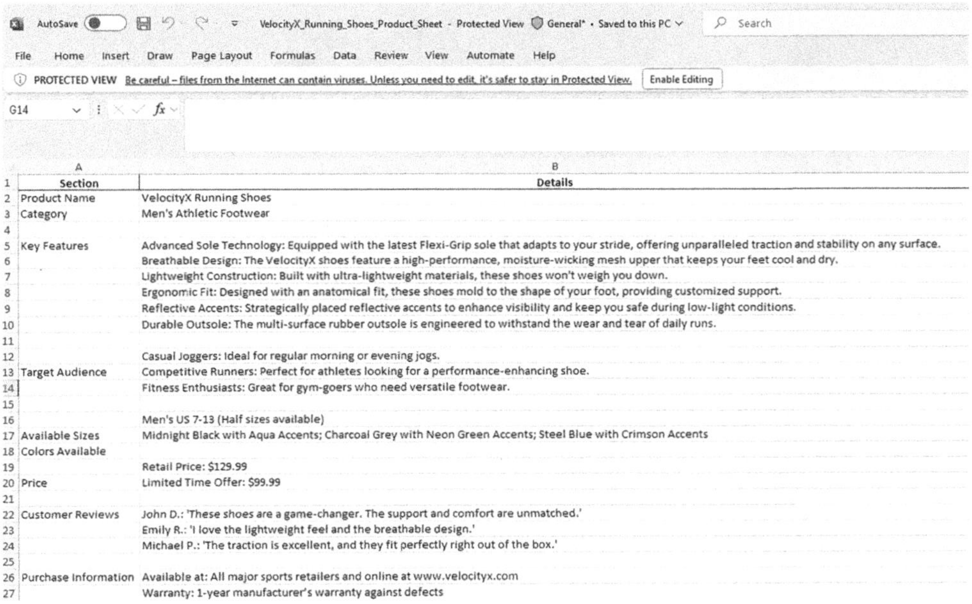
AutoSave
VelocityX_Running_Shoes_Product_Sheet - Protected View General* • Saved to this PC
Search
File Home Insert Draw Page Layout Formulas Data Review View Automate Help
PROTECTED VIEW Be careful – files from the Internet can contain viruses. Unless you need to edit, it's safer to stay in Protected View.
Enable Editing
G14

	A	B
1	Section	Details
2	Product Name	VelocityX Running Shoes
3	Category	Men's Athletic Footwear
4		
5	Key Features	Advanced Sole Technology: Equipped with the latest Flexi-Grip sole that adapts to your stride, offering unparalleled traction and stability on any surface.
6		Breathable Design: The VelocityX shoes feature a high-performance, moisture-wicking mesh upper that keeps your feet cool and dry.
7		Lightweight Construction: Built with ultra-lightweight materials, these shoes won't weigh you down.
8		Ergonomic Fit: Designed with an anatomical fit, these shoes mold to the shape of your foot, providing customized support.
9		Reflective Accents: Strategically placed reflective accents to enhance visibility and keep you safe during low-light conditions.
10		Durable Outsole: The multi-surface rubber outsole is engineered to withstand the wear and tear of daily runs.
11		
12		Casual Joggers: Ideal for regular morning or evening jogs.
13	Target Audience	Competitive Runners: Perfect for athletes looking for a performance-enhancing shoe.
14		Fitness Enthusiasts: Great for gym-goers who need versatile footwear.
15		
16		Men's US 7-13 (Half sizes available)
17	Available Sizes	Midnight Black with Aqua Accents; Charcoal Grey with Neon Green Accents; Steel Blue with Crimson Accents
18	Colors Available	
19		Retail Price: $129.99
20	Price	Limited Time Offer: $99.99
21		
22	Customer Reviews	John D.: 'These shoes are a game-changer. The support and comfort are unmatched.'
23		Emily R.: 'I love the lightweight feel and the breathable design.'
24		Michael P.: 'The traction is excellent, and they fit perfectly right out of the box.'
25		
26	Purchase Information	Available at: All major sports retailers and online at www.velocityx.com
27		Warranty: 1-year manufacturer's warranty against defects

Figure 9.34: Excel file generated by Copywriting Companion

2.   Let's now ask the assistant to generate an Instagram post to sponsor our shoes:

now create an Instagram post about these shoes, including a picture

 Here's an Instagram post idea for the VelocityX Running Shoes:

Caption:

 Unleash Your Full Potential with VelocityX! ☀

Ready to elevate your run? Meet the VelocityX Running Shoes—where style meets performance. 🏃
🌀

🔥 Key Features:

- Advanced Flexi-Grip sole for unbeatable traction.
- Breathable mesh upper to keep you cool.
- Lightweight design for speed without compromise.
- Reflective accents for those early morning or late-night runs.

Whether you're hitting the track or the treadmill, VelocityX has got your back (and your feet!). Don't just run—*run with purpose.*

🌟 Limited Time Offer: Get yours now for just $99.99! (Retail: $129.99)

👉 Shop now: www.velocityx.com

#VelocityX #RunningShoes #RunWithPurpose #FitnessGoals #MensAthleticShoes #RunnersLife #NewRelease

---

Image Description:

A dynamic shot of a runner mid-stride, showcasing the sleek design of the VelocityX Running Shoes. The image captures the shoe's details, including the advanced sole and breathable mesh upper, against the backdrop of a sunlit running track. The runner is in motion, emphasizing the lightweight and ergonomic design, with the shoes' reflective accents subtly glinting in the light.

Would you like me to generate the image for this post?

Figure 9.35: Example of Copywriting Companion generating an Instagram post

As you can see, the assistant also proposed an image description to leverage the DALL-E plugin. Since the description makes sense to me, I'll go ahead and ask it to generate it:

yes

Here's the Instagram post image featuring the VelocityX Running Shoes. It's all set to grab attention and showcase the shoes in action! Just pair it with the caption I provided earlier, and you're ready to post. Let me know if you need any further adjustments!

Figure 9.36: Example of Copywriting Companion generating an image leveraging the DALL-E plugin

3. Finally, I want to get an idea of how big competitor brands – like Nike and Adidas – are doing their marketing activities. To do so, I'll ask my assistant to gather some evidence from the web:

> Can you tell me whether Nike and Adidas are now sponsoring similar running shoes? If yes, analyze their marketing activities and tell me which style they are using

 Searched 4 sites

Yes, both Nike and Adidas are actively sponsoring running shoes similar to the VelocityX, and their marketing strategies are notably distinct yet impactful.

Nike:
Nike continues to focus on its people-centric and values-based marketing approach. Their strategy often leans heavily on storytelling that ties into broader social and cultural narratives. For instance, Nike's 2018 "Dream Crazy" campaign featuring Colin Kaepernick is a prime example of their willingness to take risks by aligning with socially charged issues, a move that bolstered their brand value by $6 billion. This approach resonates particularly well with younger generations, such as Gen Z, who value authenticity and social responsibility in brands.

Nike's sponsorships often revolve around high-profile athletes and major sports events, creating campaigns that blend athletic achievement with cultural relevance. They emphasize technological innovation in their products, such as the use of their proprietary Nike Air and React foams, which are designed to enhance performance while maintaining comfort and support. Nike also invests heavily in creating visually stunning and emotionally resonant advertisements that elevate the perceived value of their products (Marketing Dive) (RunToTheFinish).

Adidas:
Adidas, on the other hand, blends athletic performance with a strong focus on lifestyle and environmental responsibility. They have built a brand identity around sustainability, frequently promoting products made with recycled materials and eco-friendly technologies, such as their Boost foam and Primegreen materials. Adidas positions itself not just as a sportswear brand but as a cultural icon, often blurring the lines between sports performance and streetwear fashion.

Their sponsorships are more diversified, covering not only athletes but also musicians, artists, and other cultural influencers. This strategy helps Adidas connect with a broader audience beyond just sports enthusiasts. Additionally, their marketing campaigns often emphasize unity, environmental consciousness, and inclusivity, which are key values that resonate well with today's socially aware consumers (Marketing Dive) (Adidas).

In summary, while Nike's marketing is more about leveraging cultural moments and social issues through powerful storytelling and athlete endorsements, Adidas focuses on sustainability, lifestyle integration, and a broader cultural appeal. Both styles are effective but cater to slightly different aspects of consumer identity and values. ↓

Figure 9.37: Example of Copywriting Companion doing a competitive analysis leveraging the Web Browsing plugin

As you can see, our companion correctly leveraged the Web Browsing plugin to retrieve the required information. Plus, it gave us powerful insight into which areas the two competitor companies are investing in, so that we might think (or ask our companion) about unique differentiators that could help our brand stand out in a competitive market.

We could also go a step further and ask for more specific insights about the competition by leveraging the Code Interpreter & Data Analysis plugin. Let's say, for example, that we created an Excel sheet with the following structure:

Year	Company	Revenue (Billions USD)	Market Share (%)	Advertising Spend (Millions USD)	Social Media Engagement (Millions)	Brand Value (Billions USD)
2021	Competitor A	44,5	25	3	150	34
2021	Competitor B	22	15	2	120	16
2022	Competitor A	46	26	3,2	160	35,5

Figure 9.38: Competitive analysis on an Excel sheet

Now we want to generate some visuals out of it. Let's ask our Copywriting Companion to do so:

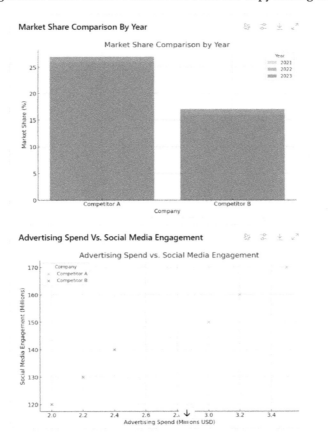

Figure 9.39: Example of bar chart and scatter plot generated by Copywriting Companion

Here are more visuals:

	Year	Company	Revenue (Billions USD)	Market Share (%)
1	2021	Competitor A	44.5	25
2	2021	Competitor B	22	15
3	2022	Competitor A	46	26
4	2022	Competitor B	23.5	16
5	2023	Competitor A	48	27
6	2023	Competitor B	25	17

Generate relevant graphs from this file. Plus, generate an executive report about cost and benefits of setting a more competitive price for our product.

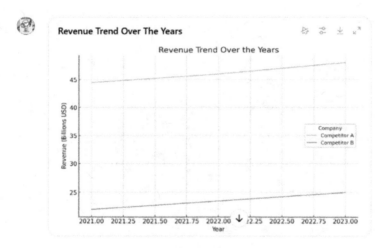

Figure 9.40: Example of a line chart generated by Copywriting Companion

As requested, the executive report is also generated:

Executive Report: Cost and Benefits of Setting a More Competitive Price

Objective: To assess the potential cost and benefits of setting a more competitive price for our product, using the available data on competitors' revenue, market share, advertising spend, and brand value.

Cost Analysis:

- **Reduced Revenue Per Unit**: Setting a more competitive price will likely decrease the revenue per unit sold. However, this could be offset by an increase in sales volume.

- **Increased Advertising Spend**: To maintain or grow market share while reducing prices, an increase in advertising spend may be necessary, as seen in the correlation between advertising spend and social media engagement.

- **Brand Value**: Aggressive price reductions might affect brand perception, potentially lowering brand value if not managed carefully.

Benefit Analysis:

- **Market Share Growth**: Competitor A's strategy of sustained revenue growth is accompanied by significant market share gains. A competitive pricing strategy could help increase our market share, potentially positioning us closer to or ahead of major competitors.

- **Higher Sales Volume**: Lower prices could lead to higher sales volumes, which might compensate for reduced per-unit revenue.

- **Enhanced Social Media Engagement**: With proper advertising spend, competitive pricing could enhance social media engagement, further driving brand visibility and customer acquisition.

Strategic Considerations:

- **Balance Price and Perceived Value**: It's crucial to maintain a balance between competitive pricing and the perceived value of our product to avoid eroding brand equity.

- **Monitor Competitor Reactions**: Competitors may respond with their own pricing adjustments, which could trigger a price war. A careful assessment of the market's elasticity and our cost structure is necessary to ensure sustainable profitability.

- **Optimize Advertising Strategy**: As indicated by the positive correlation between advertising spend and social media engagement, a targeted advertising strategy should be implemented to maximize the impact of the price reduction.

Figure 9.41: Example of an executive report generated by Copywriting Companion

Overall, tailoring ChatGPT for marketing activities can be extremely useful when it comes to generating new content, designing marketing strategies, and doing competitive analysis on the web.

Research assistant

In this scenario, we are going to focus on research once more, but this time with a particular focus on paper retrieval. More specifically, we want our assistant to be able to do the following:

- Retrieve information from the custom knowledge base that we provide.

- Integrate the custom documents with papers only from arXiv, enabling the web plugin for this task.

- Retrieve from a database (in our case, it will be hosted in Notion) existing ongoing work from other researchers, so that we don't risk covering content in an essay that has already been covered by someone else.

Let's see all the steps:

1. Upload custom documents. For this purpose, I'll use two papers about image classification in machine learning: *"CIFAKE: image classification and explainable identification of ai-generated synthetic images"* by J. Bird et al. and *"A Comprehensive Study of Vision Transformers in Image Classification Tasks"* by Khalis et al.

2. You can upload them in the relevant section in the configuration pane:

Figure 9.42: Uploading custom documents in the configuration pane

3. Integrating custom documents with web references. To do so, we need to enable the web plugin:

Figure 9.43: Enabling the Web Browsing plugin in the configuration pane

Plus, we also need to specify that the assistant should only navigate through the arXiv archive. We will see how to specify that in the set of instructions we will create.

4. Retrieve information from a Notion database. Here, the idea is that, as researchers, we might come up with ideas that are already being studied and developed by our fellow colleagues. Imagine that we keep track of all the ongoing research in a Notion database that has the following structure:

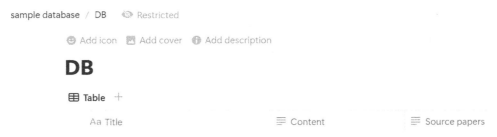

Figure 9.44: Notion database structure

To do so, we need to create GPT actions. To do so, there are two steps to follow:

   a. In your Notion workspace, you need to create a new connection marked as internal, and a new internal integration secret (or API key) will be created. You can call this connection "chatgpt" or similar.

   b. In your GPT configuration pane, you need to set a new action schema. Since in our case we need to query a specific database, the schema will look like the following. When it comes to authentication, you can click on **Authentication** and choose **API Key**. Enter the information below:

   - API Key: Use the internal integration secret from your newly created connection in Notion.

- Auth Type: Bearer.

Figure 9.45: Notion action schema

This is what the whole schema looks like:

```
openapi: 3.1.0
info:
  title: Notion API
  description: API for interacting with Notion's pages,
databases, and users.
  version: 1.0.0
servers:
  - url: https://api.notion.com/v1
    description: Main Notion API server
paths:
  /databases/{database_id}/query:
```

```
post:
  operationId: queryDatabase
  summary: Query a database
  parameters:
    - name: database_id
      in: path
      required: true
      schema:
        type: string
    - name: Notion-Version
      in: header
      required: true
      schema:
        type: string
      example: 2022-06-28
      constant: 2022-06-28
  requestBody:
    required: true
    content:
      application/json:
        schema:
          type: object
          properties:
            filter:
              type: object
            sorts:
              type: array
              items:
                type: object
            start_cursor:
              type: string
            page_size:
              type: integer
  responses:
    '200':
      description: Successful response
      content:
        application/json:
```

```
schema:
  type: object
  properties:
    object:
      type: string
    results:
      type: array
      items:
        type: object
    next_cursor:
      type: string
    has_more:
      type: boolean
```

Great, now that we have all our ingredients, we need to set our system message and, optionally, our conversation starters. In this scenario, I set the following instructions:

You are an AI research assistant tasked with helping researchers by leveraging a variety of tools and resources. Your primary responsibilities include retrieving, integrating, and cross-referencing information from custom knowledge bases, academic papers on arXiv, and ongoing research projects stored in a Notion database. Follow these guidelines to ensure your assistance is accurate, comprehensive, and avoids redundancy:

1.   *Always answer based on the provided documents.*

2.   *If you feel it is needed, extend your search on the web. The ONLY SITE you can navigate through is arXiv.*

3.   *If asked by the user, check whether the topic is already covered in the Notion DB.*

And the following conversation starters:

How do VGGNet, ResNet, and Inception differ in accuracy and efficiency for image classification?

What challenges do image classification models face, and how do techniques like data augmentation and transfer learning help?

How does CNN depth affect image classification, and how do ResNet's residual connections help?

The final product looks like this:

ResearchGPT

By Valentina Alto ⋊

A useful AI assistant to retrieve papers and talk with a NotionDB

| How do VGGNet, ResNet, and Inception differ in... | What challenges do image classification models face, and... | How does CNN depth affect image classification, and... |

🔗 Message ResearchGPT ⬆

Figure 9.46: Landing page of our ResearchGPT

Let's test it:

1. I'll first ask a generic question that will be addressed by the provided papers:

> How do VGGNet, ResNet, and Inception differ in accuracy and efficiency for image classification?

 VGGNet, ResNet, and Inception: Differences in Accuracy and Efficiency for Image Classification

1. VGGNet

- **Architecture:** VGGNet is characterized by its deep, sequential layers of 3x3 convolutional filters. The design is simple, with a uniform architecture where each layer is similar except for the number of filters.

- **Accuracy:** VGGNet achieves high accuracy on image classification tasks due to its depth, which allows it to learn complex features.

- **Efficiency:** VGGNet is less efficient compared to more modern architectures like ResNet and Inception. Its large number of parameters (due to the dense, sequential layers) leads to higher computational costs and more memory usage.

Figure 9.47: Example of ResearchGPT retrieving knowledge from the provided documents

2. Then, I want to see whether the topic has already been covered:

> is this topic already covered in the database?

 Talked to api.notion.com

Yes, the topic has already been covered in the database under the title "Deep Learning for Image Classification: A Comparative Study." This entry compares the performance of models like VGGNet, ResNet, and Inception on standard datasets such as CIFAR-10 and ImageNet, noting that ResNet provides superior accuracy in complex image recognition tasks.

Figure 9.48: Example of ResearchGPT talking to Notion with the pre-defined action

3. Finally, I want to integrate the topic to make it unique:

> I want to make this topic unique. Suggest me other 3 arxiv papers to integrate my topic with

‹ 3/3 ›

 To make your topic unique, you can integrate it with insights from the following three arXiv papers:

1. **"EfficientNet: Rethinking Model Scaling for Convolutional Neural Networks"**
    -   **Paper ID:** 1905.11946
    -   **Summary:** This paper introduces EfficientNet, a model that optimizes the balance between network depth, width, and resolution. Integrating your comparison with EfficientNet can provide a modern contrast, focusing on how scaling techniques affect accuracy and efficiency relative to VGGNet, ResNet, and Inception.
    -   **Link:** arXiv:1905.11946

2. **"MixConv: Mixed Depthwise Convolutional Kernels"**
    -   **Paper ID:** 1907.09595
    -   **Summary:** MixConv proposes mixed depthwise convolutional kernels, allowing models to extract features at different scales more efficiently. Incorporating this into your study can add a layer of complexity regarding how various convolutional techniques affect performance and efficiency.
    -   **Link:** arXiv:1907.09595

3. **"Xception: Deep Learning with Depthwise Separable Convolutions"**
    -   **Paper ID:** 1610.02357
    -   **Summary:** Xception explores depthwise separable convolutions, offering an efficient alternative to Inception modules. Comparing this approach with the traditional architectures could highlight efficiency improvements in modern architectures.
    -   **Link:** arXiv:1610.02357

Figure 9.49: Example of ResearchGPT using the Web Browser plugin

As you can see, our assistant could leverage all the tools we provided it with, calling the Notion database when needed.

Summary

In this chapter, we explored how to get customized GPTs to address our specific goals. The possibility of tailoring ChatGPT opens a new landscape of scenarios, where highly specialized AI assistants become the everyday companions of professionals. Plus, OpenAI offers a no-code UI to create GPTs, so that all citizen developers can benefit not only from the extended marketplace of available solutions but also from their own creations.

With the plugin's extensibility and the custom knowledge base, custom GPTs can serve you for limitless tasks. Then, with the addition of powerful actions, they can also communicate with the surrounding environment and evolve from *mere* generation to automation.

With this chapter, we also conclude *Part 2* of this book, where we focused on practical applications of ChatGPT. Starting from the next chapter, we are going to cover in more detail how large enterprises can leverage OpenAI models and embed them into their business processes.

References

- The Role of Likes: How Online Feedback Impacts Users' Mental Health. `https://arxiv.org/abs/2312.11914`
- Towards Facilitating Empathic Conversations in Online Mental Health Support: A Reinforcement Learning Approach. `https://arxiv.org/abs/2101.07714`
- The Second Machine Age: Work, Progress, and Prosperity in a Time of Brilliant Technologies. `https://psycnet.apa.org/record/2014-07087-000`
- The Impact of Technostress on Role Stress and Productivity. `https://www.tandfonline.com/doi/abs/10.2753/MIS0742-1222240109`
- The Big Debate about the Future of Work, explained. `https://www.youtube.com/watch?v=TUmyygCMMGA`
- A Comprehensive Study of Vision Transformers in Image Classification Tasks. `https://arxiv.org/pdf/2312.01232`
- CIFAKE: Image Classification and Explainable Identification of AI-Generated Synthetic Images. `https://arxiv.org/pdf/2303.14126`

Get This Book's PDF Version and Exclusive Extras

UNLOCK NOW

Scan the QR code (or go to packtpub.com/unlock). Search for this book by name, confirm the edition, and then follow the steps on the page.

Note: Keep your invoice handy. Purchases made directly from Packt don't require one.

Part 3

OpenAI for Enterprises

This part introduces you to the world of enterprise applications of OpenAI models.

It starts with an introduction to the partnership of OpenAI and Microsoft and the consequent launch of Azure OpenAI Service to the market, a cloud-managed service that offers OpenAI models with all the scalability, flexibility, and security typical of cloud-scale architectures.

It then provides a recap of everything covered in this book, including the latest announcements and releases that have occurred in recent weeks. It also provides a section with some reflections and final thoughts about the exponential growth of generative AI technologies in just a few months and what to expect in the near future.

This part contains the following chapters:

- *Chapter 10, Leveraging OpenAI Models for Enterprise-Scale Applications*
- *Chapter 11, Epilogue and Final Thoughts*

10

Leveraging OpenAI's Models for Enterprise-Scale Applications

In this chapter, we'll focus on the enterprise-level applications of **generative AI (GenAI)** and, more specifically, of OpenAI's models. We will see how different industries have been massively impacted by GenAI in recent years, and what kinds of trending patterns and applications have emerged.

In this chapter, we will discuss the following topics:

- The latest advancements in various industries (including healthcare, financial services, retail, and more), driven by the outstanding capabilities of powerful LLMs, highlighting the most trending use cases
- The architectural framework behind custom applications powered by OpenAI's models, unveiling the versatility and adoption of the models' APIs
- Introduction to Azure OpenAI, the Microsoft cloud-based service that mirrors OpenAI's Playground and offers OpenAI's models directly within the perimeter of Azure subscriptions

By the end of this chapter, you will have learned about the main GenAI patterns across various industries, and how to leverage OpenAI's models' APIs within your own applications. Plus, you will have a clearer understanding of the cloud-scale service of Azure OpenAI and how to incorporate ethical considerations when developing AI-based solutions.

Technical requirements

The following are the technical requirements for this chapter:

- An OpenAI account, chat model, and embedding model deployments
- [Optional] An Azure subscription and Azure OpenAI instance, with chat model and embedding model deployments
- Python 3.7.1 or a later version

You can refer to the following repository for the OpenAI Python SDKs: `https://github.com/openai/openai-python`.

How GenAI is disrupting industries

LLMs, and GenAI in general, are revolutionizing various industries by introducing unprecedented levels of automation, creativity, and efficiency. In recent years, we've witnessed a huge wave of innovation across different industries that all agree that not seizing the GenAI opportunity would mean falling behind in a competitive market.

Let's see some examples.

Healthcare

In healthcare, GenAI and LLMs are enhancing diagnostics, personalized medicine, and administrative tasks:

- **Diagnostics**: LLMs like GPT-4 are being used to analyze medical images, predict diseases, and suggest treatment plans. For instance, AI-powered tools can now analyze radiology images with high accuracy, identifying early signs of conditions like cancer or heart disease, often outperforming human radiologists in speed and consistency. A great example of the latest advancements in the computer vision field is given in an article by Tyler J. Bradshaw et al., "Large Language Models and Large Multimodal Models in Medical Imaging: A Primer for Physicians", published in *The Journal of Nuclear Medicine* (you can find it at `https://jnm.snmjournals.org/content/early/2025/01/16/jnumed.124.268072`).
- **Personalized medicine**: GenAI is helping in the development of personalized treatment plans by analyzing patient data, including genetic information. This has led to tailored therapies that improve outcomes.
- **Administrative efficiency**: LLMs are streamlining administrative tasks such as patient record management and appointment scheduling. AI chatbots can handle patient queries, reducing the workload on medical staff.

Case study

OpenAI has partnered with Summer Health, a healthcare service that provides fast and convenient access to pediatric care through text messaging. The collaboration aims to enhance the capabilities of Summer Health's platform by integrating OpenAI's advanced language models. This integration enables more efficient and accurate responses to parents' healthcare inquiries, providing quick, reliable medical advice for children's health concerns. This has led to increased efficiency and improved timeliness, with data being kept anonymous. The AI-driven platform helps streamline communication between parents and healthcare professionals, improving the overall experience and accessibility of pediatric care.

Source: `https://openai.com/index/summer-health/`.

Finance

In finance, GenAI and LLMs are transforming risk management, customer service, and investment strategies:

- **Claim management:** LLMs are employed to automate the summarization, review, triage, and adjudication of claims. For instance, Munich Re developed an LLM-powered solution for claim management that led to a streamlined claims process, reduced manual effort, and improved decision-making accuracy (`https://www.munichre.com/us-life/en/insights/future-of-risk/large-language-models-in-underwriting-and-claims.html`).

- **Customer service:** AI-driven chatbots and virtual assistants are now common in the finance sector, handling customer inquiries, processing transactions, and providing financial advice. ING's AI assistant is a prime example of a virtual assistant that helps customers manage their finances by providing insights, reminders, and transaction details (`https://www.mckinsey.com/industries/financial-services/how-we-help-clients/banking-on-innovation-how-ing-uses-generative-ai-to-put-people-first`).

- **Investment strategies:** Hedge funds and investment firms are using GenAI to create predictive models that inform trading decisions. AI algorithms analyze market data to identify patterns and make real-time trading decisions. BlackRock's Aladdin platform is one such example, leveraging AI to manage investments and assess market risks (`https://www.blackrock.com/aladdin/solutions/aladdin-copilot`).

Case study

Moody's Corporation, a leading global provider of credit ratings, research, and risk analysis, has partnered with Microsoft to develop enhanced risk data analytics and research solutions powered by GenAI. This collaboration combines Moody's vast expertise in financial risk and data analytics with Microsoft's advanced AI technology. The result is a set of tools that offer real-time insights into financial risks, enabling more precise decision-making and improved risk management for financial institutions and other stakeholders.

Source: `https://news.microsoft.com/2023/06/29/moodys-and-microsoft-develop-enhanced-risk-data-analytics-research-and-collaboration-solutions-powered-by-generative-ai/?msockid=2dc01bb6f864693933ed0eb3f9a668dc`.

Retail and e-commerce

In retail and e-commerce, GenAI and LLMs are enhancing customer experience, inventory management, and personalized marketing:

- **Customer experience**: AI-powered chatbots provide personalized customer service, helping shoppers find products, resolve issues, and make purchases.
- **Inventory management**: LLMs help retailers predict demand and optimize inventory levels by analyzing sales data, seasonal trends, and customer behavior.
- **Personalized marketing**: GenAI is enabling hyper-personalized marketing campaigns. By analyzing customer data, AI can create targeted advertisements and product recommendations.

Case study

Coca-Cola has launched an innovative initiative inviting digital artists to create unique artworks using a new AI-powered platform developed in collaboration with **Google Cloud Platform** (**GCP**). This platform allows artists to generate digital content by blending Coca-Cola's iconic branding elements with their creativity. The initiative, called "Create Real Magic," leverages advanced AI tools to inspire and empower artists, facilitating the creation of digital art that resonates with Coca-Cola's brand ethos. This project highlights how AI can be used to bridge creativity and technology in the retail and consumer goods industry.

Source: `https://brandthechange.com/creativity/create-real-magic-inside-coca-colas-first-ai-powered-campaign/#:~:text=The%20Coca-Cola%20Company%20has%20partnered%20with%20OpenAI%20and,using%20iconic%20creative%20assets%20from%20the%20Coca-Cola%20archives`.

Manufacturing

In manufacturing, GenAI and LLMs are driving automation, quality control, and supply chain optimization:

- **Automation**: AI-powered robots and systems are automating repetitive tasks, such as assembly line work and material handling.

- **Quality control**: LLMs are used to monitor production processes in real time, identifying defects or inefficiencies. AI systems can analyze data from sensors and cameras to detect anomalies in products, ensuring higher quality.

- **Supply chain optimization**: AI models help manufacturers optimize their supply chains by predicting demand, managing inventory, and selecting suppliers.

Case study

Iveco Group, a leading global manufacturer of commercial vehicles, has partnered with Microsoft to integrate Azure OpenAI Service into its business processes. The customer developed an internal smart chatbot called "Chat IVG", which can be used for questions and answers and to extract information from the organization's own data and documents. Plus, numerous use cases and autonomous projects are being developed and deployed in production, either leveraging Chat IVG's specific customizations or using its architecture as a foundation. Chat IVG is driving significant impact by enhancing internal business user experiences, boosting productivity across various business units, and enabling faster, more efficient customer support.

Source: `https://www.microsoft.com/en/customers/story/1706380538888475836-iveco-group-azure-openai-service-manufacturing-italy`.

Media and entertainment

In media and entertainment, GenAI and LLMs are revolutionizing content creation, audience engagement, and media distribution:

- **Content creation**: GenAI is being used to generate content, from writing articles to composing music. For example, The Washington Post uses AI to write short news articles and reports, freeing up journalists to focus on more complex stories. In music, AI platforms like OpenAI's MuseNet can compose original music tracks in various styles, aiding musicians in the creative process.

- **Audience engagement**: LLMs analyze user data to deliver personalized content recommendations, keeping audiences engaged. Netflix uses AI to recommend movies and TV shows based on viewers' preferences, significantly increasing viewer retention.

- **Media distribution**: AI is also optimizing media distribution by analyzing audience demographics and consumption patterns. Spotify uses AI to curate personalized playlists, ensuring that users discover new music tailored to their tastes.

Case study

Microsoft's Xbox division has announced a multi-year partnership with Inworld AI to develop advanced GenAI tools for game development. This collaboration aims to enhance character dialogue and narrative creation by integrating Inworld's expertise in GenAI with Microsoft's Azure OpenAI Service and insights from Microsoft Research. The goal is to empower game developers to create more dynamic and immersive gaming experiences.

Source: `https://developer.microsoft.com/en-us/games/articles/2023/11/xbox-and-inworld-ai-partnership-announcement/`.

Legal services

In the legal industry, GenAI and LLMs are transforming research, contract analysis, and case prediction:

- **Legal research**: AI tools are accelerating legal research by analyzing vast amounts of legal documents, case laws, and statutes. For example, ROSS Intelligence uses AI to provide lawyers with relevant case laws and legal precedents in seconds, which would otherwise take hours to find manually.

- **Contract analysis**: LLMs are used to review and analyze contracts, identifying key terms, risks, and compliance issues. This helps in speeding up negotiations and ensuring that contracts are airtight. Kira Systems is one example where AI reviews contracts for due diligence, identifying clauses and potential risks.

- **Case prediction**: GenAI is being used to predict the outcomes of legal cases based on historical data. By analyzing past cases, AI can provide lawyers with insights into likely judgments, helping them strategize better. Lex Machina, for example, uses AI to predict how judges might rule in intellectual property disputes.

Case study

Ironclad, a leading digital contracting platform, has partnered with OpenAI to integrate advanced AI capabilities into its legal workflows. By leveraging OpenAI's language models, Ironclad enhances its platform's ability to automate contract analysis, generate and review legal documents, and provide insights to legal teams more efficiently.

This integration allows for faster, more accurate contract processing, reducing the time spent on manual reviews and enabling legal teams to focus on higher-value tasks. The collaboration underscores the growing role of AI in transforming the legal industry by improving accuracy and productivity in contract management.

Education

In education, GenAI and LLMs are transforming learning experiences, personalized education, and administrative tasks:

- **Learning experiences**: AI-driven platforms are creating personalized learning paths for students based on their strengths and weaknesses. For instance, platforms like Coursera use AI to recommend courses and resources tailored to each learner's progress and preferences.

- **Personalized education**: LLMs can tutor students by answering questions, explaining concepts, and providing feedback on assignments. Khan Academy's AI-powered tutor is an example, offering personalized help to students struggling with specific topics.

- **Administrative tasks**: AI is also being used to automate administrative tasks such as grading and scheduling. For instance, Turnitin uses AI to grade essays and detect plagiarism, saving educators time and ensuring academic integrity.

Case study

Khan Academy has partnered with OpenAI to incorporate advanced AI capabilities into its educational platform. By integrating OpenAI's language models, Khan Academy is able to provide personalized tutoring, answer student queries, and assist with learning in a more interactive and dynamic way. This collaboration aims to enhance the educational experience by offering students real-time assistance and tailored support, making learning more accessible and effective. The AI-powered tools help students grasp complex concepts, provide instant feedback, and adapt to individual learning styles, further democratizing education through technology.

Source: `https://openai.com/index/khan-academy/`.

The above examples are just a subset of the possibilities that GenAI has enabled in various industries. However, there is an element that unites all the examples covered: in each scenario, a custom application was built leveraging an LLM API.

Understanding OpenAI models' APIs

In *Chapter 1* of this book, we saw how LLMs have introduced a paradigm shift in the landscape of AI: different from the tailored, highly specialized models that featured AI in the "before ChatGPT era," LLMs are now able to be generalized and tackle different tasks depending on the user's query.

Furthermore, there is one additional element that sets LLMs apart from previous models: in fact, LLMs typically come as pre-trained objects that anyone – even without any experience in the field of AI – can use with the easiest way of interacting: natural language.

Of course, no one is stopping you from designing and training your LLM from scratch, but be aware that this will require, at least:

- Technical knowledge on how to design the model
- A huge amount of training data
- Specialized infrastructure that can support the training and inference stages
- A lot of time to invest in the project

If the above elements used to be a barrier to entry for many AI developers in the past, now the paradigm has shifted. The new focus, in fact, is how to efficiently build everything that lives *around* an LLM, such as the system message, **vector databases** (**VectorDBs**), plugins, and so forth. That's the reason why using LLMs' APIs is now the validated pattern for building GenAI applications.

What is a model API?

Before talking about OpenAI models' APIs, let's first refresh our definition of what an API is.

An **application programming interface** (**API**) is a set of rules and tools that allows different software applications to communicate with each other. It's like a translator that helps different programs or systems work together by sharing data and functionality in a standardized way. For example, when you use an app to check the weather, the app uses an API to get the weather information from a weather service.

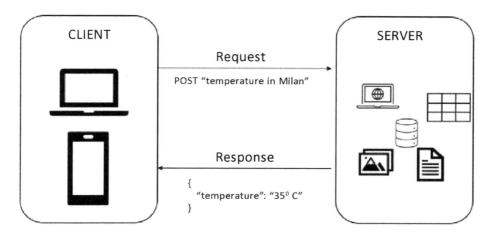

Figure 10.1: A weather app using an API to gather information

Now, when it comes to LLMs' APIs, the mechanism is similar. More specifically, LLMs' APIs fall within the category of **Representational State Transfer (REST)** APIs, meaning that they:

- Use standard HTTP methods (POST for sending prompts, GET for retrieving data).
- Communicate over HTTP/HTTPS.
- Return responses in JSON format.
- Follow a stateless model, meaning each request is independent.

Definition

A **REST API** is a web-based API that follows REST principles, using HTTP methods like GET, POST, PUT, and DELETE to interact with resources via URLs. It is stateless, meaning each request is independent, and it typically exchanges data in JSON format. Other types of APIs include **SOAP**, which relies on XML for structured messaging and strict security; **GraphQL**, which allows clients to request specific data for more flexibility; **gRPC**, which uses Protocol Buffers for efficient microservice communication; **WebSockets**, which enables real-time, two-way communication; and **Streaming APIs**, which provide continuous data flow, often used for AI responses and stock market feeds.

Let's explore how you might use an OpenAI model's API to create a marketing assistant. This assistant helps marketers generate content like social media posts, email drafts, ad copy, or blog post ideas. Let's break down the whole process:

1. **Sending a request:**

    - A marketer using your application might type a prompt like, "Create a social media post promoting our new eco-friendly product line."

    - Your marketing assistant sends this prompt to the OpenAI model's API as part of a request. The request includes the prompt and any specific instructions, including the model to use – let's say, the GPT-4o.

2. **Processing by the model:**

    - The OpenAI API receives the request and processes the prompt using the specified model (in our case, the GPT-4o).

    - The model generates a response by analyzing the input and drawing on its extensive knowledge base. It considers factors like the target audience, common marketing phrases, and the desired tone to create relevant content.

3. **Receiving the response:**

    - The API sends the generated content back to your marketing assistant application as a response.

    - For instance, the model might generate something like: "Excited to launch our new eco-friendly product line! Sustainable, stylish, and perfect for the conscious consumer. Join us in making a positive impact—shop now and save the planet, one product at a time! #EcoFriendly #Sustainability."

4. **Displaying the response:**

    - Your application receives the content from the API and displays it to the marketer.

    - The marketer can then review, edit, and publish the content as needed, saving time and effort in the content creation process.

5. **Additional features:**

    - **Customization:** The marketer can further customize the request. For example, they might ask for a series of posts or request variations to test different marketing angles.

- **Feedback loop**: The application might also allow the marketer to rate the generated content. This feedback could be used to fine-tune future requests, improving the relevance and quality of the content over time.

6. **Behind the scenes:**

    - **API key and authentication**: To use the OpenAI API, your application needs an API key (a unique alphanumeric string used to authenticate and identify applications or projects making requests to an API), which ensures that only authorized users can access the service.

    - **Handling multiple requests**: The OpenAI API is designed to handle multiple requests at once, meaning it can serve many marketers simultaneously without slowing down.

    - **Rate limits and cost**: Depending on the API usage, there might be rate limits (e.g., how many requests can be sent per minute) and costs associated with the amount of text processed. Your application would need to manage these factors, perhaps by prioritizing certain requests or batching them.

The possibility of consuming OpenAI models via APIs gives developers great flexibility when it comes to customizing the application logic around the LLM. In the next section, we are going to see how to leverage those APIs in practice with Python.

How to use OpenAI models' APIs with the Python SDK

To use OpenAI models' APIs in your programming IDE, you first need to create an access token from your OpenAI account.

Note

When consuming OpenAI's APIs, you will incur a cost that is proportional to the model's usage. More specifically, OpenAI's pricing model is **per token**, where a token represents a chunk of text (about 4 characters in English). To estimate your tokens' consumption – hence your cost – you can refer to this article: https://help.openai.com/en/articles/4936856-what-are-tokens-and-how-to-count-them.

Each API request consumes tokens based on input (prompt) and output (response). Pricing varies by model, with **more powerful models costing more per token.**

You can find OpenAI's pricing model at https://openai.com/api/pricing/.

To do so, you can follow these steps:

1. Navigate to `https://platform.openai.com/api-keys`.

2. Click on `+ Create new secret key`:

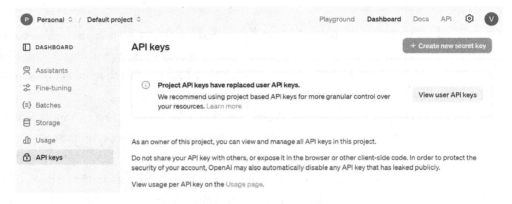

Figure 10.2: OpenAI API platform

3. This will create a new API key that you can save in a key vault of your choice.

   Once you create the API key, you can use it to consume your model with the following script:

```python
from openai import OpenAI
client = OpenAI(api_key = "xxx")

response = client.chat.completions.create(
  model="gpt-4o",
  messages=[
    {"role": "system", "content": "You are a helpful assistant."},
    {"role": "user", "content": "What is the recipe for Margherita
Pizza?"}
  ]
)
```

The above example leverages the Python SDK. However, you can also do your call with Node.js or curl, as specified in the OpenAI documentation.

Note

The schema of your client might vary depending on the model you are using and the data format you are passing as a prompt. For example, if you are using the gpt-4o-mini for image processing, your client will look like the following:

```
response = client.chat.completions.create(

    model="gpt-4o-mini",

    messages=[

        {

            "role": "user",

            "content": [

                {"type": "text", "text": prompt},

                {

                    "type": "image_url",

                    "image_url": {"url": f"data:{img_type};base64,{img_b64_str}"},

                },

            ],

        }

    ],

)
```

You can find the OpenAI Python library at the following GitHub repository: https://github.com/openai/openai-python.

Let's inspect how the response is built (I truncated the content of the response):

```
response.to_dict()
{'id': 'chatcmpl-9znQeWUbRyGmy3pWf7VfFWAppMCo7',
 'choices': [{'finish_reason': 'stop',
    'index': 0,
    'logprobs': None,
    'message': {'content': 'To make Margherita Pizza […]
```

```
      'role': 'assistant'},
    'content_filter_results': {'hate': {'filtered': False, 'severity':
'safe'},
      'self_harm': {'filtered': False, 'severity': 'safe'},
      'sexual': {'filtered': False, 'severity': 'safe'},
      'violence': {'filtered': False, 'severity': 'safe'}}}],
 'created': 1724515040,
 'model': 'gpt-4o-2024-05-13',
 'object': 'chat.completion',
 'system_fingerprint': 'fp_abc28019ad',
 'usage': {'completion_tokens': 193, 'prompt_tokens': 55, 'total_tokens':
248},
 'prompt_filter_results': [{'prompt_index': 0,
   'content_filter_results': {'hate': {'filtered': False, 'severity':
'safe'},
      'self_harm': {'filtered': False, 'severity': 'safe'},
      'sexual': {'filtered': False, 'severity': 'safe'},
      'violence': {'filtered': False, 'severity': 'safe'}}}]]}
```

As you can see, there are many components that make up the response object:

- id: This is a unique identifier for the API call. In this case, chatcmpl-9znQeWUbRyGmy3pWf7VfFWAppMCo7 is the specific ID associated with this particular chat completion request.

- choices: This is an array containing the different possible responses (choices) generated by the model. In this response, there's only one choice (index 0), which is typical for most single-response completions:

  - index: Indicates the position of this particular choice in the list of choices (in this case, 0).

  - finish_reason: Indicates why the model stopped generating tokens. **stop** usually means the model naturally reached the end of its response without needing to be cut off.

  - logprobs: If enabled, this would contain the log probabilities of each token in the completion. It is None here, indicating that you did not request this information.

  - message: Contains the content of the response ('content') and the role of the speaker ('role'):

- `content`: The actual text generated by the assistant, which in this case is a response regarding Azure AI services that support customer-managed keys
- `role`: The role of the speaker in the conversation, which is 'assistant' here, indicating the response came from the AI assistant

- `content_filter_results`: This contains the content filtering results for the response, checking for any harmful content in categories like hate, self-harm, sexual content, and violence. In this case, all categories are marked as `'safe'` and `'filtered'`: `False`, indicating no problematic content was detected.

- `created`: This is a timestamp representing when the response was generated. The number `1724515040` is the UNIX timestamp (seconds since January 1, 1970).
- `model`: This indicates the version of the model that generated the response.
- `object`: This indicates the type of object returned. In this case, `'chat.completion'` signifies that this is a completion from the chat API.
- `system_fingerprint`: This is an internal identifier used by OpenAI for tracking or diagnosing the system that handled the request. `'fp_abc28019ad'` is the specific fingerprint for this transaction.
- `usage`: This object tracks the token usage for the API call:

  - `completion_tokens`: The number of tokens used in the generated response (193 tokens)
  - `prompt_tokens`: The number of tokens used in the input prompt (55 tokens)
  - `total_tokens`: The total number of tokens consumed in the request, which is the sum of the prompt and completion tokens (248 tokens)

- `prompt_filter_results`: This array contains the results of content filtering applied to the input prompt before generating the response. It ensures that the prompt does not contain harmful content. Like the `content_filter_results` in the choices section, it includes checks for hate, self-harm, sexual content, and violence. All are marked as `'safe'` and `'filtered'`: `False`, indicating no issues were found.

Among all the output parameters, the `content_filter_results` might be particularly relevant when it comes to managing potentially harmful results. In fact, you might want to enforce a more conservative approach when it comes to potentially harmful content, in either input or output. If this is the case, you could simply enforce a deterministic rule that prevents the model from further processing any request that triggers a given level of risk.

This is a meaningful example of how leveraging OpenAI models' APIs allows for great flexibility when it comes to building application logic around LLMs.

Architectural patterns to build applications with models' APIs

The rise of GenAI and LLMs paved the way for a revolution in the field of software development. In fact, from "modern applications" – referring to microservices-based architectures and rapid innovation with CI/CD – we now talk about "intelligent applications" that are infused with GenAI models defined by natural language interaction, data-driven experience, and velocity of adaptation to new models' releases.

An intelligent app can be described with the following illustration:

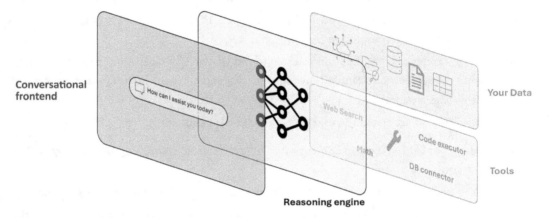

Figure 10.3: Anatomy of an intelligent application powered by an LLM

In the above architecture, we depict the anatomy of an intelligent application with the following features:

- It has a natural language interface (it might be text- or voice-based).
- It is powered by an LLM that acts as the "brain" of the app.
- It has a knowledge base that the model can query, typically with **retrieval augmented generation (RAG)** techniques.
- It has a set of tools or plugins that it can use to interact with the external environment.

This new paradigm of software development brings a set of new application components that are typical of AI-powered applications. Let's explore these new components in more detail.

New application components

The main shift in terms of AI development refers to the way we work with models: from producing models, now the trend is consuming models that, as we mentioned several times, are nothing but APIs.

This shift leads to a series of new software components (or adjustments of existing components) in the landscape of development:

- **Models**: The model is simply the type of LLM we decide to embed in our application. There are two main categories of models:

    - **Proprietary LLMs**: Models that are owned by specific companies or organizations. Examples include GPT-4o, developed by OpenAI, or Gemini, developed by Google. As their source code and architecture are not available, those models cannot be re-trained from scratch on custom data, but they can be fine-tuned if needed.

    - **Open-source**: Models with code and architecture freely available and distributed, hence they can also be trained from scratch on custom data. Examples include Falcon LLM, developed by Abu Dhabi's **Technology Innovation Institute** (TII), and Llama, developed by Meta.

- **System message**: This is the set of instructions that we provide the model with, and that influence the style and behavior of our AI app. There are many features that we can shape directly within the meta-prompt, including:

    - Reducing hallucination by specifying that the model only refers to the provided knowledge base (this process is called "grounding")

    - Implementing responsible AI practices by specifying, for example, not to respond to malicious queries or not to generate potentially harmful responses

    - Instructing the model to always ask an additional question to consolidate the context before answering

- **Memory and VectorDB**: When we talk about memory in the context of AI apps, we need to differentiate between two types of memory:

    - **Short-term memory**: This is the capability of the app to keep the interactions between the user and LLMs in a context window. It means that each message feeds the existing meta-prompt of the model, without the user repeating something already mentioned.

- **Long-term memory**: This type of memory refers to the external knowledge base we provide the model with using embeddings. When this is the case, we typically leverage VectorDBs, a new type of database (or new feature of an existing database) that stores the numerical representations of the provided documents.

> **Definition**
>
> A VectorDB is a type of database that stores and retrieves information based on vectorized embeddings, the numerical representations that capture the meaning and context of text. By using a VectorDB, you can perform semantic search and retrieval based on the similarity of meanings rather than keywords. Some examples of a VectorDB are Chroma, FAISS, Elasticsearch, Milvus, Pinecone, Qdrant, and Weaviate.

- **Tools/plugins**: These can be seen as additional modules or components that can be integrated into the LLM to extend its functionality or adapt it to specific tasks and applications. These plugins act as add-ons, enhancing the capabilities of the LLM beyond its core language generation or comprehension abilities.

  The idea behind plugins is to make LLMs more versatile and adaptable, allowing developers and users to customize the behavior of the language model for their specific needs. Plugins can be created to perform various tasks, and they can be seamlessly incorporated into the LLM's architecture.

The following is an illustration of the main components of an LLM-powered application:

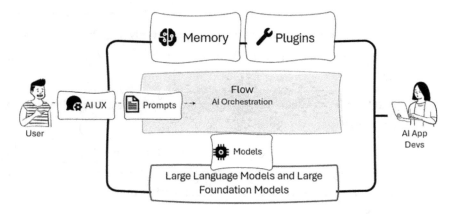

Figure 10.4: High-level architecture of LLM-powered applications

As you can see from the picture above, the core of the high-level architecture is the **AI orchestrator**. With the AI orchestrator, we refer to lightweight libraries that make it easier to embed and orchestrate LLMs within applications.

AI orchestrators

Since LLMs went viral toward the end of 2022, many libraries have begun to arise in the market. In the next sections, we are going to focus on three of them: LangChain, Semantic Kernel, and Haystack.

LangChain

LangChain was launched as an open-source project by Harrison Chase, in October 2022. It can be used in both Python and JS/TS.

LangChain is a framework for developing applications powered by language models, making them data-aware (with grounding) and agentic – meaning able to interact with external environments.

LangChain provides modular abstractions for the components necessary to work with language models that we previously mentioned, such as prompts, memory, and plugins. Alongside those components, LangChain also offers pre-built **chains**, which are structured concatenations of components. These chains can be pre-built for specific use cases or be customized.

Overall, LangChain has the following core modules:

- **Models**: These are the LLMs or large foundation models that will be the engine of the application. LangChain supports proprietary models, such as those available in OpenAI and Azure OpenAI, and open-source models consumable from the **Hugging Face Hub**.

Definition

Hugging Face is a company and a community that builds and shares state-of-the-art models and tools for **natural language processing (NLP)** and other machine learning domains. It developed the Hugging Face Hub, a platform where people can create, discover, and collaborate on machine learning models and LLMs, datasets, and demos. The Hugging Face Hub hosts over 120k models, 20k datasets, and 50k demos in various domains and tasks, such as audio, vision, and language.

Alongside models, LangChain also offers many prompt-related components that make it easier to manage the prompt flow.

- **Data connections**: These refer to the building blocks needed to retrieve the additional non-parametric knowledge we want to provide the model with. Examples of data connections are document loaders or text embedding models.

- **Memory**: It allows the application to keep references to the user's interactions, in both the short and long term. It is typically based on vectorized embeddings stored in a VectorDB.

- **Chains**: These are predetermined sequences of actions and calls to LLMs that make it easier to build complex applications that require chaining LLMs with each other or with other components. An example of a chain might be: take the user query, chunk it into smaller pieces, embed those chunks, search for similar embeddings in a VectorDB, use the top three most similar chunks in the VectorDB as context to provide the answer, generate the answer.

- **Agents**: Agents are entities that drive decision-making within LLM-powered applications. They have access to a suite of tools and can decide which tool to call based on the user input and the context. Agents are dynamic and adaptive, meaning that they can change or adjust their actions based on the situation or the goal.

Haystack

Haystack is a Python-based framework developed by *deepset*, a startup founded in 2018 in Berlin by Milos Rusic, Malte Pietsch, and Timo Möller. deepset provides developers with the tools to build an NLP-based application, and with the introduction of Haystack, they are taking it to the next level.

Haystack has the following core components:

- **Nodes**: These are components that perform a specific task or function, such as a retriever, a reader, a generator, a summarizer, etc. Nodes can be LLMs or other utilities that interact with LLMs or other resources. Among LLMs, Haystack supports proprietary models, such as those available in OpenAI and Azure OpenAI, and open-source models consumable from the Hugging Face Hub.

- **Pipelines**: These are sequences of calls to nodes that perform natural language tasks or interact with other resources. Pipelines can be querying pipelines or indexing pipelines, depending on whether they perform searches on a set of documents or prepare documents for search. Pipelines are predetermined and hardcoded, meaning that they do not change or adapt based on the user input or the context.

- **Agent:** This is an entity that uses LLMs to generate accurate responses to complex queries. An agent has access to a set of tools, which can be pipelines or nodes, and it can decide which tool to call based on the user input and the context. An agent is dynamic and adaptive, meaning that it can change or adjust its actions based on the situation or the goal.

- **Tools:** There are functions that an agent can call to perform natural language tasks or interact with other resources. Tools can be pipelines or nodes that are available to the agent and they can be grouped into toolkits, which are sets of tools that can accomplish specific objectives.

- **DocumentStores:** These are backends that store and retrieve documents for search. DocumentStores can be based on different technologies, including VectorDBs (such as FAISS, Milvus, or Elasticsearch).

Haystack is renowned for its simplicity and ease of use, featuring a modular architecture that allows developers to construct customizable pipelines for tasks like semantic search and question-answering. This design makes it particularly suitable for **RAG** applications, where efficient data retrieval is crucial.

Semantic Kernel

Semantic Kernel is the third open-source SDK we are going to explore in this chapter. It was developed by Microsoft, originally in C#, and is now also available in Python.

This framework takes its name from the concept of a "kernel," which, generally speaking, refers to the core or essence of a system. In the context of this framework, a kernel is meant to act as the engine that addresses users' input by chaining and concatenating a series of components into pipelines, encouraging **function composition.**

Definition

In mathematics, function composition is a way to combine two functions to create a new function. The idea is to use the output of one function as the input to another function, forming a chain of functions. The composition of two functions, f and g, is denoted as $(f \circ g)$, where the function $(f \circ g)$ is applied first, followed by the function $f \rightarrow (f \circ g)(x) = f(g(x))$.

Function composition in computer science is a powerful concept that allows for the creation of more sophisticated and reusable code by combining smaller functions into larger ones. It enhances modularity and code organization, making programs easier to read and maintain.

Semantic Kernel has the following main components:

- **Models:** These are the LLMs or large foundation models that will be the engine of the application. Semantic Kernel supports proprietary models, such as those available in OpenAI and Azure OpenAI, and open-source models consumable from the Hugging Face Hub.

- **Memory:** This allows the application to keep references to the user's interactions, in both the short and long term. Within the framework of Semantic Kernel, memories can be accessed in three ways:

  - **Key-value pairs:** This consists of saving environment variables that store simple information, such as names or dates.

  - **Local storage:** This consists of saving information to a file that can be retrieved by its filename, such as a CSV or JSON file.

  - **Semantic memory search:** This is similar to LangChain's and Haystack's memory, as it uses embeddings to represent and search for text information based on its meaning.

- **Functions:** Functions can be seen as skills that mix LLM prompts and code, with the goal of making users' requests interpretable and actionable. There are two types of functions:

  - **Semantic functions:** These are basically a templated prompt, which is a natural language query that specifies the input and output format for the LLM, also incorporating prompt configuration, which sets the parameters for the LLM.

  - **Native functions:** These refer to the native computer code that can route the intent captured by the semantic function and perform the related task.

  To give an example, a semantic function could ask the LLM to write a short paragraph about AI, while a native function could actually post it on social media like LinkedIn.

- **Plugins:** These are connectors toward external sources or systems that are meant to provide additional information or the ability to perform autonomous actions. Semantic Kernel offers out-of-the-box plugins, such as the Microsoft Graph connector kit, but you can build a custom plugin by leveraging functions (both native and semantic, or a mix of the two).

- **Planner:** As LLMs can be seen as reasoning engines, they can also be leveraged to auto-create chains or pipelines to address new users' needs. This goal is achieved with a planner, which is a function that takes as input a user's task and produces the set of actions, plugins, and functions needed to achieve the goal.

Below is an illustration of the anatomy of Semantic Kernel:

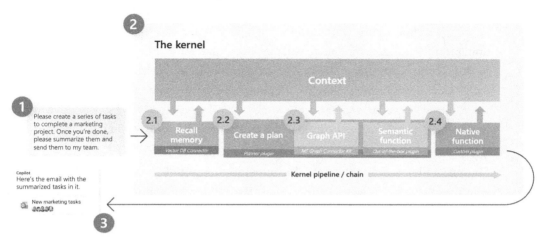

Figure 10.5: Anatomy of Semantic Kernel. Source: https://learn.microsoft.com/en-us/semantic-kernel/overview/

Overall, the three frameworks offer more or less similar core components, sometimes called a different taxonomy, yet covering all the blocks illustrated within the concept of the copilot system. So, a natural question might be, "Which one should I use to build my LLM-powered application?"

Below are some criteria you might want to consider:

- **The programming language you are comfortable with or prefer to use**. Different frameworks may support different programming languages or have different levels of compatibility or integration with them. For example, Semantic Kernel supports C#, Python, and Java, while LangChain and Haystack are mainly based on Python (even though LangChain also introduced JS/TS support). You may want to choose a framework that matches your existing skills or preferences, or that allows you to use the language that is most suitable for your application domain or environment.

- **The type and complexity of the natural language tasks you want to perform or support**. Different frameworks may have different capabilities or features for handling various natural language tasks, such as summarization, generation, translation, reasoning, etc. For example, LangChain and Haystack provide utilities and components for orchestrating and executing natural language tasks, while Semantic Kernel allows you to use natural language semantic functions to invoke LLMs and services. You may want to choose a framework that offers the functionality and flexibility you need or want for your application goals or scenarios.

- **The level of customization and control you need or want over the LLMs and their parameters or options**. Different frameworks may have different ways of accessing, configuring, and fine-tuning the LLMs and their parameters or options, such as model selection, prompt design, inference speed, output format, etc. For example, Semantic Kernel provides connectors that make it easy to add memories and models to your AI app, while LangChain and Haystack allow you to plug in different components for the Document-Store, retriever, reader, generator, summarizer, and evaluator. You may want to choose a framework that gives you the level of customization and control you need or want over the LLMs and their parameters or options.

- **The availability and quality of the documentation, tutorials, examples, and community support for the framework**. Different frameworks may have different levels of documentation, tutorials, examples, and community support that can help you learn, use, and troubleshoot the framework. For example, Semantic Kernel has a website with documentation, tutorials, examples, and a Discord community; LangChain has a GitHub repository with documentation, examples, and issues; Haystack has a website with documentation, tutorials, demos, blog posts, and a Slack community. You may want to choose a framework that has the availability and quality of documentation, tutorials, examples, and community support that can help you get started and solve problems with the framework.

Well, there is no right or wrong answer! All three orchestrators discussed above are extremely valid. However, some features might be more relevant to specific use cases or developers' preferences. Make your choice based on that.

Introducing the public cloud: Azure OpenAI

In 2016, OpenAI agreed to leverage Microsoft's Azure cloud infrastructure to run its AI experiments, which led, in 2019, to a $1 billion investment from the tech giant into Sam Altman's company (`https://news.microsoft.com/2019/07/22/openai-forms-exclusive-computing-partnership-with-microsoft-to-build-new-azure-ai-supercomputing-technologies/`).

This marked the beginning of a strategic partnership between the two companies, aiming at developing AI models and technologies that can be used for the benefit of humanity. This partnership is based on the following three main pillars:

- Microsoft and OpenAI will jointly build new Azure supercomputing infrastructure to train AI models.
- OpenAI will make its models and technologies consumable from the Azure cloud.
- Microsoft will become OpenAI's preferred partner for commercializing new AI solutions to the market.

Since then, the two companies kept investing and researching, and finally, in January 2023, OpenAI models were made available on Microsoft Azure as a managed service: **Azure OpenAI Service** (in short, **AOAI**).

With the general availability of the AOAI Service, a new milestone was reached, and the Microsoft AI portfolio has been extended with the powerful LLMs of OpenAI.

AOAI Service

The AOAI Service is a product of Microsoft that provides both a playground and APIs to interact and consume all of OpenAI's powerful language models. It is important to highlight that the models are exactly the same: the only difference is that, if you are consuming them via AOAI, you are leveraging your own Azure subscription and automatically inheriting all the enterprise features that are typical of the Microsoft public cloud, including security, role-based access control, data privacy, and so on.

To create your AOAI resource, follow these instructions:

- Navigate to your Azure portal at `https://ms.portal.azure.com`.
- Click on **Create a Resource**.
- Type *azure openai* and click on **Create**.
- Fill in the required information and click on **Review + create**.

This is shown in the following screenshot:

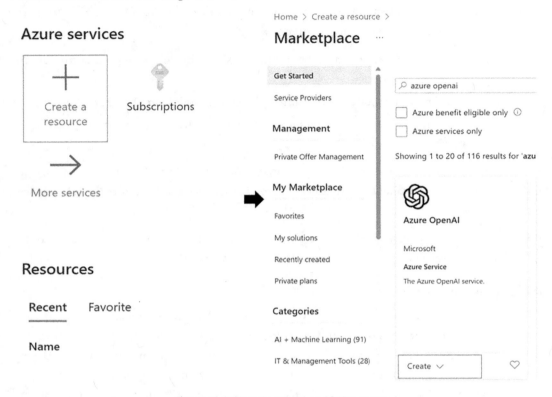

Figure 10.6: Steps to create an AOAI resource

This process might take a few minutes. Once it is ready, you can directly jump to its user-friendly interface, the AOAI Studio, to test your models before deploying them:

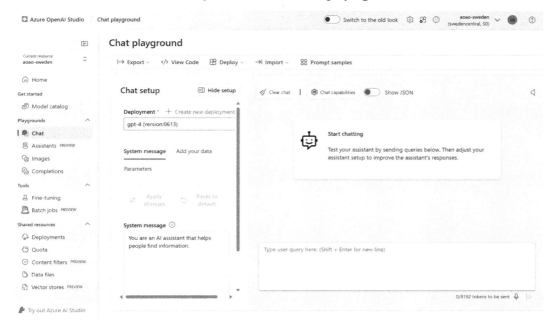

Figure 10.7: AOAI Studio and chat playground

To use AOAI models, you have to initiate a deployment, which is a serverless compute instance you can attach to a model.

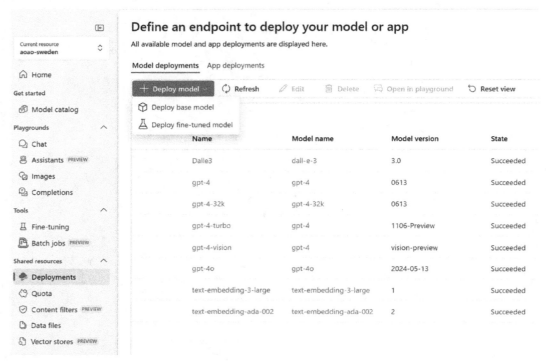

Figure 10.8: Creating a new AOAI deployment via the Azure OpenAI portal

Lastly, exactly like we did for OpenAI models' APIs in the previous section, from the AOAI Studio, you can consume your deployed models via APIs. For a quick start, you can navigate to the **Chat playground** and click on the **View Code** button. A script will be ready to be copied and pasted into your favorite programming IDE, along with the secret keys needed to access the resource:

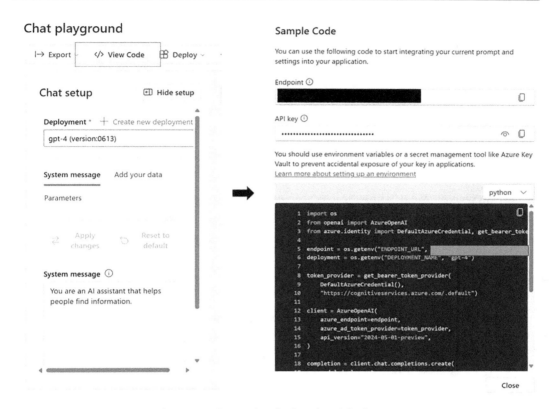

Figure 10.9: Consuming deployed models via APIs

By doing so, you can seamlessly incorporate your Azure OpenAI's LLMs within your own application.

Summary

At the beginning of this chapter, we had an overview of how GenAI is disrupting industries, from increasing the efficiency of internal processes to enhancing customers' journeys with personalized experiences. Many of these applications can be achieved through a high margin of customization, and pre-built, consumer-facing applications like ChatGPT might not be enough.

That's why we introduced OpenAI models' APIs. With the models' APIs, you can leverage the power of the model behind ChatGPT within your own application, tailored to your own industry and scenarios. Developing AI-powered applications, however, requires a new set of components that have also marked a new paradigm in software development.

Finally, we saw how, from 2023, OpenAI models (both in Playground and via APIs) have been made available through Microsoft Azure as a managed service: Azure OpenAI. This has paved the way for a new wave of adoption from large enterprises that benefit from all the security and governance layers that already exist within the public cloud (which is, by design, enterprise-ready).

In the next chapter, we will provide a recap of everything covered in this book, including the latest announcements and releases that have occurred. We will also focus on reflections and final thoughts about the exponential growth of generative AI technologies in just a few months and what to expect in the near future.

References

- OpenAI Forms Exclusive Computing Partnership with Microsoft to Build New Azure AI Supercomputing Technologies: `https://news.microsoft.com/2019/07/22/openai-forms-exclusive-computing-partnership-with-microsoft-to-build-new-azure-ai-supercomputing-technologies/`
- General Availability of Azure OpenAI Service Expands Access to Large, Advanced AI Models with Added Enterprise Benefits: `https://azure.microsoft.com/en-us/blog/general-availability-of-azure-openai-service-expands-access-to-large-advanced-ai-models-with-added-enterprise-benefits/`
- Microsoft CEO Satya Nadella: Humans and A.I. Can Work Together to Solve Society's Challenges: `https://slate.com/technology/2016/06/microsoft-ceo-satya-nadella-humans-and-a-i-can-work-together-to-solve-societys-challenges.html`
- Microsoft Calls for Government Regulation of Facial Recognition Technology: `https://www.geekwire.com/2018/microsoft-calls-government-regulation-facial-recognition-technology/`
- Six Principles to Guide Microsoft's Facial Recognition Work: `https://blogs.microsoft.com/on-the-issues/2018/12/17/six-principles-to-guide-microsofts-facial-recognition-work/`
- Responsible AI Principles and Approach: `https://www.microsoft.com/en-us/ai/principles-and-approach`
- Microsoft Responsible AI Toolbox: `https://responsibleaitoolbox.ai/`

- Human Parity on CommonsenseQA: Augmenting Self-Attention with External Attention: https://www.microsoft.com/en-us/research/publication/human-parity-on-commonsenseqa-augmenting-self-attention-with-external-attention/

- Customize a Model with Azure OpenAI Service: https://learn.microsoft.com/en-gb/azure/cognitive-services/openai/how-to/fine-tuning?pivots=programming-language-studio#openai-cli-data-preparation-tool

- Moody's and Microsoft Develop Enhanced Risk, Data, Analytics, Research and Collaboration Solutions Powered by Generative AI: https://ir.moodys.com/press-releases/news-details/2023/Moodys-and-Microsoft-Develop-Enhanced-Risk-Data-Analytics-Research-and-Collaboration-Solutions-Powered-by-Generative-AI/default.aspx

- Increasing Accuracy of Pediatric Visit Notes: https://openai.com/index/summer-health/

- Coca-Cola Invites Digital Artists to 'Create Real Magic' Using New AI Platform: https://www.coca-colacompany.com/media-center/coca-cola-invites-digital-artists-to-create-real-magic-using-new-ai-platform

- IVECO Group Uses Azure OpenAI Service to Transform Manufacturing: https://customers.microsoft.com/en-us/story/1706380538888475836-iveco-group-azure-openai-service-manufacturing-italy

- Ironclad and OpenAI Partnership: https://openai.com/index/ironclad/

- Inworld AI and OpenAI Collaboration: https://openai.com/index/inworld-ai/

- Khan Academy and OpenAI Partnership: https://openai.com/index/khan-academy/

Subscribe for a free eBook

New frameworks, evolving architectures, research drops, production breakdowns—AI_Distilled filters the noise into a weekly briefing for engineers and researchers working hands-on with LLMs and GenAI systems. Subscribe now and receive a free eBook, along with weekly insights that help you stay focused and informed. Subscribe at https://packt.link/80z6Y or scan the QR code below.

11

Epilogue and Final Thoughts

You've made it up to this point – congratulations! I hope you found the book interesting and that it helped you toward your goals.

Writing the second edition of this book gave me food for thought, as the number of changes and achievements that have occurred between the two editions is insane, considering that only a little over one year has passed.

Even while writing this edition, things have been changing rapidly, which makes the job of writing a final chapter very hard.

So, I'd like to use this chapter as a compendium of the current landscape of **large foundation models** (**LFMs**) beyond OpenAI, as well as the most promising areas of research in the field of generative **artificial intelligence** (**AI**) and the concerns that are arising around these new powerful models.

More specifically, we will cover the following topics:

- An overview of what we have learned so far
- It's not all about OpenAI
- Ethical implications of generative AI and why we need responsible AI
- What to expect in the near future

By the end of this chapter, you will have a broader picture of the state-of-the-art developments within the domain of generative AI, how it is impacting industries, and what to expect in terms of new developments and social concerns.

An overview of what we have learned so far

We started this book with an introduction to the concept of generative AI and its various applications. We saw how generative AI is about not only text but also images, video, and music.

In *Chapter 2*, we moved on to look at the company that brought generative AI to its greatest popularity: OpenAI. Founded in 2015, OpenAI mainly focuses its research on a particular type of generative model, **Generative Pre-trained Transformer (GPT)**. Then, in November 2022, OpenAI released ChatGPT, a free web app of a conversational assistant powered by GPT models. It gained immense popularity, reaching one million users in just five days!

ChatGPT has been a game-changer. Its impact on daily productivity, as well as in various industry domains, is huge. We also saw, in *Chapter 3*, how to properly design the most important element when using generative models such as ChatGPT: the prompt. Prompts are the user's input, nothing more than instructions in natural language. Designing prompts is a pivotal step to getting the maximum value from your generative models to the point where **prompt engineering** has become a new domain of study.

Once we got familiar with ChatGPT and prompt design, we moved on to *Chapter 4*, where we finally got concrete examples of how ChatGPT can boost your daily productivity and become your daily assistant. From email generation to improving your writing skills, we saw how many activities can be improved thanks to the generative power of ChatGPT.

But we didn't stop there. With *Chapters 5, 6, 7*, and *8*, we saw how ChatGPT can boost not only daily productivity but also domain-specific activities – for developers, from code generation and optimization to interpreting machine learning models; in the case of marketers, from new product development to improving **search engine optimization (SEO)**; for researchers, from experiment design to the generation of a presentation based on a study; and for those needing an assistant for visual creativity, from design suggestions to images and canvas creation.

Furthermore, in *Chapter 9*, we explored how all the previous ChatGPT capabilities (code generation, marketing research, and so on) can be further tailored by building highly specialized assistants called GPTs, leveraging OpenAI's GPT Store. With GPTs, users can build personal assistants that leverage the power of the model behind ChatGPT, yet benefit from a more specialized and scoped behavior, leveraging knowledge bases, plugins, and precise instructions provided by users themselves – all without writing a single line of code!

With *Chapter 10*, we shifted the conversation to the enterprise level, exploring how OpenAI's models can also be consumed via APIs and embedded in custom applications. This allows both individuals and organizations to build powerful AI-infused apps, which benefit from OpenAI's LLMs yet offer great flexibility in terms of backend application logic and frontend UI.

This journey was meant to provide you with greater clarity about what we are talking about when we refer to popular buzzwords such as ChatGPT, OpenAI, and LLMs.

However, in the next section, we will see how the incredibly fast AI developments in recent months are bringing brand-new technologies on top of what we have learned so far.

It's not all about OpenAI

Throughout this book, we have covered "all things OpenAI." It's well known that OpenAI was the first entrant in the landscape of generative AI. It is hard to argue that the launch of ChatGPT was the milestone that marked the so-called paradigm shift in the AI field, from two angles:

- From a technological perspective, ChatGPT (or, more precisely, the model behind it – GPT-3.5-turbo) was the most powerful LLM out there by the time it was live (November 2022). This gave a competitive advantage to OpenAI, which was hard to benchmark for competitors.
- From a behavioral perspective, ChatGPT "broke the internet" in the sense that almost everyone was shocked by its ease of use and its extraordinary capabilities. This led to a new wave of users who, even though not AI experts, became interested in the matter and started exploring the endless capabilities of the product, raising the expectation bars more and more over the months.

Nevertheless, soon after November 2022, many other players entered the market and started populating the landscape of LFMs with new entries, both proprietary and open source.

Let's explore some of the key players as of today.

Mistral AI

This France-based company has made significant strides in the generative AI landscape with its open-source models. Mistral AI is known for its Mistral 7B and Mixtral models, which have been praised for their performance and efficiency. The company focuses on creating highly capable models that are accessible to the broader AI community, promoting innovation through open-source contributions. Their models are designed to handle a variety of tasks, from text generation to code completion, making them versatile tools in the AI toolkit.

Meta

Meta has been a key player in advancing LLMs, particularly with its **Large Language Model Meta AI (LLaMA)** series. These models have been instrumental in pushing the boundaries of what LLMs can achieve, particularly in terms of scalability and efficiency. Meta's research has focused on optimizing the infrastructure needed to train these massive models, ensuring they can be deployed effectively across various applications. Their work has also emphasized the importance of open-source models, allowing developers worldwide to build on their innovations.

Microsoft

As we covered in *Chapter 10*, Microsoft has leveraged its Azure platform to support the development and deployment of OpenAI through a multi-year partnership. Microsoft has also made an entire catalog of other LLMs available via an API (both proprietary and open source) on its Azure platform.

In addition to its partnerships, Microsoft has developed its own family of models known as the Phi series. The Phi-3 models, including Phi-3-mini, Phi-3-small, and Phi-3-medium, are designed to be highly efficient and cost-effective. These models excel in various benchmarks, outperforming larger models in tasks such as language understanding, reasoning, coding, and mathematics. The Phi-3-mini, for instance, supports a context window of up to 128K tokens, making it highly versatile for different applications. Microsoft's focus on optimizing these models for deployment across various platforms, including Azure AI, Hugging Face, and local environments, ensures that they are accessible and practical for a wide range of users. This commitment to developing robust, scalable, and efficient models highlights Microsoft's significant contributions to the field of GenAI.

Google

Google has been at the forefront of GenAI with its Gemini models, designed for multi-modal applications. These models can process and generate content across various formats, including text, images, and videos. Google's innovations in **retrieval-augmented generation** (**RAG**) have improved the accuracy and reliability of LLM outputs by integrating real-time data from cloud databases. This approach helps mitigate issues like hallucinations, ensuring that the generated content is both relevant and accurate.

Anthropic

Anthropic has developed the Claude family of LLMs, which are known for their safety and ethical considerations. Claude models are designed to minimize biases and promote fairness, making them suitable for a wide range of applications.

Anthropic's focus on responsible AI development has set a high standard in the industry, ensuring that its models are not only powerful but also aligned with ethical guidelines. This commitment to safety and transparency has made Claude a trusted name in the GenAI community.

The proliferation of LLMs in the market of GenAI is increasing exponentially. However, it is important to acknowledge that our choice of the "best LLM for our app" shouldn't be routed toward the biggest (on average) highest-performing model available. As of the time of writing, there are many LLMs that have been trained in a specific domain or expertise (like mathematical reasoning, code generation, specific languages, and so on) that, on average, perform way worse than general-purpose models like OpenAI's o1. Nevertheless, we might consider different variables when it comes to developing our application.

For example, we might be interested in a model that has a very specific comprehension of an industry-specific taxonomy. If this is the case, we might want to leverage LLMs that have been trained and fine-tuned for this purpose, like Microsoft's BioGPT. Or, we might need to run our model locally, in disconnected scenarios (think about an offshore plant in the middle of the ocean); if this is the case, we couldn't run, let's say, GPT-4o – firstly, because it is a proprietary model and cannot be "downloaded"; secondly, would we have a supercomputer that is capable of hosting more than 100 trillion parameters?

There are many scenarios where models other than the "state of the art" are needed, and it's part of the job of the new GenAI-related jobs to assess the type of model needed for specific use cases.

Ethical implications of generative AI and why we need responsible AI

The previous section highlighted how, alongside the widespread knowledge and adoption of generative AI technologies, a general concern is rising.

The rapid advancement of AI technologies brings forth a plethora of ethical considerations and challenges that must be carefully addressed to ensure their responsible and equitable deployment. Some of them are listed here:

- **Data privacy and security**: As AI systems rely heavily on data for their learning and decision-making processes, ensuring data privacy and security becomes paramount. In the context of generative AI, this is a topic that affects the data that is used to train the model in the first instance. Even though the knowledge base used by ChatGPT to generate responses is public, where is the threshold of the consent of involved users whose information is used to generate responses?

- **Bias and fairness**: AI models often learn from historical data, which might inadvertently introduce biases. Addressing bias and fairness in AI systems involves the following:

    - **Diverse datasets**: Ensuring that training data is diverse and representative of various demographics can help reduce biases in AI models

    - **Algorithmic fairness**: Developing algorithms that prioritize fairness and do not discriminate against specific demographic groups is essential

    - **Monitoring and auditing**: Regular monitoring and auditing of AI systems can help identify and rectify biases, ensuring that the outcomes are equitable

- **Transparency and accountability**: As AI systems become more complex, understanding their decision-making processes can be challenging. This involves the following two important aspects:

    - **Explainable AI**: Developing AI models that can provide clear explanations for their decisions can help users understand and trust the system.

    - **Responsibility and liability**: Establishing clear lines of responsibility and liability for AI systems is crucial to hold developers, organizations, and users accountable for the consequences of AI-driven decisions.

- **The future of work**: AI-driven automation has the potential to displace jobs in certain sectors, raising concerns about the future of work. Throughout this book, we have seen how ChatGPT and OpenAI models are able to boost productivity for individuals and enterprises. However, it is also likely that some repetitive tasks will be definitively replaced by AI, which will impact some workers. This is part of the change and development process, and it is pivotal to embrace the change rather than fight it.

Some actions in this direction could be reskilling and upskilling programs – governments, organizations, and educational institutions should invest in reskilling and upskilling programs to help workers adapt to the changing job market and acquire new skills required for emerging roles.

Most importantly, human-AI collaboration should be encouraged. Developing AI systems that complement and augment human capabilities can help create new job opportunities and foster collaborative work environments.

By addressing these ethical considerations and challenges, we can work in the right direction to ensure that AI technologies are developed and deployed responsibly, promoting a better and more equitable future for all.

Now, the next logical question might be: given the tremendous acceleration of AI technologies in recent months, what should we expect in the near future?

What to expect in the near future

The acceleration of AI research and developments in recent months has been incredible. From November 2022 up to the time of writing (February 2025), we have seen the following occur:

- November 2022: OpenAI releases ChatGPT, a conversational AI model based on GPT-3.5, which quickly gains widespread attention for its human-like text generation capabilities.

- December 2022: ChatGPT reaches over one million users within five days of its launch, highlighting the public's rapid adoption of AI-driven conversational tools.

- January 2023: Microsoft announces a multibillion-dollar investment in OpenAI, aiming to integrate advanced AI technologies into its products and services. This is the foundation for the Copilot system.

- March 2023: OpenAI unveils GPT-4, an advanced multimodal AI model capable of processing both text and image inputs, marking a significant leap in AI's understanding and generation capabilities.

- May 2023: Google introduces Gemini, a multimodal LLM developed by Google DeepMind, designed to process various data types simultaneously, including text, images, audio, and video.

- December 2023: Google launches Gemini 1.0, integrating it into products like Bard and Pixel devices, and plans for broader applications across its services.

- February 2024: OpenAI introduces Sora, a text-to-video model capable of generating realistic videos from textual descriptions, expanding the horizons of AI-generated content.

- May 2024: OpenAI releases GPT-4o, a multimodal model that processes and generates text, images, and audio, setting new benchmarks in AI performance across various tasks.

- June 2024: Anthropic unveils Claude 3.5 Sonnet, an AI model demonstrating enhanced performance in coding, multistep workflows, and image analysis, contributing to the diversification of AI applications.

- July 2024: OpenAI introduces GPT-4o mini, a more accessible version of GPT-4o, aimed at making advanced AI capabilities available to a broader audience.

- September 2024: OpenAI releases the o1-preview and o1-mini models, designed to enhance reasoning accuracy, particularly in scientific, coding, and complex reasoning tasks.

- December 2024: OpenAI unveils o3 and o3-mini, successors to the o1 model, focusing on improved reasoning and efficiency, and begins testing these models with select users.
- January 2025: Chinese AI start-up DeepSeek releases its R1 model, an open-source AI assistant that rivals leading models in performance while being significantly more cost-effective. The launch causes a substantial impact on global tech markets, leading to significant stock fluctuations among major U.S. tech companies.

Plus, in January 2025, a new breakthrough initiative was announced: the Stargate Project. The project is a large-scale initiative focused on developing next-generation AI infrastructure in the U.S. Backed by OpenAI, SoftBank, Oracle, and MGX, the project is set to receive up to $500 billion in investment over the next four years. The first phase involves a $100 billion initial investment, with plans to expand as demand grows.

This initiative aims to build cutting-edge data centers and power facilities, ensuring the U.S. remains competitive in AI development. Major technology players like Microsoft, NVIDIA, and Arm are contributing expertise and resources. The project is expected to create hundreds of thousands of jobs and drive economic growth, with Texas selected as the first construction site and additional locations under review. Beyond the economic impact, Stargate is positioned as a strategic effort to bolster AI infrastructure and enhance national security.

This incredible pace makes it hard to predict what will come next. As we have seen, this velocity has also raised concerns among institutions, companies, and public figures because of the lack of regulation for these new technologies. At the same time, companies and institutions will inexorably need to adapt to this new landscape in order to keep up with competitors.

As we look ahead, the trajectory of generative AI points toward increasingly autonomous and collaborative systems. AI agents – autonomous entities capable of performing complex tasks without human intervention – are evolving rapidly. These agents are expected to manage intricate processes across various sectors, from automating business operations to enhancing personal productivity. The integration of multi-agent systems, where multiple AI agents collaborate to achieve shared objectives, is poised to revolutionize problem-solving by mimicking effective human teamwork.

Summary

The rapid development of generative AI technologies is ushering in a new era of innovation and transformation. With the immense potential to revolutionize industries and reshape day-to-day life, these advancements are rewriting the rules of human-machine interaction.

As we stand on the brink of this AI-driven future, it is our collective responsibility to ensure that these technologies are used responsibly and ethically. By embracing opportunities and addressing challenges, we can foster a world where AI empowers humanity and elevates our potential to new heights.

The GenAI era began "only" two years ago and, if you think about the impact it had over this timeframe, we cannot help imagine all the great achievements we might witness in the near future.

References

- LangChain documentation: `https://python.langchain.com/v0.1/docs/get_started/quickstart/`
- Semantic Kernel documentation: `https://learn.microsoft.com/en-us/semantic-kernel/whatissk`
- Pinecone documentation: `https://www.pinecone.io/`

Get This Book's PDF Version and Exclusive Extras

UNLOCK NOW

Scan the QR code (or go to packtpub.com/unlock). Search for this book by name, confirm the edition, and then follow the steps on the page.

Note: Keep your invoice handy. Purchases made directly from Packt don't require one.

12

Appendix

In the main chapters of this book, we explored the power of OpenAI's models through the lens of ChatGPT, diving into its conversational interface and understanding how it can revolutionize the way we interact with AI. However, the world of OpenAI extends beyond ChatGPT's familiar chat-based experience. To fully harness the potential of these models, it's crucial to understand the broader tools and interfaces OpenAI provides.

This appendix is dedicated to exploring one such tool: the **OpenAI Playground**. The Playground offers a versatile environment to experiment with OpenAI's models, granting more control over parameters, outputs, and behaviors. Whether you want to fine-tune responses, test different use cases, or simply gain a deeper understanding of the models' capabilities, the Playground is an invaluable resource.

In this appendix, we will:

- Walk through the Playground interface and its key features.
- Illustrate how to interact with OpenAI models directly from the Playground.
- Offer tips and best practices to maximize your outcomes when using the Playground.

By the end of this appendix, you'll have the knowledge and confidence to use OpenAI's Playground and its models, going beyond ChatGPT.

Trying OpenAI models in the Playground

To access an OpenAI Playground, you need to create an OpenAI account and navigate through to `https://platform.openai.com/playground`. This is how the landing page looks:

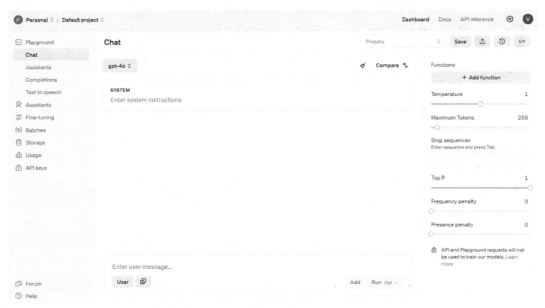

Figure 1: OpenAI Playground at https://platform.openai.com/playground

As you can see from *Figure 1*, the Playground offers a UI where the user can start interacting with the model, which you can select at the top of your chat interface. Note that, whenever consuming models via the OpenAI Playground, you will be charged a fee depending on the amount of interactions. You can find the pricing page at `https://openai.com/api/pricing/`.

Before diving deeper into the main sections of the Playground, let's first define some jargon you will see in this chapter:

- **Tokens**: Tokens can be considered as word fragments or segments that are used by the API to process input prompts. Unlike complete words, tokens may contain trailing spaces or even word segments. As a general rule of thumb, one token in English is approximately equivalent to four characters, or three-quarters of a word (you can refer to the following link to convert words to tokens in the context of OpenAI models: `https://platform.openai.com/tokenizer`).

- **Prompt:** In the context of **natural language processing (NLP)** and Generative AI, a prompt refers to a piece of text that is given as input to an AI language model to generate a response or output. The prompt can be a question, a statement, or a sentence, and it is used to provide context and direction to the language model.

- **Context:** In the field of GPT, context refers to the words and sentences that come before the user's prompt. This context is used by the language model to generate the most probable next word or phrase, based on the patterns and relationships found in the training data.

- **Model confidence:** Model confidence refers to the level of certainty or probability that an AI model assigns to a particular prediction or output. In the context of NLP, model confidence is often used to indicate how confident the AI model is in the correctness or relevance of its generated response to a given input prompt.

- **Tools:** With tools, we provide the model with an extra skill that it can invoke to accomplish the user's task. A function will always have a description in natural language so that the model knows when to invoke it.

In the Playground, there are four main sections to interact with the models. Let's explore them in the next sections.

Chat

Here, you can test all the chat models available today, including both text-only models (like GPT-3.5) and multimodal models (like GPT-4o). You can provide a system message – the set of instructions that you provide your model with – all in natural language.

Definition

In the context of LLMs, the system message is an instruction provided at the beginning of a conversation to establish the model's role, behavior, and response guidelines. This message sets the overarching context, guiding the model's interactions to align with specific objectives or constraints. For example, a system message might specify that the model should act as a friendly travel advisor or maintain a formal tone. This configuration can be set at the backend level by the AI developer, so that the end user will not have access to it and, henceforth, will not be able to "force" the model to behave differently.

You can also compare the output of two different models, given the same question. The following is an example of how to do that:

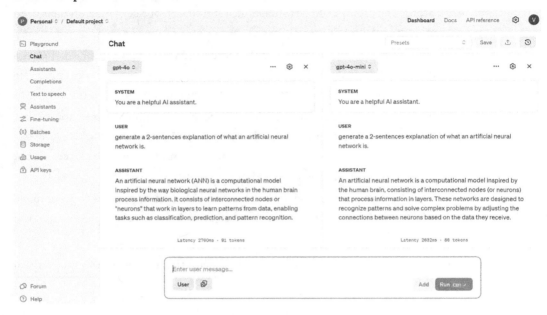

Figure 2: An example of comparison between two models

For each model, you can also play with some parameters that you can configure. Here is a list:

- **Temperature** (ranging from 0 to 2): This controls the randomness of the model's response. A low-level temperature makes your model more deterministic, meaning that it will tend to give the same output to the same question. For example, if I ask my model multiple times *What is OpenAI?* with the temperature set as 0, it will give, most of the time, the same answer. On the other hand, if I do the same with a temperature greater than 0, it will try to modify its answers each time, in terms of wording and style.

- **Max tokens:** This controls the length (in terms of tokens) of the model's response to the user's prompt.

- **Stop sequences** (user input): This makes responses end at the desired point, such as the end of a sentence or list.

- **Top probabilities** (ranging from 0 to 1): This controls which tokens the model will consider when generating a response. This means that the model will select from the smallest set of tokens whose cumulative probability adds up to 90% of the distribution.

- **Frequency penalty** (ranging from 0 to 1): This controls the repetition of the same tokens in the generated response. The higher the penalty, the lower the probability of seeing the same tokens more than once in the same response. The penalty reduces the chance proportionally, based on how often a token has appeared in the text so far (this is the key difference from the following parameter).

- **Presence penalty** (ranging from 0 to 2): This is similar to the previous parameter but stricter. It reduces the chance of repeating any token that has appeared in the text at all so far. As it is stricter than the frequency penalty, the presence penalty also increases the likelihood of introducing new topics in a response.

Assistants

OpenAI Assistants can be seen as a way to develop AI agents faster and more easily. In fact, Assistants can be defined as entities powered by an LLM, with a set of instructions to follow and a set of tools or plugins to use.

In the case of OpenAI Assistants, they come with three pre-built tools:

- **File Search**: This allows the user to upload custom documents so that the Assistant can navigate through them to accomplish the user's query. It operates with a RAG-based framework.

- **Function Calling**: This allows the user to define a set of custom functions that can be invoked by the Assistant to accomplish a given task.

- **Code Interpreter**: This refers to the capability of the Assistant to run code either against provided documents (for example, in the case of spreadsheets or analytical papers that require mathematical computations) or simply to solve complex tasks provided by the user (for example, complex mathematical problems).

In the following screenshot, you can see an example of an Assistant called **Chat with PDF**, which specializes in responding to provided documents (in my case, I uploaded the paper *LLaMA: Open and Efficient Foundation Language Models* by Hugo Touvron et al.).

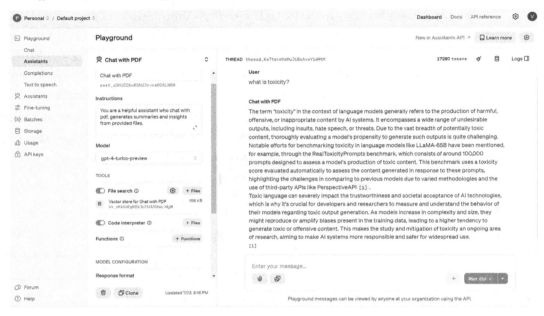

Figure 3: Example of an OpenAI Assistant

As you can see from the preceding screenshot, the Assistant was able to answer my question, retrieving knowledge from the provided document. In fact, my question was pretty vague, since the term *toxicity* can refer to multiple domains; nevertheless, the Assistant knows to watch over the provided documents as the primary source of information.

Completions

This section refers to a class of models called **base models**, like GPT-3. They are the basis on which the so-called "assistant models" (or chat models, as we saw previously) are built. For example, the chat model GPT-3.5 Turbo (the model behind ChatGPT) is a fine-tuned version of the base model GPT-3.

Definition

Completions (base) models are designed for generating single responses to prompts, making them suitable for tasks like text generation and summarization without maintaining context over multiple interactions. Chat (assistant) models, on the other hand, are optimized for interactive conversations, capable of maintaining context across multiple turns, and are ideal for applications like chatbots and virtual assistants.

Below you can see an example of a typical completion task in the Playground:

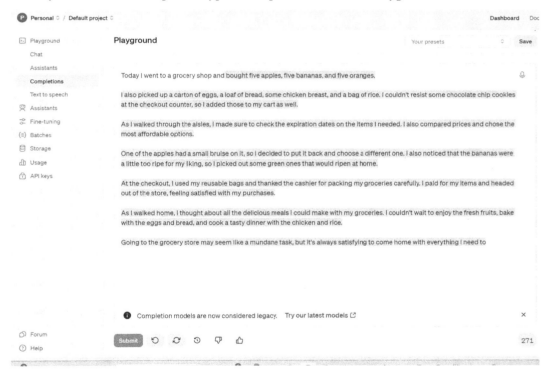

Figure 4: Example of completion task in OpenAI Playground

As you can see, using my words "Today I went to a grocery store and" the model completed the sentence with the most likely words.

Today, completion models are rarely used as they are outperformed by chat models, yet they can be further fine-tuned to tailored use cases (we will cover fine-tuning later on in this section).

Text to speech

In addition to *Whisper*, the aforementioned speech-to-text model, OpenAI also released a **text-to-speech (TTS)** model that can be tested directly in the Playground.

Let's see an example:

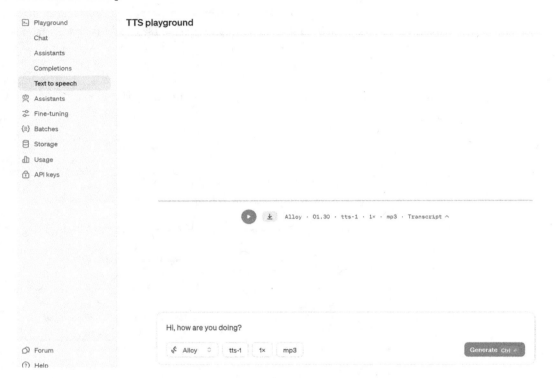

Figure 5: Example of using OpenAI's TTS models in the Playground

As you can see from the above screenshot, you can select the voice, model, speed, and format of the generated audio.

All the previous models come pre-built, in the sense that they have already been pre trained on a huge knowledge base.

However, there are some ways you can make your model more customized and tailored for your use case.

Customizing your model

The first method of tailoring your model for your use case is embedded in the way the model is designed, and it involves providing your model with the context in the few-shot learning approach.

For example, you could ask the model to generate an article whose template and lexicon recall another one you have already written. For this, you can provide the model with your query of generating an article and also with the former article as a reference or context, so that the model is better prepared for your request.

Here is an example of it:

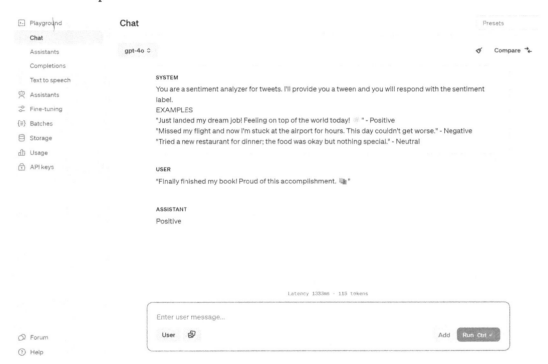

Figure 6: An example of a conversation within the OpenAI Playground with the few-shot learning approach

In the previous example, I instructed the model to output only the label of the tweet's sentiment, providing it with three examples of how to do that.

The second method of customizing your model is more sophisticated and is called **fine-tuning**. Fine-tuning is the process of adapting a pre trained model to a new task.

In fine-tuning, the parameters of the pre trained model are altered, either by adjusting the existing parameters or by adding new parameters, to better fit the data for the new task. This is done by training the model on a smaller labeled dataset that is specific to the new task. The key idea behind fine-tuning is to leverage the knowledge learned from the pre trained model and fine-tune it to the new task, rather than training a model from scratch. Have a look at the following figure:

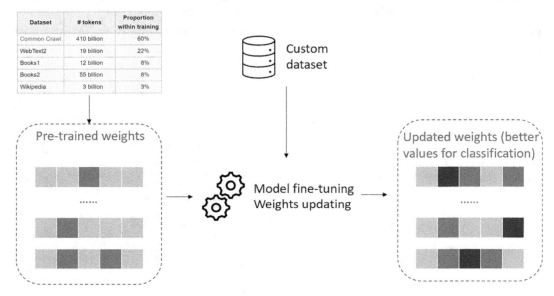

Figure 7: Model fine-tuning

In the preceding figure, you can see a schema on how fine-tuning works on OpenAI pre-built models. The idea is that you have available a pre trained model with general-purpose weights or parameters. Then, you feed your model with custom data, typically in the form of *key-value* prompts and completions, as shown here:

```
{"prompt": "<prompt text>", "completion": "<ideal generated text>"}
{"prompt": "<prompt text>", "completion": "<ideal generated text>"}
{"prompt": "<prompt text>", "completion": "<ideal generated text>"}
```

Once the training is done, you will have a customized model that performs particularly well for a given task, for example, the classification of your company's documentation.

The nice thing about fine-tuning is that you can make pre-built models tailored to your use cases, without the need to re-train them from scratch, yet leveraging smaller training datasets and hence needing less training time and computing. At the same time, the model keeps its generative power and accuracy learned via the original training, the one that was carried out on the massive dataset.

Summary

The OpenAI Playground presents a powerful tool for experimenting with advanced AI models through zero- or few-shot learning and fine-tuning techniques. The Playground allows users to interact directly with pre trained models, making it easier to customize and enhance them for specific tasks, such as sentiment analysis or document classification.

For developers looking to build AI applications that leverage OpenAI's API, mastering these techniques is crucial to ascertain whether a specific model's configuration will meet a specific application's requirements.

Despite the focus of this book being mainly on ChatGPT, enterprise-scale scenarios (which we covered in *Chapter 10*) require more customized approaches when it comes to AI use cases; that's why familiarizing yourself with the concept of the Playground and OpenAI models' APIs is of a great value to embrace the mindset of this new wave of AI-powered application development.

Subscribe for a free eBook

New frameworks, evolving architectures, research drops, production breakdowns—AI_Distilled fi lters the noise into a weekly briefi ng for engineers and researchers working hands-on with LLMs and GenAI systems. Subscribe now and receive a free eBook, along with weekly insights that help you stay focused and informed. Subscribe at `https://packt.link/8Oz6Y` or scan the QR code below.

13

Unlock Your Exclusive Benefits

Your copy of this book includes the following exclusive benefits:

- ⌂ Next-gen Packt Reader
- 🗎 DRM-free PDF/ePub downloads

Follow the guide below to unlock them. The process takes only a few minutes and needs to be completed once.

Unlock this Book's Free Benefits in 3 Easy Steps

Step 1

Keep your purchase invoice ready for *Step 3*. If you have a physical copy, scan it using your phone and save it as a PDF, JPG, or PNG.

For more help on finding your invoice, visit https://www.packtpub.com/unlock-benefits/help.

Note: If you bought this book directly from Packt, no invoice is required. After *Step 2*, you can access your exclusive content right away.

Step 2

Scan the QR code or go to packtpub.com/unlock.

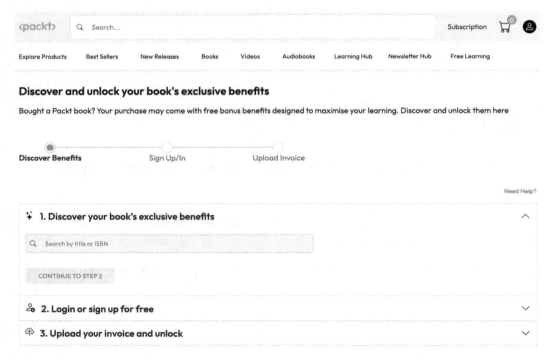

On the page that opens (similar to *Figure 13.1* on desktop), search for this book by name and select the correct edition.

Figure 13.1: Packt unlock landing page on desktop

Step 3

After selecting your book, sign in to your Packt account or create one for free. Then upload your invoice (PDF, PNG, or JPG, up to 10 MB). Follow the on-screen instructions to finish the process.

Need help?

If you get stuck and need help, visit `https://www.packtpub.com/unlock-benefits/help` for a detailed FAQ on how to find your invoices and more. This QR code will take you to the help page.

 Note: If you are still facing issues, reach out to `customercare@packt.com`.

packt.com

Subscribe to our online digital library for full access to over 7,000 books and videos, as well as industry leading tools to help you plan your personal development and advance your career. For more information, please visit our website.

Why subscribe?

- Spend less time learning and more time coding with practical eBooks and Videos from over 4,000 industry professionals
- Improve your learning with Skill Plans built especially for you
- Get a free eBook or video every month
- Fully searchable for easy access to vital information
- Copy and paste, print, and bookmark content

At www.packt.com, you can also read a collection of free technical articles, sign up for a range of free newsletters, and receive exclusive discounts and offers on Packt books and eBooks.

Other Books You May Enjoy

If you enjoyed this book, you may be interested in these other books by Packt:

Generating Creative Images With DALL-E 3

Holly Picano

ISBN: 9781835087718

- Master DALL-E 3's architecture and training methods
- Create fine prints and other AI-generated art with precision
- Seamlessly blend AI with traditional artistry
- Address ethical dilemmas in AI art
- Explore the future of digital creativity
- Implement practical optimization techniques for your artistic endeavors

Building AI Applications with OpenAI APIs

Martin Yanev

ISBN: 9781835884003

- Develop a solid foundation in using the OpenAI API for NLP tasks
- Build, deploy, and integrate payments into various desktop and SaaS AI applications
- Integrate ChatGPT with frameworks such as Flask, Django, and Microsoft Office APIs
- Unleash your creativity by integrating DALL-E APIs to generate stunning AI art within your desktop apps
- Experience the power of Whisper API's speech recognition and text-to-speech features
- Find out how to fine-tune ChatGPT models for your specific use case
- Master AI embeddings to measure the relatedness of text strings

Packt is searching for authors like you

If you're interested in becoming an author for Packt, please visit authors.packtpub.com and apply today. We have worked with thousands of developers and tech professionals, just like you, to help them share their insight with the global tech community. You can make a general application, apply for a specific hot topic that we are recruiting an author for, or submit your own idea.

Share your thoughts

Now you've finished *Practical Generative AI with ChatGPT, Second Edition*, we'd love to hear your thoughts! Scan the QR code below to go straight to the Amazon review page for this book and share your feedback or leave a review on the site that you purchased it from.

https://packt.link/r/1836647859

Your review is important to us and the tech community and will help us make sure we're delivering excellent quality content.

Join our Discord and Reddit space

You're not the only one navigating fragmented tools, constant updates, and unclear best practices. Join a growing community of professionals exchanging insights that don't make it into documentation.

Stay informed with updates, discussions, and behind-the-scenes insights from our authors. Join our Discord space at `https://packt.link/z8ivB` or scan the QR code below:	Connect with peers, share ideas, and discuss real-world GenAI challenges. Follow us on Reddit at `https://packt.link/0rExL` or scan the QR code below:

Index